Your Church
EXPERIENCING
G⊕D
TOGETHER

1112

HENRY T. BLACKABY
— AND —
MELVIN D. BLACKABY

ISBN 0-6330-8818-8

This book is the text for course CG-0808 in the Church category of the Christian Growth Study Plan.

Dewey Decimal Classification Number: 262.7
Subject Headings: CHURCH MEMBERSHIP \ GOD

Editor in Chief: Betty Hassler
Art Director: Jon Rodda
Cover Photo: Chad Rutherford
Editor: Gena Rogers
Copy Editor: Beth Shive

Unless otherwise indicated, all New Testament Scripture quotations are from the *Holman Christian Standard Bible,* © Copyright 2001 Holman Bible Publishers, Nashville, TN. All rights reserved.

Unless otherwise indicated, all Old Testament Scripture quotations and New Testament Scripture Quotations marked NASB are from the NEW AMERICAN STANDARD BIBLE, © copyright 1960, 1962, 1963, 1968, 1971, 1972, 1973, 1975, 1977, 1995 Used by permission.

Scripture quotations identified KJV are from the *King James Version* of the Bible.

Scripture quotations identified as NIV are from the Holy Bible, *New International Version,* copyright © 1973, 1978, 1984 by International Bible Society.

Scripture quotations identified AMP are from *The Amplified New Testament* © The Lockman Foundation 1954, 1958, 1987. Used by permission.

To order additional copies of this resource, write to LifeWay Church Resources Customer Service; One LifeWay Plaza; Nashville, TN 37234-0013; fax (615) 251-5933; phone toll free (800) 458-2772; email *customerservice@lifeway.com;* order online at *www.lifeway.com;* or visit the LifeWay Christian Store serving you.

Printed in the United States of America

Leadership and Adult Publishing
LifeWay Church Resources
One LifeWay Plaza
Nashville, TN 37234-0175

CONTENTS

ABOUT THE AUTHORS

Henry T. Blackaby is president of Henry Blackaby Ministries. He is a popular speaker and writer whose workbook study *Experiencing God: Knowing and Doing the Will of God* has sold more than 3,000,000 copies. Now retired, Blackaby pastored numerous churches in Canada and served as Director of Missions in Vancouver, Canada, before coming to the United States as special assistant to the presidents of the International Mission Board, North American Mission Board, and LifeWay Christian Resources. He and his wife, Marilynn, are the parents of five adult children and live in Rex, Georgia.

Melvin D. Blackaby is the third son of Henry and Marilyn Blackaby. He holds a Ph.D. in theology degree from Southwestern Baptist Theological Seminary with his dissertation on the Church and the Kingdom. Mel has served as senior pastor for churches in the United States and Canada. He is currently pastor of Bow Valley Baptist Church in Cochrane, Alberta, where he lives with his wife Gina and their three children, Christa, Stephen, and Sarah. Mel enjoys outdoor sports and ice hockey.

Amy T. Summers wrote the personal learning activities and the leader guide. Amy has written extensively for LifeWay adult Sunday School member and leader materials. She holds a Master of Arts in Religious Education degree from Southwestern Baptist Theological Seminary. A pastor's wife and mother, Amy lives with her husband Stephen and their children, Aaron, Rachel, and Philip, in Arden, North Carolina.

VIEWER GUIDE

❧

(For use in each session.)

Session No. ___   Session Title _____

Henry Blackaby's Teaching

_____

_____

_____

_____

_____

Mel Blackaby's Teaching

_____

_____

_____

_____

_____

Decisions/Actions you will take from this session:

_____

_____

_____

_____

ABOUT THIS STUDY

Welcome to this study. Over the next eight weeks of study you will be expanding your understanding of God's plan for His church. His church is a living organism with Christ as its Head, the Spirit as its Power, the world as its mission and the kingdom as its focus. The church is held together by covenant expressed as koinonia—a loving, caring ministry to the body.

You may say this description fits your church beautifully, or you may not recognize your church in many of these descriptors. Whatever the case, this study will help you build on the foundation He has laid to strengthen and mature the fellowship. This process will be achieved through several ways:

Daily Workbook Studies ✳ Each week contains five study segments which you can read daily or spread over seven days. We do not recommend your reading the material in one day's sitting. You will not retain the material in the flurry to finish.

Bible Activities ✳ You may be asked to look up Scriptures that are not in the margin. Finding these verses will strengthen your Bible study skills and enrich your life.

Learning Activities ✳ The activities which you complete help you personalize the study. They may ask you to choose between several options, tell a personal experience, or put a mark where you find yourself on a continuum of opposites.

Group Experience ✳ Come to your weekly group meeting ready to discuss the material you read and ask questions. Did you know that participation is the best way to learn?

ABOUT THE VIDEO

After you have discussed the previous week's topic, you will watch a 25 minute video while writing on the viewer guide (the front side of this sheet). The video will have 4 components.

Introduction ✳ Mel Blackaby introduces each segment. These segments were filmed in the breathtaking Canadian Rockies.

Seminar Teaching ✳ Both Henry and Mel teach at a "Your Church Experiencing God Together Conference" at First Baptist Church, Jonesboro, Georgia. Some of the sessions include a question-answer period that followed each conference session.

Documentary ✳ Henry believes the church that practices the principles embodied in this book most closely is Bow Valley Baptist Church in Cochrane, Alberta, Canada. Our video crew went to Cochrane and interviewed Mel, his wife Gina, and key leaders in the church to hear how this church functions.

Closing Prayer ✳ Mel closes each session in prayer.

INTRODUCTION

I am amazed to see how God has used *Experiencing God: Knowing and Doing the Will of God* to help people know and do His will. As important as this book has been to many people, *Your Church Experiencing God Together* is a necessary sequel. Christians must make the transition from knowing and doing the will of God as an individual to knowing and doing the will of God within a corporate body of believers. *Experiencing God* helped people get on track with God; this book will guide their journey within the family of God.

I asked my son Mel to co-author this work with me. Not only does he have much practical experience as a pastor of an exciting church, but he has also earned his Ph.D., focusing a great deal of study on the nature of the church and its relationship to the kingdom of God. Although I will guide you through this study, Mel and I have worked very closely on this project. You will enjoy wonderful anecdotes from Mel's ministry that we have inserted to illustrate the truths we seek to communicate.

This book will deal with many significant questions:
- *What did God have in mind when He chose to save us?*
- *Although He saved us individually, what is the corporate nature of God's great salvation?*
- *What does it mean to be born into the family of God?*
- *How does God want us to relate to other Christians around the world?*

We will also ask some reflective questions.
- *When people attend our churches, do they experience a well-run organization or the presence of God?*
- *Do our churches reveal the collective knowledge of people or the manifest (obvious) wisdom of God?*
- *Does the world see our churches as places where good people do good things for God, or do they see the power of God working through His people to do what only He can accomplish?*
- *How can God use our churches to touch a world in need of God's great salvation?*

Each week of *Your Church Experiencing God Together* will unpack specific dimensions of God's great salvation and the purposes of God for our lives. When God's ideal is realized, the impact upon an individual, a church, a community, or a nation, will be enormous.

I can't tell you how many times I hear Christians crying out for something more in their relationship with God. They have accepted Christ into their lives, but they don't know what to do next. They hear others talking about abundant life in Christ, but abundant life seems to be just beyond their grasp. They become frustrated and depressed, even to the point of desperation. Their struggle tends to come from the fact that they have never understood the nature of God's great salvation. More specifically, they have never understood the corporate nature of salvation and their significant place within the people of God.

We often read the simple record of the first church in Jerusalem described in Acts 2:46-47. "Every day they devoted themselves to meeting together in the temple complex, and broke bread from house to house. They ate their food with gladness and simplicity of heart, praising God and having favor with all the people. And every day the Lord added those being saved to them." Oh, how the early believers were overwhelmed with the grace of God and the power of the Holy Spirit in their midst! They were hungry to grow in their knowledge of God, and they experienced love for one another in a way they had never known.

THE CHURCH LIFE GOD HAS PLANNED FOR YOU

As a pastor, I earnestly sought for our church to experience the fullness of life that I knew was available. I longed for the manifest presence of God in our midst and a quality of love that could only come from Him. It was amazing what we experienced as a church, and it seemed to grow from year to year. Even in the midst of trials, we knew the joy of the Lord as we walked together as a church. I can recount much heartache that people endured, but they never endured it alone. We were a family.

I have fond memories of a church that was open seven days a week, simply because people liked to be there. I can still see the cars that lined the street, the students coming to our theological college, and the constant laughter in the foyer. I remember many visitors recounting that when they first approached the building, they had a sense of God's presence. As they entered, they immediately saw joy and excitement on people's faces. Often at the close of a service there would be people deep in conversation, others weeping, still others praying. Nobody was in a hurry to go home; they would rather linger in the presence of God with their church family. People hesitated to take trips over the weekend, because they didn't want to miss what God would do on Sundays as we gathered for worship. And God added regularly those who were being saved.

Sound too good to be true? Sound like something you have longed for? I have also known times when this wasn't true, but once I tasted what God could do in and through a church, I didn't want to settle for anything less. I have come to realize that God's purpose for the church is much grander than many people have experienced or even know is possible. God has provided everything we need in Christ, "who is the head over every ruler and authority" (Col. 2:10). What He has planned for His people is far beyond us—it is infinite in dimension.

We must remember that God's purposes and ways are from eternity to eternity. He seeks to bring salvation to mankind and expand the kingdom of God through His people. God is creating for Himself a people through whom He can accomplish His purposes in our world. His eyes go " 'to and fro throughout the earth that He may strongly support those whose heart is completely His' " (2 Chron. 16:9). Jesus established the church as a divine institution for the proclamation and extension of the kingdom.

The church is not need-centered or people-centered, but God-centered. When the church is God-centered, the people will know His awesome presence. When God grants His presence to a church, He expresses His wisdom, His power, and His activity to accomplish His purposes.

RE-CAPTURING THE FEAR OF GOD
How do we come to experience God in this way? Listen to what the Lord says in Proverbs 2:1-5:

> My son, if you will receive my saying,
> And treasure my commandments within you,
> Make your ear attentive to wisdom,
> Incline your heart to understanding;
> For if you cry for discernment,
> Lift your voice for understanding;
> If you seek her as silver,
> And search for her as for hidden treasures;
> Then you will discern the fear of the Lord,
> And discover the knowledge of God.

According to the Scriptures, the "fear of the Lord is the beginning of wisdom" (Prov. 9:10). Have you studied in order that you might fear the Lord? Almost everything in the evangelical community is against that. We have been told that we should have a good time, celebrate, praise, and shout to God, but don't fear Him. In fact, what we need more than at any other time in human history is to fear the Lord our God.

To lose the fear of God is to lose the fear of sin. To lose the fear of sin is to lose the relationship with God. Don't let anybody tell you that to fear the Lord just means to have an awe of Him. It means far more than that. It takes much more than one little word to describe the fear of the Lord.

We may choose to play games with God, but " 'the fear of the Lord' " indicates that God is not playing games with us. He expects that we " 'fear the Lord your God, to walk in all His ways and love Him, and to serve the Lord your God with all your heart and with all your soul, and to keep the Lord's commandments' " (Deut. 10:12-13). When we choose to take God seriously, when we begin to fear the Lord, He will grant us wisdom beyond our human capacity to understand. He will show us the way of more abundant life. Let me finish the wonderful passage I started earlier by quoting Proverbs 2:6-11:

> The Lord gives wisdom;
> From His mouth come knowledge and understanding.
> He stores up sound wisdom for the upright;
> He is a shield to those who walk in integrity,
> Guarding the paths of justice,
> And He preserves the way of His godly ones.
> Then you will discern righteousness and justice
> And equity and every good course.
> For wisdom will enter your heart,
> And knowledge will be pleasant to your soul;
> Discretion will guard you,
> Understanding will watch over you.

God desires to give you wisdom and show you His purpose for your life. Be prepared to receive all that God teaches you through the Holy Spirit. The fear of the Lord is the beginning of wisdom, so seek to know God as He has made Himself known in the Scriptures. Through *Your Church Experiencing God Together*, Mel and I pray that God will reveal Himself, His purposes, and His ways to you in a much deeper way as you go through this study.

Bow Valley Baptist Church
Cochrane, Alberta

Henry Blackaby Ministries
Atlanta, Georgia

God Has No Orphans

By obedience to the truth, having purified yourselves for sincere love of the brothers,
love one another earnestly from a pure heart, since you have been born again—
... through the living and enduring word of God.

1 PETER 1:22-23

Frank enjoys outdoor activities such as camping, fishing, and hunting. These activities take him away from church two to three weekends a month. Frank says he needs the R&R from his high-pressure job. Besides, a person can worship God on a river bank just as easily as in a church building.

As Marge has grown older, she has developed the Sunday morning habit of curling up on her couch to watch her favorite television preacher rather than going to the trouble of getting dressed for church. True, no one in her Sunday School class calls much anymore, and she does miss her church friends. However, she tells herself that the main thing is to get spiritually fed, and that dynamic TV preacher certainly does feed her!

Frank and Marge consider church attendance optional. They apparently feel no responsibility for fellow church members. They sense no call from God on their time or resources to accomplish God's purpose for their church.

Is it possible to be a committed, growing Christian and not be an active part of His body, the local church? This week we will discuss God's plan for every Christian's life. As you read, look for the answers to these key questions:

1. What is the difference between being saved and experiencing the full measure of God's great salvation?
2. How does God's great salvation relate to your involvement in a local church?
3. Can an individual experience the fullness of God's great salvation outside the fellowship of a church family?
4. How does the love between Christians impact the effectiveness of evangelism?
5. Have you been so focused on your church that you have neglected your responsibilities within the larger kingdom of God?

Placed into a Love Relationship

As a pastor, I saw more than my share of heart-wrenching life situations. I recall one in particular. The husband had been an alcoholic most of his adult life. Although he had become a Christian, he still struggled to stay away from drinking. I was glad that he chose to join our church, for I knew he would benefit from the genuine love in our fellowship.

One day the man got word that both of his parents had died suddenly. He was alone when he heard the devastating news and turned to alcohol to hide his pain. While driving home, he hit another car but drove on without stopping. Fortunately nobody was hurt, but he was arrested and jailed. A small group of deacons from our church drove to the jail to minister to him. They secured his release and offered help through a difficult time.

I drove to his wife's workplace to tell her what had happened and that several of our men were with her husband. I reassured her of the church's love for her family and that her Savior's love was ever present in times of need. I took her home, and a group of us prayed together. The Lord graciously redeemed this man and his wife. As far as I know, he never drank again. In fact, he later found a place of service in our church.

Years later the couple's son approached me at a conference. Although he recalled the pain of growing up in the home of an alcoholic, he said, "You will never know what the love of your church did for my dad and mom and for me as their son. Because of the love I saw in your church, I responded to God's call into the ministry and am serving Him in my own church. Thank you! I've always wanted to tell you what your church meant to my family."

On the figures below, write the names of church members who ministered to you in times of need. Thank God for the way they demonstrated love to you.

God intends your local church family to care *for* you and *about* you. If you are not a member of a caring local church, ask God to guide you to begin the process of becoming a caring church.

No matter what mistakes we have made, God cares for those who have chosen to enter a love relationship with Him. God has no orphans—only family. He has made Christ the Head of the churches He has established, in order that He might bring healing through His people who have come to know His saving grace. That is the strategy of God's redemptive plan to touch a world.

If you are a member of a local church, by the direction and will of God, you are exactly where God wants you and where God will unfold to you the fullness of salvation. And it is here that God will cause you to reach out to a lost world for His glory.

SALVATION FROM GOD'S PERSPECTIVE

The deepest longing of our hearts is to have a relationship with God. When God saved us, what was on His heart? What did He do to accomplish it? How does He implement His purposes in our lives? To answer these questions is to unfold the heart of God's message in the Bible, for the Scriptures reveal God, His purposes, and His ways so that we don't miss His activity in our lives. To experience God daily as He intended, we must have a thorough understanding of the greatness of salvation from God's perspective.

> *"This is eternal life: that they may know You, the only true God, and the One You have sent— Jesus Christ."*
>
> ❧ JOHN 17:3 ❧

Read Hebrews 2:1-3 in the margin. It would be tragic for people to receive the riches of the gospel and then live as spiritual paupers, to accept such great love from Christ and then resent what He asks in return. Have we neglected God's great salvation and lived our lives far below what God purposed when He chose to save us?

Many Christians accept the gift of salvation because they want to go to heaven when they die, but they don't understand God's total plan and purpose in salvation and the unparalleled cost to God to grant it. Consequently, they neglect major dimensions of the Christian life and don't experience the incredible relationship with God made possible by His salvation. They live in black and white without seeing the full spectrum of colors in all their beauty.

> *We must therefore pay even more attention to what we have heard, so that we will not drift away. For if the message spoken through angels was legally binding, and every transgression and disobedience received a just punishment, how will we escape if we neglect such a great salvation?*
>
> ❧ HEBREWS 2:1-3 ❧

Which phrase best describes your spiritual life?
- ❑ I am a spiritual pauper, living far below what God purposed for me when He chose to save me.
- ❑ I live in the spiritual middle-class, not quite poor but definitely not rich.
- ❑ I live as a child of the King, enjoying the full riches of salvation.

I hear non-Christians say, "I feel there's something more to life than I am currently experiencing." What they are missing is God's great salvation. But I also hear Christians say, "I feel there's something more to the *Christian* life than I am currently experiencing." What they are missing is God's great salvation! They have not understood what God accomplished on their behalf. Their hearts have never been opened to understand what motivated God when He chose to save them from their sins and caused them to be born again into the family of God. This study will take us back into the heart of God and His purpose for our lives.

At a conference in southern California, I encountered a couple who had driven almost six hundred miles simply to say, "Thank you." They had studied one of my previous books, *Experiencing God: Knowing and Doing the Will of God,* when suddenly they were overwhelmed by the fullness of life that God promised to them. As tears ran down this man's face, he explained that he had taught theology in a well-known Bible college, but he had never understood what it meant to walk with God in real and practical ways. He also expressed the need to ask God's forgiveness for having taught many young students about God without helping them know how to walk with God. Now in their late 60s, this couple had a renewed joy and excitement concerning their relationship to God and an enthusiasm to serve Him with all their hearts.

I have heard stories similar to this far too often—of individuals who were content to gather information about God and to feel secure in their eternal reward but who missed out on the greatness of God's salvation and the love relationship He sought to develop with us. If we do not understand the extent of God's accomplished work on our behalf, we will never experience abundant life, nor will we fulfill God's purpose for our lives. God is not primarily interested in making us successful; instead, His heart desires for us to experience the full measure of His great salvation.

> God is not primarily interested in making us successful; instead, His heart desires for us to experience the full measure of His great salvation.

Read the following Scriptures and draw a line to match the reference with the actions God took to initiate and cultivate a love relationship with humanity.

Deuteronomy 7:6	God demonstrated His love by sending Christ to die for sinners.
Isaiah 43:1	God chose His people to be His treasured possession.
Romans 5:8	God saved sinners out of His mercy, love, and kindness.
Titus 3:4-5	God redeemed and called His people by name.

Can you recall a time when you were overwhelmed by the greatness of God's salvation as you studied the Scriptures?

❏ Yes ❏ No   If so, in the margin briefly describe that time.

CHARACTERISTICS OF GOD'S GREAT SALVATION

What do I mean by God's great salvation? Today we will look at two characteristics. *First,* salvation is always granted on God's terms. One of the great truths concerning God's salvation is found in John 6:44. In the margin read what Jesus said.

Have you understood how significant that statement is concerning your life? God has called you into a love relationship with Himself through Jesus Christ. You are special. You are the object of God's calling. You did not choose Him; He chose you. You can count on it: your salvation began in the heart of God.

Fill in the blanks of John 6:44 with your name:

_____ can't come to God unless the Father
  (Your name)

who sent Me draws _____
                                    (Your name)

How do you feel about the truth that God actually chose you? Underline all that apply.

special	unworthy	overwhelmed	skeptical
grateful	like singing	confused	elated

Second, God's salvation reflects His nature. The most identifiable characteristic of salvation is the quality of our love, first toward God and then toward His people. Without a love relationship on both levels, vertically and horizontally, we have not experienced God's great salvation. If we get this basic truth wrong, we are in desperate trouble. God's strategy to touch a world is vitally linked with these two basic relationships.

Fill in the blanks on the vertical and horizontal beams of the cross below, using the concept Jesus taught in Matthew 22:37-40.

If either one of the beams is missing, is the figure a cross?
❑ Yes   ❑ No

"No one can come to Me unless the Father who sent Me draws him."
❧ JOHN 6:44 ❧

CHARACTERISTICS OF
GOD'S GREAT SALVATION
1. Granted on God's terms
2. Reflects God's nature

He said to him, "'You shall love the Lord your God with all your heart, with all your soul, and with all your mind.' This is the greatest and most important commandment. The second is like it: 'You shall love your neighbor as yourself.' All the Law and the Prophets depend on these two commandments."
❧MATTHEW 22:37-40❧

> *"'You shall love the Lord your God with all your heart, with all your soul, and with all your mind.' This is the greatest and most important commandment. The second is like it: 'You shall love your neighbor as yourself.' All the Law and the Prophets depend on these two commandments."*
>
> ✤ MATTHEW 22:37-40 ✤

If one element of a love relationship is missing, either love for God or for others, is God's salvation fully experienced?
❏ Yes ❏ No

I was in Tampa, Florida, when I received a call from my third son, Mel. He and his wife had just received news that their seven-month-old daughter had cerebral palsy. Mel is probably the most sensitive of my five children, and I knew he was hurting. He began to weep as we spoke.

After I hung up the phone, I turned to the only place I knew to go. I went into the presence of the One who created that little girl. Does God know my granddaughter? He does! Does God know my son? He does indeed! As I went through that experience, I came to know the tender love of God in a way I couldn't have known before.

I remember being in their home about two years later. She ran to me with a slight limp in her walk, put her arms around my leg, and hung on as though her life depended on it. Everywhere I went she wanted to follow me. She would look up with a big smile and say, "I love you, Grandpa!"

That child has taken to her grandpa. Do you know why? Because her grandpa has taken to her. Do you know why we love our Lord? Because He first loved us. In fact, while we were yet sinners, God loved us enough to send His only Son to die for our sins and set us free to know and experience Him. You can count on it: the more we experience God's love, the more we are drawn into His presence.

Check which statement best describes your life.
❏ I feel there is something more to life than I am currently experiencing.
❏ I feel there is something more to the Christian life than I am currently experiencing.
❏ I occasionally catch glimpses of what it means to experience God's great salvation.
❏ I fully enjoy God's great salvation.

If you checked the first choice, this course will have little meaning for you until you trust Jesus Christ as your Savior and acknowledge Him to be the Lord of your life. Turn to page 179 and discover how to become a Christian.

Placed into a Spiritual Family

According to God's divine eternal plan of salvation, those who enter a relationship with Him through Jesus Christ are automatically born into the family of God. God has no orphans! Believers now have the capacity to enjoy an intimate love relationship with the Heavenly Father and the rest of His children.

Just as God designed for a baby to be born into a family to receive love and care, so He designed for those who are born again to enter a spiritual family that will love and care for them. Without a thorough understanding of our place in the family of God, our Christian life will not be the abundant life Jesus offered.

To all who did receive Him,
He gave them the right to be
children of God,
to those who believe in His name,
who were born,
not of blood,
or of the will of the flesh,
or of the will of man,
but of God.

❧ JOHN 1:12-13 ❧

ADDITIONAL CHARACTERISTICS OF GOD'S GREAT SALVATION

In Day 1 we examined two characteristics of God's great salvation: It is granted on God's terms and reflects His nature. Today we will look at four additional characteristics.

The *third* characteristic grows out of a confusion between the words *personal* and *private*. Unfortunately, when people are challenged to become involved with the family of God in a particular church, some refuse and keep their distance. They may say, "My relationship with God is private." Although that statement may accurately reflect their experience, it's not biblical.

Our relationship with God is personal, but it was never meant to be private. Salvation is intensely personal, but God never planned for our salvation to be private.

Check the phrase that most accurately describes your relationship with God.
❑ Relationship with God? What do you mean?
❑ My relationship with God is intensely private. Religion is something best kept quiet and to one's self.
❑ My relationship with God is personal but not private. I live out that relationship through involvement with my local church congregation.
If you are discouraged by your lack of relationship with God and His people, ask God to help you listen as He speaks to you through this study.

Fourth, Everything in the Bible, Old Testament and New Testament, bears witness to the corporate life of God's children; this is by God's eternal design and purpose. New birth places a person automatically

CHARACTERISTICS OF GOD'S GREAT SALVATION
1. Granted on God's terms
2. Reflects God's nature
3. Personal but not private
4. Births us into a spiritual family

into a spiritual family with other believers. In a local church they are to be nourished, fed, protected, and guided toward spiritual maturity. Just as a child, when born into a physical family, has family, friends, and neighbors who rejoice in the birth, so it is the same when a person is born again. He or she is born into a spiritual family who has prayed for this moment, and they celebrate their entrance into the family of God.

We should not equate *spiritual* with *invisible* and *private,* for the Spirit-filled life is obvious to all who see it. The Bible describes Christians as the salt of the earth who make a recognizable difference, a candle that gives light in a dark world, and a city set on a hill that all can see. Jesus didn't say that we *have* salt and light. Jesus said that we *are* salt and light and will by our very nature impact everybody we encounter. The influence we exert is always the influence of what we are. Jesus challenges every believer to confess Him as Lord publicly and to live for Christ openly.

> We should not equate *spiritual* with *invisible* and *private.*

How important is the care of a family to the life of a child?

unnecessary   essential

How should a church care for a new believer?

_____

_____

We cannot live our faith in isolation; that would run contrary to the purpose of God's salvation. No one who served God faithfully in the Bible had a relationship to God in private. Rather, each had a significant involvement with God's people, for that is where God's heart is found. This was certainly true in Jesus' life and His relationship to the Father.

Salvation automatically makes God our Father and every other believer our brother or sister in the household of God. Today many people openly acknowledge their faith in Christ, but they have nothing to do with God's people and feel no connection to them. According to God's purpose, as revealed in the Scriptures, Christians are not in some way separated unto themselves. Together, we are "heirs of God and co-heirs with Christ"(Rom. 8:17).

> *You are no longer foreigners and strangers, but fellow citizens with the saints, and members of God's household.*
> ❧ EPHESIANS 2:19 ❧

Read Ephesians 2:19. Circle the phrase that best describes how you feel in relation to God's family:

Foreigner and stranger   Member of God's family

Read Romans 8:15. List the two types of spirits identified in this verse:

Spirit of _____   Spirit of _____

Make an X over the spirit that would cause the label of "foreigner and stranger" to characterize someone. Put a cross over the Spirit that assures believers they are God's children. Check the spirit that most often controls your life.

You did not receive a spirit of slavery to fall back into fear, but you received the Spirit of adoption, by whom we cry out, "Abba, Father!"

❧ ROMANS 8:15 ❧

A child born into my family will automatically experience many things that happen only in our family. This is true with God and His family. For example, only the Israelites experienced the joy and power of God during the time of the exodus. God's family was awestruck by the many miracles of God. But if you were not a part of His family, you did not receive the blessings of that relationship.

To the family of Israel God gave the law with a great display of power. To the family He provided manna, quail, and water. To the family He provided guidance through a cloud by day and a pillar of fire by night. As a result, the family experienced the care of the Heavenly Father.

The same is true today. God places His children in His family. He planned it this way. The local church is crucial to the life of every believer's unfolding relationship with God.

How do you view those who are in the family of God? Perhaps the proper questions to consider are how does God view your relationship to those who are in the family of God, and how does He intend for you to relate to other Christians?

Fifth, the most convincing evidence that we have received the gift of salvation is that we demonstrate Christlike love to other believers. "We have this command from Him: the one who loves God must also love his brother" (1 John 4:21). All who call Christ Lord are now our brothers or sisters, and God expects us to treat them as His family. He expects us to love other Christians just as much as He loves them. First John 3:16 says, "This is how we have come to know love: He laid down His life for us. We should also lay down our lives for our brothers." That is a powerful statement of God's love and a penetrating statement about how much we should love the family of God.

CHARACTERISTICS OF
GOD'S GREAT SALVATION
1. Granted on God's terms
2. Reflects God's nature
3. Personal but not private
4. Births us into a spiritual family
5. Demonstrated by love

Read 1 John 3:14. What is the most convincing evidence we have received the gift of salvation? Underline it.

Do you recognize how seriously God takes your relationship with other believers?   ❏ Yes ❏ No

We know that we have passed from death to life because we love our brothers. The one who does not love remains in death.

❧ I JOHN 3:14 ❧

Have you made the connection? Would you pass God's test of love for other believers? ❑ Yes ❑ No

When our daughter was born, we already had four boys. She automatically had older brothers, whether she liked it or not. We had already been nourishing, teaching, and caring for the older boys. If she was going to grow and develop in our family, our daughter would have to learn to love her brothers. If she loved her parents, she would love the other children whom her parents loved. Similarly, the rest of the family uniquely loved Carrie. Each brother would grow to love her because of our love for her. So it is with a church family. God deeply loves each one and has made a significant investment in his or her life. To love God, then, is to love each member in the family.

We must always see as God sees. For a Christian to consciously refuse to love the children of God for whom Christ died is to dishonor His death and ridicule His love. But when we walk in a loving relationship with God's people, the testimony to the world is profound.

God does things in, for, and through His family that He does nowhere else! He manifests His presence in special ways when two or three are gathered together (Matt. 18:20). We are not living life alone. Just as biological families must interact and spend significant time together, so our spiritual family must walk together in love.

> *"By this all people will know that you are My disciples, if you have love for one another."*
>
> ♣ JOHN 13:35 ♣

Read John 13:35. Circle the words you would use to describe the love you have for your Christian family. Add other words in the margin.

earnest   nonexistent   half-hearted   inconsistent

pure   inadequate   sincere   growing   affirming

In God's family we will receive strength, encouragement, and much-needed fellowship. We will grow in wisdom and maturity as we benefit from those who have walked with God for many years. We will find security in the family's watch care over our lives and respond to its comfort and accountability.

Sixth, after all God has done on our behalf, we must respond with complete submission to His will. When the family gathers, the Father is always present and active. He speaks to the family. He gives gifts in the family. He gives direction to the family. He gives His power to the family. When Christians are joined with the family, the Father is free to pour out His blessing into our lives, even as He continually does to all who are related to Him.

Does your heart desire to gather with other believers in the family where God has placed you? When you get close to the heart of your

CHARACTERISTICS OF GOD'S GREAT SALVATION

1. Granted on God's terms
2. Reflects God's nature
3. Personal but not private
4. Births us into a spiritual family
5. Demonstrated by love
6. Submitted to God's will

Heavenly Father, His love for each member will be laid over your heart as well. Are you investing your life in the people of God and joining them in fulfilling God's purposes? God has no orphans! He desires for you to walk with His family.

Place an X on the scale to indicate the degree of your desire to join with God's people in fulfilling His purposes.

0%   100%

Placed into a Living Body

The call to salvation is a call to be on mission with God, but we cannot be on mission with Him effectively unless we are vitally connected to the church. This is God's eternal strategy to touch the world. We have already seen how God the Father draws people into a love relationship with Christ the Savior. A critical Scripture that describes what Christ does upon receiving people whom the Father draws is Matthew 16:15-18. Read it in the margin. Examine carefully what the Father was doing and how Christ responded to the Father's activity.

When Jesus asked the disciples who they thought He was, Peter answered, " 'You are the Messiah, the Son of the living God!' " When Jesus heard Peter's answer, He basically said, "Peter, you are very fortunate, because flesh and blood did not reveal this to you." Now remember, Jesus was flesh and blood. He had not made known His true nature to the disciples; instead, the Heavenly Father opened Peter's understanding and revealed to him that Jesus was the Messiah, the Son of the living God.

This pattern of God's activity is consistent with what we see in other passages of Scripture. The apostle Paul described the activity of God's Spirit to reveal spiritual truth. Read 1 Corinthians 2:12-14 in the margin.

CRITERIA FOR BUILDING A CHURCH

Peter had insight into the nature of Christ, because God's Spirit revealed it to him. But as soon as the Father revealed that Jesus was the Messiah, Jesus immediately made the statement, " 'On this rock I will build My church.' " What was the rock? What was the foundation upon which He would build His church?

Jesus was essentially saying, "On the basis of My Heavenly Father's activity in the hearts of people, convincing them that I am the Messiah, the Son of the living God, I will build my church." Now when Jesus

"But you," He asked them, "who do you say that I am?"

Simon Peter answered, "You are the Messiah, the Son of the living God!"

And Jesus responded, "Blessed are you, Simon son of Jonah, because flesh and blood did not reveal this to you, but My Father in heaven. And I also say to you that you are Peter, and on this rock I will build My church, and the forces of Hades will not overpower it."

❧ MATTHEW 16:15-18 ❧

We have not received the spirit of the world, but the Spirit who is from God, in order to know what has been freely given to us by God. ... But the natural man does not welcome what comes from God's Spirit, because it is foolishness to him; he is not able to know it since it is evaluated spiritually.

❧ 1 CORINTHIANS 2:12-14 ❧

builds His church upon the Father's activity in the hearts of people, a dramatic event takes place. The Holy Spirit convinces people of truth. The gates of hell will not prevail against that group of people, for the Spirit of God is actively drawing them and guiding them to His Son, who has come to do His perfect will.

What was the rock upon which the church would be built? Cross out all that don't apply.

1. Peter, the man
2. Peter's confession of Jesus as the Messiah
3. God's activity in the hearts of people

Is it true that when Jesus builds His church, the gates of hell will not prevail against it? What is the next logical conclusion? We must ask ourselves: Has Jesus built this church or have we built this church? Has my denomination built this church? How do we know if people built our church or if Jesus built it?

Our problem is that we are capable of running a religious organization, and we have learned to do it well. But too often our standard for evaluating the success of our church is to observe how large it has become. Church growth is not the biblical standard to evaluate the health of a church. A church can grow through effective marketing, but Christ may not have had anything to do with it. Jesus said, " 'I will build My church.' " Yet we run around to church growth conferences to discover how we can build a successful church. Most conferences do not tell us how to recognize the activity of Jesus as He builds His church.

Upon which rock do you desire your church to be built?

1. Solid budget
2. Charismatic leaders
3. Well-equipped and furnished building
4. God's activity in the hearts of people

In this passage, Jesus gave two criteria for building His church.
1. The gates of hell will be coming down. God's strategy to bring down the gates of hell and to touch a world is found in the local church. So, no matter what we say, if our lives are not significantly related to the people of God in a local church, we are not effectively on mission with Him.
2. We will be using the keys to the kingdom of heaven to free people from the bondage of sin and to bring them into the

presence of God. His strategy of evangelism is the interdependence of each member related to the body and following Christ as the Head.

Do these two criteria characterize your church?
❑ Yes ❑ Partially ❑ No

If you answered *yes*, pause for a prayer of thanksgiving. If you answered *no*, pray that your church will become the church that Christ builds.

Those who resist gathering with God's people in a local congregation are not storming the gates of hell nor showing evidence of their salvation. In fact, one of the evidences of salvation is that Christians love other Christians (John 13:14,34-35; John 15:12,17; 1 John 2:9). Those who choose to stand aloof or refuse to be involved in a church have a serious heart problem.

Read the following passages and fill in the blanks:

John 13:34. " 'I give you a new commandment: that you

_____ _____ _____.' "

John 13:35. " 'By this all people will know that you are My

disciples, if you have _____ _____ _____ _____.' "

John 15:12. " 'This is My commandment: that you _____

____ _____.' "

A Christian cannot stand outside the church, mock it, laugh at it, or call it a hypocrite; it runs against every fiber of faith. Christians *love* the church and would give their lives for it.

In fact, 1 John 2:19 says that those who leave the church and never return were not really saved in the first place, for no one who has the Spirit of God can turn away from the people of God. To be on mission with God is to be involved in the church, God's strategy to touch the world.

To love God is to love God's people.

A LOVING ENVIRONMENT

Some of my best memories have come in the context of a loving church family. They were there to witness my conversion and public profession of faith through baptism. They were there to teach me

God's Word as a child and pray for me as I grew through the struggles of life. They affirmed my call into the ministry and encouraged me with opportunities to serve my Lord.

They first placed the passion for missions in my heart and taught me to share my faith with the lost. They helped me care for the poor and the broken as we went together to the rescue mission of our city. They taught me to pray as we gathered together in prayer meetings. They helped me appreciate music as we sang our praises to the God who saved us. They celebrated my marriage and cared for my children as God added them to my life. They wept with me during personal crisis and family loss. They loved me! Actually, God was loving me through them. I know that I would not be the person I am today without God's placing me into the care of His family in a local church.

On the timeline of your life, use one word descriptions of major events when God loved and cared for you through your church family.

childhood   youth   adult   senior adult

The fellowship in the early church was a constant source of joy for the believers. Every person who received the gospel and responded to Christ as Lord was immediately baptized, and God added each one to the church so they could grow in their faith.

Read Acts 2:41-47. Underline the activities of the early church.

As a result of these activities, the new believers grew in their faith as they were taught by the apostles, as they prayed with the apostles, and as they fellowshipped with their new spiritual family. Because they were together, each one benefited from the presence of God as He performed miracles in their midst.

The fellowship and love in this early church grew exponentially. They began to care for one another's physical needs, even if it meant selling their possessions so that a brother in the Lord could be blessed. The striking characteristic of this moment was that they loved to be together, for they experienced God together.

We need to understand that this was not an accident or a decision made by the believers; it was according to the divine purposes of God. Salvation brings believers into a relationship with God and His people, and both relationships are crucial.

Jesus knew this when He said, " 'I assure you: The one who receives whomever I send receives Me, and the one who receives Me receives Him who sent Me' " (John 13:20). The early believers grew

Those who accepted his message were baptized, and that day about three thousand people were added to them. And they devoted themselves to the apostles' teaching, to fellowship, to the breaking of bread, and to prayers.

Then fear came over everyone, and many wonders and signs were being performed through the apostles. Now all the believers were together and had everything in common. So they sold their possessions and property and distributed the proceeds to all, as anyone had a need. And every day they devoted themselves to meeting together in the temple complex, and broke bread from house to house. They ate their food with gladness and simplicity of heart, praising God and having favor with all the people. And every day the Lord added those being saved to them.

❧ ACTS 2:41-47 ❧

in their ability to have one mind and heart. Their fellowship moved from the temple to the homes and into the streets. As they gave God the glory, He continued to add to their number daily.

Look at your timeline on page 24. Was your church family's ministry to you similar to the ways the early Christians cared for one another? List similarities in the margin beneath the passage. Be prepared to share your response in your group time.

The Acts passage clearly pictures the incredible transformation in a believer's life. Whereas sin leads to independence and self-centeredness, salvation leads to radical interdependence and Christ-centeredness. Sin creates isolation, separation, and independence, all of which lead to utter destruction. Sin magnifies self and cuts us off from relationships that God intends for us to experience. But in God's salvation, "He has rescued us from the domain of darkness and transferred us into the kingdom of the Son" (Col. 1:13). His Son reigns in the lives of His people, and the particular expression of His reign is found in the local congregation of believers.

Whereas sin leads to independence and self-centeredness, salvation leads to radical interdependence and Christ-centeredness.

Identify how you feel about this statement by circling the appropriate words below: Believers can only fully experience God's great salvation within the fellowship of a local church family.

resistant   confused   intrigued   troubled

strengthened   humbled   convinced

The signs of a healthy Christian who has been set free from sin are first, interdependence with other believers and second, commitment to function within the body of Christ. Read Romans 12:5 in the margin. Paul gave a powerful statement of our interdependence and our corporate submission to the authority of Christ as Head of the body.

In the eternal and predetermined plan of God, He designed the local church to be the primary way for Christians to walk together and carry out the work of Christ. The fact that there are many local churches does not divide Christians; it unites them around a common purpose under the lordship of Christ. Children are born into the human race yet belong to a specific human family. In the same way, those who have been born into the kingdom of God are entrusted to the care of a loving church family.

The existence of many churches in a community does not imply a human corruption of sinful humanity; it was by God's design. The family imagery is common in Paul's writing to the church. "Like newborn infants, desire the unadulterated spiritual milk, so that you

We who are many are one body in Christ and individually members of one another.

✤ ROMANS 12:5 ✤

may grow by it in your salvation, since 'you have tasted that the Lord is good' " (1 Pet. 2:2-3). The church was intended to preach and teach the Word of God so new believers would grow into maturity.

The more we grow in our relationship to the Lord, the more intimate and loving we grow in our relationships to other believers. Just as the helplessness of a baby creates a bond with the ones who give care, so the babe in Christ develops a special bond with the church family that provides nurture and love. This response is not only natural but intentional. God designed for church families to enjoy a deep bond of love for one another.

Jesus said, " 'I will build My church' " (Matt. 16:18). Jesus calls people out of the world and gathers them together into a living body in which He lives and carries out His purpose. The Lord added to the church daily "those being saved" (Acts 2:47). God works by that pattern today. Those whom He saves, He immediately chooses to add to a local church.

DAY FOUR

Placed into the People of God

God has placed the parts, each one of them, in the body just as He wanted.

❧ 1 Corinthians 12:18 ❧

God has a purpose for every person in His family. His purpose, however, has a corporate dimension. Unless we understand the corporate dimension of salvation, we will never fulfill the purpose God had for our lives when He chose to save us.

From the beginning, God has worked through His people. Even when God chose to go to Moses, He did not go simply to bless Moses. He went to free and bless the entire people of God. The heart of God is always turned toward all of His people, because as the people of God go, so goes the redemption of the rest of the world.

Over the last few decades, the focus has shifted away from God's people to the lost. However, significant evangelism is a by-product of what God does with His people. If we bypass the people of God, we have shut down evangelism. But when we help the people of God know who they are in Christ and what God purposed for their lives through salvation, the world will be turned upside down.

The most significant statement of the Great Commission is " 'teaching them to observe everything I have commanded you. And remember, I am with you always, to the end of the age' " (Matt. 28:20). If God's people are not practicing everything Christ has commanded, they will be ineffective in evangelism. But those who are walking in an obedient love relationship with their Lord will naturally share the good news of the gospel with convincing power.

When we examine how the early apostles implemented the Great Commission, we may be surprised. The apostles were not focused on evangelizing the lost. Rather, they turned their attention to teach the people of God to obey all that Christ commanded. Acts 6 gives us another clear picture of this strategy.

Read Acts 6:2-4. What was the apostles' main priority?

_____

_____

The Twelve summoned the whole company of the disciples and said, "It would not be right for us to give up preaching about God to wait on tables. Therefore, brothers, select from among you seven men of good reputation, full of the Spirit and wisdom, whom we can appoint to this duty. But we will devote ourselves to prayer and to the preaching ministry."

✤ ACTS 6:2-4 ✤

A STORY FROM MEL BLACKABY

The Condition of God's People

I had the privilege of pastoring a small country church in west Texas while I attended seminary. I was a Canadian city boy trying to fit into small-town, cowboy country. My wife and I had a wonderful time serving the Lord in that place.

As the time drew near for us to minister in Canada, the church began the process of putting together a pastor search committee. One of the members of that committee made an interesting comment. He said, "Mel, you were an evangelistic pastor; we need to pray about the kind of pastor we should have follow you."

My response was, "Tell me what we did that was evangelistic."

"Well," he said, "we have had an incredible number of people baptized this past year; you must have been evangelistic."

True, many people had responded to the Lord and been baptized into the church, but I pointed out that my focus was not on evangelism. I taught and preached three major issues: (1) what it means to have a growing relationship with Christ, (2) the nature of the church as God intended, and (3) the absolute necessity of prayer.

When the members became excited about their walk with Christ, the community began to see a difference in their lives. When they understood the incredible potential of a healthy church that followed Christ as the Head, they found confidence to do His will. When they understood the power of prayer to transform lives, they began to cry out to God to save their friends and neighbors. Evangelism was a by-product of a people in love with their Lord.

This pattern has always been true among God's people. When the people of God were taught how to practice the truth of God's Word in their lives, evangelism was explosive. The key was the condition of God's people, not just a better church growth strategy. Who can forget the promise of God in 2 Chronicles 7:13-14, "If … My people who are called by My name humble themselves and pray, and seek My face and turn from their wicked ways, then I will hear from heaven, will forgive their sin, and will heal their land"? The key to touching our world is for the people of God to walk in a right relationship with Him and one another.

Read Acts 6:7 on page 28. What was the result of the apostles' decision to walk with God and invest in God's people?

_____

The preaching about God flourished, the number of the disciples in Jerusalem multiplied greatly, and a large group of priests became obedient to the faith.

❧ ACTS 6:7 ❧

The apostles' priority was to devote their efforts toward prayer and preaching. As a result of their decision to walk with God and invest in God's people, the number of the disciples in Jerusalem multiplied greatly.

Circle one or more of the keys to effective evangelism.

1. Inspiring evangelistic sermons
2. A church staff gifted in evangelism
3. Witnessing classes and weekly visitation
4. God's people in right relationship with Him and one another

5. Other:_____

Check the keys your church has used.

AN EXAMPLE FROM THE LIFE OF JESUS

An exciting statement of this twofold relationship with God and His people is recorded in Jesus' high priestly prayer in John 17. As you read the passage in the margin, listen to the heart of God for His people.

Jesus had an intimate relationship with His Heavenly Father. Though the relationship was thoroughly and intensely personal, it was not private. Jesus wanted them to know how deep His relationship with the Father was, so He brought the disciples to see and experience it (see John 14:7-11). Then He prayed that the disciples would have this same relationship with Him and His Father, so that their relationship with one another would be strengthened.

When this relationship was in effect, Jesus said that the world would believe that the Father had sent Him. He knew *relationship* was God's eternal strategy, and He lived it out with His disciples. Life in God's family in the local church is vital to world redemption.

*"I pray not only for these,
    but also for those
who believe in Me through
    their message.
May they all be one, just as You, Father,
are in Me and I am in You.
May they also be one in
Us, so that the world may believe
    You sent Me.
I have given them the glory that
    You have given to Me.
May they be one just as We are one.
I am in them and You are in Me.
May they be made completely one,
so that the world may know You sent Me
and that You have loved them just as
    You have loved Me."*

❧ JOHN 17:20-23 ❧

What was the most challenging statement or Scripture you read today? Explain why you found it challenging.

_____

_____

How will you obey God in responding to that challenge?

_____

_____

Placed into the Kingdom of God

Today we will study one more dimension of God's great salvation. The *seventh* characteristic of God's great salvation automatically brings us into the kingdom of God. The gospel of the kingdom of God was at the heart of Jesus' preaching. Jesus urged people to " 'seek first the *kingdom of God*' " (Matt. 6:33, italics mine), not *the church*, but He established the church as a divine institution for the proclamation and extension of the kingdom.

Check the response that most accurately reflects your experience: In my Christian journey I have focused most often on:
❏ The church ❏ The kingdom of God

Amazingly, many Christians have not been taught about the kingdom of God. They seek to follow Christ's teachings but don't realize that the kingdom was the focus of His teaching. The New Testament does not exhort people to seek the church, but to " 'seek first the kingdom of God.' " Christ did not say, "Truly, truly, I say to you, unless one is born of water and the Spirit, he cannot enter the *church*." Instead He said, "He cannot enter the *kingdom of God*" (John 3:5, italics mine). Jesus preached throughout the area around the Sea of Galilee, " 'Repent, because the kingdom of heaven has come near!' " (Matt. 3:2).

Which statement best describes your reaction when you hear the phrase "kingdom of God"?
❏ Absolutely nothing. I draw a complete blank.
❏ Some ethereal concept or place.
❏ Heaven—in the sweet by and by.
❏ Christ's rule over all that exists.
❏ Other _____

WHAT IS THE KINGDOM?

Let me take a moment to help you understand the nature of the kingdom. First of all, the kingdom is identified with the reign of Christ, who fulfilled the messianic promise of a coming King. The Scripture uses the phrases "kingdom of heaven," "kingdom of God," and "kingdom of Christ," all meaning essentially the same thing. Simply to describe the kingdom in terms of territory or even the subjects under the King does not do it justice. Kingdom is king dominion, kingly jurisdiction. The primary idea is kingly authority.

When Jesus said, " 'Repent, because the kingdom of heaven has come near!' " what did He mean? How was it right next to them?

CHARACTERISTICS OF
GOD'S GREAT SALVATION
1. Granted on God's terms
2. Reflects God's nature
3. Personal but not private
4. Births us into a spiritual family
5. Demonstrated by love
6. Submitted to God's will
7. Seeks first the kingdom

The kingdom was right in front of them because He was there. And they were about to see the rule of the King.

They saw Him rule over—

- sickness as He healed the lepers;
- nature as He calmed the storms;
- evil spirits as He cast them out of those trapped under their control;
- death as He raised the dead to life;
- all things, for there was nothing that the King could not do.

When Jesus told them that the kingdom was near, He was indicating that the King had come to invite them to live under His rule.

Deepen your understanding of the kingdom of God by completing these statements:

1. The kingdom is identified with the _____ of Christ.

2. The primary idea is kingly _____.

We need a fresh understanding of the kingdom's centrality and its powerful influence on our lives and on the churches across our world. Without such an understanding, we'll live our lives outside the purpose of God's great salvation. We won't know where we belong in the schema of God's strategy to touch the world. Remember, He desires that His kingdom come on earth as it is in heaven. Churches aren't an end to themselves; they are to build the kingdom of God. That's why Christ established the church.

Read the words you wrote in the blanks above. Most likely you recorded "reign (or rule) and authority." On the scale below, indicate with an X who has the reign (or rule) and authority over you.

me   Christ

Based on your response, is the kingdom of heaven near to you?
❑ Yes ❑ Sometimes ❑ No

KINGDOM CITIZENS

Some people struggle with the concept of the kingdom of God because it appears to be beyond them and in some way out of their control. Some find it hard enough to function in the local church, let alone function with other churches in the kingdom. However, we are kingdom citizens serving the King of kings and Lord of lords. If all we accomplish is building our church to the neglect of the kingdom, we are neglecting a major dimension of God's great salvation.

The basis for Christian unity among all believers is found in the kingdom of God. All who have been born again have entered the kingdom and are brothers and sisters in Christ, living together under the rule of their King. Everyone who responds to the gospel of the kingdom has a spiritual relationship that must be expressed through mutual love. Christ prayed for unity among God's people so that the world would see God's love in them.

Anyone doing the work of the kingdom is to be encouraged and supported. Although all churches do not structurally combine their efforts in kingdom work, all churches ought to applaud other groups and not compete with or fight against them. The key to cooperation between Christians is not whether they are like us but whether they are doing kingdom work. The kingdom provides the impetus for brotherly love and cooperation.

How should we treat other believers who are not following Jesus exactly the way we think they should? Jesus gave John a clear answer to this question. Read Jesus' answer in the margin.

How can you support someone doing kingdom work in—

1. another church in your town? _____

2. another country?_____

3. a parachurch organization?_____

John said to Him, "Teacher, we saw someone driving out demons in Your name, and we tried to stop him because he wasn't following us."

"Don't stop him," said Jesus, "because there is no one who will perform a miracle in My name who can soon afterward speak evil of Me. For whoever is not against us is for us. And whoever gives you a cup of water to drink because of My name, since you belong to the Messiah, I assure you: He will never lose his reward."

❧ MARK 9:38-41 ❧

It takes all Christians working together in God's kingdom to touch a hurting world. We will never make a difference in our world if we cannot love one another within the kingdom of God. When love and cooperation are present, God pours His Holy Spirit upon His people and the gates of hell will come down all around us.

On page 11 you were asked the question, *Is it possible to be a committed, growing Christian and not be an active part of His body, the local church?* **After a week of study, how would you answer that question?** ❑ Yes   ❑ Still thinking   ❑ No

Write the reason for your answer in the margin.

As you understand it, what is God's plan for every Christian's life? (Hint: Review the seven characteristics of God's great salvation.)

_____

_____

Koinonia:
God's Love Expressed

If we say, "We have fellowship with Him," and walk in darkness, we are lying and are not practicing the truth. But if we walk in the light as He Himself is in the light, we have fellowship with one another, and the blood of Jesus His Son cleanses us from all sin.

1 JOHN 1:6-7

One particular Sunday a woman came forward during the invitation weeping over her wayward son. I immediately guided the church family to gather around her, pray with her, share some Scriptures, and make arrangements to get involved with her. The teenagers were enlisted to pursue her son. The men were encouraged to seek him out and be a father figure to him in this time of need. The entire body was praying. He eventually did return with many tears, and the entire church was filled with joy. This is *koinonia* at work. The body loving God and one another in real and practical ways.

Contrast that story with this one: In the early days at Saskatoon, our congregation was small, around 30 people. One of the leaders decided we were not functioning as he thought we should and said so in a business meeting. His face got red, and he said, "You are all going against the will of God, He will not bless you, and I am leaving." He summoned his wife and as he was walking out said, "As of today I am resigning all my positions in the church."

Which story do you identify with the most? Have you ever been a part of a tumultuous church business meeting? Survived a church split? Been the object of the gossip mill? Felt uneasy around a fellow church member? Or has your experience in the church mostly been filled with loving examples of Christians caring for one another in practical ways?

In this week's study, we will define and illustrate the word that best describes the fellowship God envisions in a church family: *koinonia*. As you read, look for the answers to these key questions:

1. Why is it important that the local church express *koinonia?*
2. Can a church truly be a church without *koinonia?*
3. How does unforgiveness affect *koinonia* in the church?
4. How do you maintain *koinonia* in the church?

What Is *Koinonia?*

An ordinary working couple joined our church and joyfully entered into the fellowship among the people. They often commented that they had never experienced such love in any church but ours.

At a prayer meeting months later, the man began to weep. His brother had been injured and was left in a coma, not expected to live. Since his brother was not a Christian, it broke his heart to think he was about to slip into eternity without hope. If only he could get to his brother and share the gospel, but he did not have the finances to make the trip. Immediately people in the church began to respond and soon the plane fare was provided. One couple even cashed in some retirement funds to help pay his way!

As our church prayed, the man went to see his brother, hoping to have an opportunity to share the gospel with him. Miraculously, his brother suddenly came out of the coma. He was able to witness to him, and the brother prayed to receive Christ. For the first time the two men rejoiced together as brothers in Christ. Then almost as suddenly as he awoke, the brother slipped back into a coma and never recovered.

Although sad at the loss of his brother, the man came home happy in the Lord. We rejoiced together as a church family, knowing that God had been gracious to one of our own. That moment was a powerful time in this man's life. He was forever grateful to the church for walking with him, praying for him, and offering practical assistance during such a difficult time.

God's people are supposed to care for each other! We have a love that began in the heart of God and is expressed between members in the family of God. The greatest evidence that a person has been born again is love for those within the church family.

Read 1 John 3:16 in the margin. What do you need to lay down to love your fellow believers the same way Christ loved you? Symbolically lay them down by drawing an arrow from each response to the figure kneeling before the cross.

This is how we have come to know love: He laid down His life for us. We should also lay down our lives for our brothers.

✤ 1 JOHN 3:16 ✤

my rights
my space
my time
my opinions
my finances
my comfort
my physical life
other: _____

Koinonia: GOD'S LOVE IN ACTION

People all over the world recognize that there is a God, but few have experienced a love relationship with Him. Many would tell us he is unknowable to human experience. If our relationship to God were based on our ability to know Him, their assessment would be absolutely true; God would be unknowable. How can a finite creature know an infinite Creator? He can't, unless, of course, the Creator makes Himself known to the creature.

The truth is that God has made Himself known, and He is active in the world today. He has revealed Himself to us in many different ways. The greatest revelation is found in the person of His Son, Jesus Christ. While talking to His disciples, "Jesus told him, 'I am the way, the truth, and the life. No one comes to the Father except through Me. If you know Me, you will also know My Father. From now on you do know Him and have seen Him' " (John 14:6-7). God loved us so much that He sent His Son to show us who He truly is and how we can know Him.

We do not serve a God who watches from a distance. We serve a God who desires a love relationship with us that is real and personal. So how do we relate to God and experience a love relationship with Him in practical ways?

Koinonia expresses God's love toward His people in practical ways. I want us to become well acquainted with this word, because it is how God's love manifests itself in real life. *Koinonia* is *agape* or unconditional love in action. Through *koinonia,* we experience the fullness of God's love *for* His people and *in* His people. In a real sense *koinonia* is the essence of God's great salvation.

> **Which phrase best describes your response to the term *koinonia*?**
> ❑ It's Greek to me.
> ❑ Coin collecting?
> ❑ It has something to do with fellowship.
> ❑ It describes how Christians relate to each other and to God.
> ❑ It's a term I need to think about and study more.

What can be known about God is evident among them, because God has shown it to them. From the creation of the world His invisible attributes, that is, His eternal power and divine nature, have been clearly seen, being understood through what He has made. As a result, people are without excuse.

❧ ROMANS 1:19-20 ❧

Koinonia: GOD'S LOVE RETURNED

Koinonia is not a new and innovative word. It's a New Testament Greek word rich with meaning and therefore not easily translated into English. Usually translated as "fellowship," "partnership," "sharing," or even "stewardship," it takes on much greater significance when applied to God's relationship with His people.

What an awesome realization to know that we have literally become *partners* with God—that is, a bonding of two lives for a common purpose. Nothing is withheld in a true partnership, but the resources of each one are shared with the other.

Koinonia Implies:
Partnership
Sharing
Stewardship

In Philippians 1:3-7 Paul used the term as he talked to the other believers about their partnership with him in the gospel. They shared his suffering, his poverty, his message, and their very lives with him as partners in the gospel. The term *sharing* also applies to the *koinonia* relationship with God. It is the release of everything in you to the one with whom you are sharing.

Second Peter 1:3-4 illustrates this principle beautifully. Read these verses in your Bible and fill in the blanks.

God's divine power has given believers everything they need

for _____ and _____.

Through these God has given believers His very great and

precious _____.

In some way, we receive that which is divine into our lives. This thought is too grand to comprehend but true nonetheless.

God has withheld nothing from you. Are you withholding anything from Him? ❏ Yes ❏ No
If you answered yes, what must you release so you can enjoy true

koinonia **with the Lord?**_____

_____

Koinonia also means *stewardship*. You have been entrusted with a relationship to God and now you are a good steward of all that God has brought to you. You are taking all the resources of God and letting them flow through you to the rest of the people of God.

A good steward receives not what is his but what is someone else's. God has a purpose for what He has given to us. The apostle Paul admonished us not to "receive the grace of God in vain" (2 Cor. 6:1). That is, we must not receive all the resources of God into our lives and then do nothing with them. Paul put it this way in 1 Corinthians 15:10, "By God's grace I am what I am, and His grace toward me was not ineffective. However, I worked more than any of them, yet not I, but God's grace that was with me."

Koinonia receives the grace of God with a grateful heart and lets the resources of God flow through your life into the rest of God's family. Paul said, "Working together with Him, we also appeal to you: 'Don't receive God's grace in vain' " (2 Cor. 6:1).

I give thanks to my God for every remembrance of you, always praying with joy for all of you in my every prayer, because of your partnership in the gospel from the first day until now. I am sure of this, that He who started a good work in you will carry it on to completion until the day of Christ Jesus. It is right for me to think this way about all of you, because I have you in my heart, and you are all partners with me in grace, both in my imprisonment and in the defense and establishment of the gospel.

❧ PHILIPPIANS 1:3-7 ❧

Circle the picture that best illustrates what you are doing with the gifts of God's divine nature and grace.

Koinonia: THE ESSENCE OF THE CHURCH

Koinonia expresses the essence of the church. We fellowship with God intimately. We partner with God in His activity. We share in God's nature. We come to know God experientially! To describe an encounter with the living God defies human language, yet such an encounter is at the heart of what the New Testament writers were trying to convey through the word *koinonia*.

You just read marvelous truths about *koinonia*. Have you grasped those truths yet? Fill in the blanks to complete the phrases:

1. We _____ with God intimately.

2. We _____ with God in His activity.

3. We _____ in God's nature.

4. We come to _____ God experientially.

Now read those realities out loud. Go ahead and burst into a song of praise! It's worth singing about!

The apostle John said, "We testify and declare to you the eternal life that was with the Father and was revealed to us—what we have seen and heard we also declare to you, so that you may have fellowship [koinonia] along with us; and indeed our fellowship [koinonia] is with the Father and with His Son Jesus Christ."

❧ I JOHN I:2-3 ❧

True *koinonia*, in its fullest expression, can only be found in one place—the local church. Nowhere else is God's love displayed and experienced more deeply than in the midst of His people. Oh, how God loves the church. He delights to see His children gathering for worship, helping each member grow in Christlikeness, joining with one heart yet from different backgrounds and interests serving their common Lord. When a church demonstrates to a watching world the love that comes from Him, God receives the glory and honor.

Koinonia with God

God's great salvation is nothing less than His desire to fellowship with human beings. However, without practical expression, God's love is irrelevant. God's love must be experienced in real life in order for it to be of any value. Fortunately, God chooses to enter a personal love relationship with us. In fact, without a personal relationship with God, there is no salvation nor eternal life.

GOD'S LOVE IS AN INTERNAL RESPONSE

Many people have difficulty at this very point. Eternal life is based not on religion but on a relationship with God. Our relationship with God is not essentially about external acts of ritual; it is an internal response of the heart. God's great salvation frees us from sin in order that we might be free to know Him. Some think that we are freed from sin so that we might *act* right, yet God's desire is that we *be* right. Being right speaks of the heart, the core of our existence. What we need is to be in a right relationship with God. Herein is the significance of *koinonia,* the personal interaction between God and His people.

Fill in the blanks to identify contrasting approaches to attaining eternal life. Use these words: right, relationship, acts, response. Words may be used more than once.

Religion vs. _____with God

External _____ vs. internal _____

Acting _____ vs. being _____

Circle the word above that describes the only way a person can experience *koinonia* with God now and eternally.

Read Deuteronomy 6:5 and Matthew 22:37. What is the first and

greatest commandment? _____

The Amplified Bible may help us to see the extensiveness of salvation described in John 17:3. "This is eternal life: [it means] to know (to perceive, recognize, become acquainted with, and understand) You, the only true and real God, and [likewise] to know Him, Jesus [as the] Christ (the Anointed One, the Messiah), Whom You have sent." Salvation is a personal love relationship with God through His Son.

"You shall love the Lord your God with all your heart and with all your soul and with all your might."
❧ DEUTERONOMY 6:5 ❧

He said to him, " 'You shall love the Lord your God with all your heart, with all your soul, and with all your mind.' "
❧ MATTHEW 22:37 ❧

Do you recognize the presence of Christ in your everyday routine? ❑ Yes ❑ No Describe a recent instance when your intimate knowledge of Christ enabled you to perceive His presence in a very real way.

_____

_____

Are you becoming better acquainted with Christ on a daily basis? Is your understanding of Christ growing? ❑ Yes ❑ No **Explain.**

_____

_____

❧ A STORY FROM MEL BLACKABY ❧

A Father's Love

On January 25, 1985, my father was to fly to Hawaii to be the main speaker at a large conference. What made this assignment especially inviting was that we were having a bitterly cold winter that year. So my father decided to take my mother and make a vacation out of it.

On January 24, however, I was severely injured in a logging accident and was flown out of the back country to Edmonton, Alberta, for surgery. I was in bad shape; my femur had been shattered, some muscles had been torn, and I was hurting. As I lay in the hospital, I remember talking to my father on the phone. He said, "Your mother is already on her way to see you, and if you need me, I will call and cancel my trip to Hawaii." I thought to myself, *Hawaii versus Edmonton? Warm sun versus 40 degrees below zero? Beautiful beaches versus a hospital room?* All that my father thought about was his son. He is my father! He loves me!

I know my father would do anything he could to help me. But I also know he is limited. He can't always be there. He has limited resources. We live a long way from each other. Nobody can separate us from the love of our Heavenly Father. Knowing how much our earthly fathers love us, how much more does our Heavenly Father? That is *koinonia*, God's love expressed toward His children.

GOD'S LOVE IS UNSTOPPABLE

The apostle Paul had come to know the love of God in his life. He wrote one of the most impassioned statements about God's love toward His children in the Scriptures.

If God is for us, who is against us? Who can separate us from the love of Christ? Can affliction or anguish or persecution or famine or nakedness or danger or sword? No, in all these things we are more than victorious through Him who loved us. For

I am persuaded that neither death nor life, nor angels nor rulers, nor things present, nor things to come, nor powers, nor height, nor depth, nor any other created thing will have the power to separate us from the love of God that is in Christ Jesus our Lord! (Rom. 8:31,35,37-39).

Make this promise your very own. Fill in the blanks as directed.

If God is for me, who is against me? Who can separate me from the love of Christ?

Can _____ or _____ (Fill in these blanks with things that are troubling or afflicting you)

_____ or _____ or

_____? (What issues of life or death are you struggling with?)

No, in all these things I am more than victorious through Him who loves me.

(What do you fear about the future?)

For I am persuaded that neither _____ nor

_____, nor angels or rulers, nor

_____, nor _____, nor powers, (What causes you the greatest heartache or struggle?)

nor height, nor depth, nor _____
will have the power to separate me from the love of God that is in Christ Jesus our Lord!

Now read God's personal promise of *koinonia* out loud. Pause to thank God for His marvelous love for you.

DAY THREE

Koinonia with Each Other

God expects us to love one another in exactly the same way that He has loved us. Some will undoubtedly cry, "Impossible!" Humanly speaking, it is impossible. But with God all things are possible. Fortunately for us, God placed His Spirit within us to enable us to love as He loves. This is part of His great salvation. When we are walking in fellowship with God, He gives us the ability to walk in fellowship with all of His people.

A STORY FROM MEL BLACKABY

The *Koinonia* Connection

While attending seminary in Texas, I pastored my first church in a small town that boasted a population of 250. Being the pastor of the only Baptist church in the town, I quickly became known in the community.

One day I noticed a moving truck and furniture being unloaded. So I went to introduce myself to the newcomers with the intention of inviting them to church. The man was pleasant and quickly revealed that he was a Christian. Even more, the man was a Baptist! I was hot on the trail of a potential addition to our little congregation. So I pursued even further by asking where the man's church membership belonged.

"I belong to Bluff Dale Baptist Church," he proudly replied.

I was a little perplexed and simply responded, "Well I am the pastor of Bluff Dale Baptist Church, and I have never seen you before!"

"Well I don't attend," he acknowledged, "but I was married in that church five years ago."

It was clear that this man had been brought up in a Christian culture but did not have a concept of a personal relationship with God and, therefore, a relationship with God's people.

Many people are not sure what it means to be a Christian, not sure how to relate to God, and not sure how to relate to God's people. According to the Scriptures, it's spiritually impossible to have fellowship with God and, at the same time, be out of fellowship with God's people.

If we are not experiencing true *koinonia* with God's people—or any one of God's people—we are not enjoying *koinonia* with God or walking in the light as He is in the light. The deeper the relationship to God, the deeper the relationship becomes with God's people. The two are eminently connected.

"I am the light of the world. Anyone who follows Me will never walk in the darkness, but will have the light of life."

❧ JOHN 8:12 ❧

In John 8:12 did Jesus mean we would never have to turn the lights on? Explain how light relates to *koinonia*.

_____

You discovered earlier this week that *koinonia* is almost impossible to describe with language. Seek to deepen your understanding of *koinonia* with a picture.

Label one of the figures "ME." Draw a box around yourself to create a barrier between you and God's people.

GOD'S PEOPLE

From whom else are you separated when you are detached from

God's people? _____

THE SOURCE OF BROKEN RELATIONSHIPS

If a person claims to be in fellowship with God yet has broken relationships with other believers, what does the Bible call that person? A liar! Broken relationships with God's people are a symptom of a broken relationship with God.

If you see people at odds with one another, what is their problem? Their primary need is to be reconciled with God, and then God will help them to be reconciled with one another. How do you have fellowship in the church? Help people to have fellowship with God. Then the life of God in them will affect every relationship they have with other people.

If a husband and wife have a broken relationship, what is their problem? It is spiritually impossible to walk in the light as He is in the light and not have fellowship with one another. The same is true between parents and children.

How do you help a family member come back to God? *You* come back to God! We had a son who gave us great difficulty during his teenage years. I remember when my son was having trouble in school, when he ran with the wrong crowd of friends, when he slipped away from the Lord. I remember how broken I became. Late one night I slipped into the living room of our home and cried out to God to change the heart of my son. But God said, "No, I am going to change the heart of his father."

That was a blow; it caught me off guard. At that time I was a director of missions. How much closer to God can you get? If only our ministry was an indication of our heart, but it is not. God needed to draw me closer to Him in order that I might be closer to my son. What God began to speak to me was exactly what the Scripture says. If I walk in the light as He is in the light, I will have *koinonia* with my son. That applies in every area of life.

When our relationship with our son was strained, we had to get *our* lives right with God. But if your relationship to God is basically religious activity, you will drive your kids away.

We confuse religious busyness with having fellowship with God, but they are not the same. In fact, our activity for God can often replace fellowship with God. And that will be reflected in the relationships we have with others.

Mark an X on the scale to indicate which phrase most closely describes your life:

I base my relationship with God on religious activities.

I base my relationship with God on fellowship with Him.

Broken relationships with God's people are a symptom of a broken relationship with God.

If we say, "We have not sinned," we make Him a liar, and His word is not in us.

♣ 1 JOHN 1:10 ♣

We confuse religious busyness with having fellowship with God, but they are not the same.

Does your relationship with God affect your relationships with others? Place an X on the scale to indicate the usual weather pattern of your friendships.

cloudy skies   blue skies

The Source of Right Relationships

First John 1:3-7 tells us that fellowship with God results in fellowship with God's people. John is careful to use the same word for both relationships, indicating that the fellowship we have with God is the same quality of fellowship we have with one another.

We have said that a good working definition of *koinonia* is *agape love* or *God's love in action.* How has He expressed *koinonia* in your life? How has God loved you? What have you received from God because He loves you?

He has forgiven you. He has been merciful to withhold what you, as a sinner, deserve. He has been gracious to give you what you don't deserve. He has given you protection. He has given you discipline in order that He might shape your character. He has given you direction. He has been your friend. He has expressed His love in a thousand different ways.

Read John 13:34-35 in your Bible. Our love for each other should

equal whose love for us? _____

Circle the number that best describes how fully you are obeying Jesus' command, with 1 being not at all and 10 signifying completely.

1   2   3   4   5   6   7   8   9   10

Do you understand why we need to ask how God has loved us? It helps us understand how we should love one another.

Forgiveness: A Key to *Koinonia*

God expects us to forgive others exactly as He forgives us. Jesus said in the Lord's Prayer, " 'Forgive us our debts, as we also have forgiven our debtors' " (Matt. 6:12). If there was any doubt about what Jesus meant by that statement, He gave a commentary on it just two verses later. Read it in the margin on page 43.

Is there someone you have not forgiven? Make Matthew 6:14-15 personal. On page 43 write that person's initials in the blanks.

"If you forgive people their wrongdoing, your heavenly Father will forgive you as well. But if you don't forgive people, your Father will not forgive your wrongdoing."

❧ Matthew 6:14-15 ❧

If I forgive _____ 's wrongdoing, my Heavenly Father

will forgive me as well. But if I don't forgive _____, my Father will not forgive my wrongdoing.

How do you feel knowing your unforgiveness impacts your fellowship with God? Circle any that apply.

ashamed   frightened   convicted   doubtful

determined   repentant   confused   unconcerned

Can you see how important it is that we are forgiving in our relationships with others? If we refuse to forgive a brother, the Lord will not forgive us. We can plead with God all we want, but He will not forgive our sin against Him unless we are also willing to forgive those who have sinned against us. God is seeking to reveal Himself through us, and for us not to forgive is to give a wrong picture of God to a watching world.

I am convinced that many among God's people today are still carrying years of sin on their shoulders because they have been unwilling to forgive others. Furthermore, their growing accumulation of sin has created a barrier between them and God. That barrier has left them feeling distant from God, and that distance from God has brought deadness to their Spirit. That spiritual deadness has left them void of any real joy in life.

Read 1 John 1:7 in the margin. Fellowship with one another and forgiveness of one another allows for forgiveness of our sins and a right relationship with God.

If we walk in the light as he himself is in the light, we have fellowship with one another, and the blood of Jesus his Son cleanses us from all sin.

❧ 1 John 1:7 ❧

Unforgiveness: An Affront to God

Let me drop forgiveness into the corporate arena. What happens when a church splits? I believe that if a church ever has a split, the members need to go back and reconcile with their brothers if they ever want to see the blessings of God again. But the tragedy is that a church will split and the very next Sunday both groups will pray, "O God, will you bless us today?"

That behavior is an affront to a holy God, for they have just broken fellowship with their brothers because they would not forgive. They treat relationships in the church the way many are treating the marriage relationship: irreconcilable differences. There are no irreconcilable differences among God's people. If there were, that would mean there was a limit to God's ability to forgive you as well. The cross would be void of its meaning. We must forgive as Christ has forgiven us—totally, forever.

Since God's salvation provided His Son to live His life in us, "the one who says he remains in Him should walk just as He walked. The one who loves his brother remains in the light, and there is no cause for stumbling in him" (1 John 2:6,10). That is what God's salvation looks like! Christ living His life in us and ministering to others through us.

Perhaps the Lord is using this study to convict you of a person or group of believers from whom you need to seek or offer forgiveness. Read Matthew 5:23-24 in the margin. Ask God for the strength, courage, and opportunity to seek reconciliation soon.

"If you are offering your gift on the altar, and there you remember that your brother has something against you, leave your gift there in front of the altar. First go and be reconciled with your brother, and then come and offer your gift."

♣ MATTHEW 5:23-24 ♣

DAY FOUR

Koinonia in the Church

God's desire for *koinonia* among His people is directly related to His strategy to touch a world. It's seen most clearly in the local congregation. The basic meaning of the word translated *church* in the English Bible is a rendering of the Greek word *ekklesia*. The word never denotes a building or a structure in which worshippers assemble; instead, it denotes the people themselves. The translation of this compound word is literally, *the called-out ones*.

The New Testament reveals that the first Christians were called out of the world and gathered together into religious assemblies; they acted as organized bodies. The word *church* is used for a congregation of believers who are committed to one another under the lordship of Jesus Christ and who are united through the bond of His Spirit. The fellowship *[koinonia]* among the people of God is a powerful force in the purposes of God.

THE TEST OF FELLOWSHIP

I have never known a Christian to be walking in true fellowship with God who was not at the same time walking in true fellowship with God's people. Similarly, every time I have been involved with broken love relationships in a church, in a marriage, in a family, or in God's kingdom work, I have witnessed someone who was out of fellowship with God.

Many think that broken relationships among God's people result in a broken relationship with God. I have found it to be the other way around; broken relationships with one another are a symptom of a previous broken relationship with God. Our relationship with God determines all other relationships in our lives.

Our relationship with God determines all other relationships in our lives.

THE TRUE EXPRESSION OF FELLOWSHIP

The apostle Paul has given us a wonderful prayer to pray for our church family. If you are a leader, this prayer should be on your lips regularly for the members of your church. It lays the foundation for *koinonia* in the church.

As you read Paul's prayer, underline what you would like to pray for your church family.

I pray that He may grant you, according to the riches of His glory, to be strengthened with power through His Spirit in the inner man, and that the Messiah may dwell in your hearts through faith. I pray that you, being rooted and firmly established in love, may be able to comprehend with all the saints what is the breadth and width, height and depth, and to know the Messiah's love that surpasses knowledge, so you may be filled with all the fullness of God (Eph. 3:16-19).

You probably noted that Paul prayed that each one would be strengthened by the power of the Holy Spirit and rooted and grounded in love. He prayed that all the saints, all the believers in the church, would come to know the love of Christ.

What would happen if your church was filled with the love of Christ?

_____

_____

Did you note that your church would then be filled with the fullness of God? Can you imagine that? He is talking to the church!

When Paul talks about knowing the love of Christ, what does he mean? What does it look like when God brings His love through Jesus Christ into every member of the church? He then displays in that church the *breadth* of His love. How long does His love hold on to you? He displays the *width* of His love. How wide will His love reach, and how many people will it include? He displays the *height* of His love. How high does He lift and encourage every individual when He loves them? He displays the *depth* of His love. How far will His love go to reach the fallen sinner? Where sin abounds, grace does much more abound. It doesn't matter how deep a person has gone in sin; God's love will go deeper.

The one who experiences great mercy and forgiveness from God expresses mercy and forgiveness to others. To experience the patience of God in our lives causes us to have patience with others. To have a

"Just as you want others to do for you, do the same for them. Be merciful, just as your Father also is merciful."

✤ LUKE 6:31,36 ✤

conscious awareness of God's faithfulness leads us instinctively to express faithfulness to God and His people. As we grow in our relationship with God, we automatically grow in our relationship with other believers.

What power is found in the church that is experiencing *koinonia* with God and one another! It is explosive! If the "hand" is not listening to or speaking with the "eye," the entire activity of God through the body is hindered. God chose to make us mutually interdependent in our church family; we are spiritually connected in the body. When Christ has a mature body of believers who are in fellowship with Him and one another, He can effectively do the work of the Father to touch a lost world.

Koinonia between the members is absolutely vital to the nature of the church and to the purposes God has for the church. Jesus prayed that the fellowship He had with the Father would be replicated among His people. Their love for one another would then demonstrate to the world that Christ was the Son of God, and they would see His glory. Examine carefully Jesus' prayer below with a fresh understanding of *koinonia*.

> "I pray not only for these, but also for those
> who believe in me through their message.
> May they all be one, just as you, Father,
> are in me and I am in you.
> May they also be one in Us,
> so that the world may believe You sent Me.
> I have given them the glory that You have given to Me.
> May they be one just as We are one.
> I am in them and You are in Me.
> May they be made completely one,
> so that the world may know You sent Me
> and that You have loved them just as You have loved Me.
> Father, I desire those You have given Me to be with Me where I am.
> Then they may see My glory, which You have given Me
> because You loved Me before the world's foundation.
> Righteous Father! The world has not known You.
> However, I have known You,
> and these have known that You sent Me.
> I made Your name known to them and will make it known,
> so that the love with which You have loved Me may be in them,
> and that I may be in them" (John 17:20-26).

Why is Christ so concerned about our relationships with other

believers?_____

When Christ has a mature body of believers who are in fellowship with Him and one another, He can effectively do the work of the Father to touch a lost world.

We are to experience the same love Christ had with His Father within our relationships in the family of God. His love is in us!

If His love is in every believer, how would that look in a church family? Sketch or describe that church family in the space below.

If God's love was present in church families, would the world believe the gospel of reconciliation?

❑ No way.

❑ I wish it were so, but I don't see much hope.

❑ Maybe a few people would believe.

❑ Absolutely!

❑ Additional comments? _____

I tried my best as a pastor to teach our people to love God with all their hearts. I opened the Scriptures, especially the Gospels, and demonstrated how Jesus loved the Father and sought to do what was pleasing to Him. I then taught them what it meant to love one another as Christ has loved us. As people responded to God during our worship services, I helped the entire congregation come alongside those who were struggling and love them through their brokenness.

THE MOST POWERFUL FORCE IN THE WORLD

God's great salvation lived out among His people is the most powerful force in the world. That is what is on the heart of God for our churches today. When the church is experiencing *koinonia* as God intended, there is no limit to what He can do through them to touch the world.

We have looked at Paul's prayer for the church (p. 45). But notice the very next verses in Ephesians 3:20-21: "Now to Him who is able to do above and beyond all that we ask or think—according to the power that works in you—to Him be glory in the church and in Christ Jesus to all generations, forever and ever. Amen." When a church receives and distributes the love of God, they will experience above and beyond all that they could have imagined.

Love in Action

A poor family who literally lived on the other side of the tracks in a run-down trailer began to visit our church. They had five young children, and the father was out of work. They had a hard time trusting people and were therefore hesitant to get too involved, but they eventually joined fellowship with us.

Almost the very next week, I heard that the man had run out of gas and was stuck on the highway. I called Rob, one of our older deacons, and the two of us went out to pick him up. We drove on into the next town to get some gas to take back to his van.

While in town, Rob decided to take us to lunch. The man was a little hesitant but didn't have much of a choice; he was riding with us! There Rob pulled out his wallet and handed the man a one-hundred-dollar bill. "Whatever you have left after filling your vehicle, get something nice for the kids."

The man couldn't believe his eyes. He didn't want to take it. He finally asked, "Why are you doing this?" Rob answered, "You are part of the family, and we take care of our family."

I will never forget the look on the man's face. He had never experienced that kind of love.

What feelings do you have when you consider the statement, "You are part of the family, and we take care of our family"? Circle any that apply. Add other words in the margin.

disbelief	deep joy	lump in my throat
regret	wonder	warm
skepticism	gratitude	regret

Perhaps Mel's story brought to mind someone in your church whom you could help. How will you take care of your family member? Write your answer in the margin.

DAY FIVE

Keeping *Koinonia* in the Church

Busyness that leads to the neglect of relationships will affect a marriage, a business partnership, or a family, and it can ultimately be fatal. When we are busy doing things for God and yet we neglect time with God, the relationship falters. When our relationship with God falters, we have turbulence in the church.

I am aware of a pastor who was troubled over two couples in his church who were going through the process of divorce because there was an adulterous relationship between the husband of one couple and the wife of another. The pastor essentially said, "These two couples were the most active people in the church. They served as deacons and leaders, taught Sunday school, and were at the church whenever the doors were open. How could these people have marriages that were falling apart?"

Yet in asking the question, he heard the answer. They were so busy doing things for God that they neglected their relationship to Him. They were so busy in their church activities that they never had time to spend with their own families. We must learn to release our people from burdensome busyness so that they can build healthy and strong relationships.

Koinonia, like love, cannot be taken for granted. Proverbs warns us, "Watch over your heart with all diligence, for from it flow the springs of life" (Prov. 4:23). What is happening in our lives, whether in the church or in the home, is a reflection and expression of what is happening in our hearts. If our love for the Lord is neglected and we let the fire go out, it will soon be seen in our lives, especially our love relationships to others. This is true in every relationship in life.

What flows out of your heart? Underline all that apply.

hurry, hurry	serenity	complaints
anger	stress	joy
gratitude	criticism	heavy sighs
laughter	encouragement	AAAAHH!

How to Lose *Koinonia*

Three parables of Jesus express three ways we can lose that which is important to us in our churches. The parable of the lost sheep demonstrates how distraction may cause us to lose *koinonia*. People in the church can get distracted and unknowingly wander off into that which is dangerous. Leaders must be careful to keep watch over those who seem to be straying.

The parable of the lost coin shows carelessness. Churches can simply be careless, not paying attention to what God has already given them. Each person sent by God is precious and ought to be protected as such.

Ways to Lose *Koinonia*
1. Distraction
2. Carelessness
3. Disobedience

The parable of the lost son illustrates how we can choose to disobey God or to overlook sin that has crept into the fellowship. As a result, we walk away from the blessings of God. When we lose *koinonia* in the church, we have lost our very lives.

Read what Jesus said to the church at Ephesus in Revelation 2:4-5. What did He have against this church body?

_____

_____

"I have this against you: you have abandoned [lost] the love you had at first. Remember then how far you have fallen; repent, and do the works you did at first. Otherwise, I will come to you and remove your lampstand from its place—unless you repent."

❧ Revelation 2:4-5 ❧

List other reasons a church might lose its first love.

_____

_____

When we lose our love for God and one another, we no longer have a message of good news to give the world. We can't talk about reconciliation between God and man if we are not reconciled with one another. Without a vital relationship with God and His people, we have lost the essence of God's great salvation.

HOW TO MAINTAIN *Koinonia*

Do you recall what Jesus said in Revelation 3:20 (see margin)? Who was He talking to? The church at Laodicea.

"I stand at the door and knock. If anyone hears My voice and opens the door, I will come in to him and have dinner with him, and he with Me."

❧ REVELATION 3:20 ❧

He was saying, "If you want to have Me come into your church, just open the door." It's not that difficult; just let Him in! For those who may be thinking, *I need to go find a church that's enjoying true koinonia,* you may need to stay where you are and be the one to open the door for your church. God may have put you in your church so that He could work through you to express His love to the rest of the church. If one person recognizes it is Jesus who is knocking, and that one person opens the door, He will come in. Once He is in, He will begin to affect every part of the church through that one person's life.

Don't leave the church; the church needs you. If you have fellowship with the Father, and you have fellowship with the Son, and you are filled with the Holy Spirit, and you are walking in the light as He is in the light, what do you think will happen? That *koinonia* love will begin to touch everybody in the church. I have watched that happen. I have watched God do it. Could you be that one? Are you willing to be that one?

> **Thank God for the particular church body in which He has placed you. On a separate sheet of paper, list prayer requests for your church. Pray about those requests faithfully. Consider sharing some of them with your group so you can pray together. Keep this sheet updated in your member book or in a prayer journal. You will refer to it throughout this study.**

The secret to building deeper relationships in the church is not more activities; it is not more potlucks; it is not more entertainment and fun. All of these may be a part of a strong church, but *koinonia* is a by-product of a vibrant and living relationship with God through Jesus Christ. *Koinonia* can't be conjured up by human activity; the working of the Holy Spirit produces it.

Koinonia can't be conjured up by human activity.

How to Grow *Koinonia*

Let me give one more word concerning *koinonia* in the church. Read Luke 6:38 in the margin. This verse describes a principle of the kingdom of God. The measure by which you measure to others will be measured back to you. If you have received much from God and give only a little to others, then God says He will give only a little to you. He will not respond to you in a way contrary to how you respond to others.

"Give, and it will be given to you; a good measure, pressed down, shaken together, and running over will be poured into your lap. For with the measure that you use, it will be measured back to you."

♣ LUKE 6:38 ♣

Underline the measure you use when you give to family and close friends. Circle how you give to the larger church family.

teaspoon   cup   quart   gallon

How then should you love one another? If God did not hold back His blessings to you, you should not hold back anything from others. The Scripture says: "Although He was rich, for your sake He became poor, so that by His poverty you might become rich" (2 Cor. 8:9). If you see a need in the church, you should do all you can to help meet it. The early church in Jerusalem did, and the world didn't understand that kind of love. What produced that kind of love? If we walk in the light as He is in the light, we have the same *koinonia* with our brother as we have with Him.

First John 3:14 says, "We know that we have passed from death to life because we love our brothers. The one who does not love remains in death." According to that verse, if a person does not love his brother, he remains in death. That is an absolute with God. So what should you do when you see members of your church at odds with one another?

As a pastor, I always prayed and then if I saw them not walking with Him, I would risk everything to go and talk with them. But if I watched their lives and they remained in death because they never showed evidence of love, I would go talk to them again.

If they got offended, I knew that when they stood before God they would at least know that their pastor loved them enough to show them what the Scripture said: if a person does not love his brother, he or she may be abiding in death, and that is an eternal consequence.

How to Express *Koinonia*

I remember preaching in a large church that was led by a well-known pastor. I delivered a message on repentance, and when I had finished, the pastor remained in his seat weeping. I turned the service over to him, but he just sat there for about five minutes. When he eventually got up, he said to the congregation, "In my life, I have heard many people preach on repentance, but this is the first time I have ever heard a message on repentance that was not spoken in anger."

I couldn't believe my ears. How could a person preach on repentance with anger? I preach repentance with a broken heart because I know the consequences when a person doesn't repent. We must speak the truth in love, and God's love will break down the heart of the person who is not walking with Him.

Let me illustrate what I am talking about by telling the rest of the second story you read in the introduction to Week 2 (see page 32). After the man and his wife got out the door, I said to the group, "Will someone second that motion?" They said, "What motion?" I said, "He just resigned from his positions, and his attitude indicated that he should. A deacon should not act that way. But don't you vote on this unless you make a pledge to love him the way Christ loved you. I will not have you vote to remove him from all positions unless you at the same time vote to give your life to help redeem him." I don't have the right to criticize people unless I am willing to come alongside them and encourage them to become what God desires.

So the next week I went to this man and said, "I am the only pastor you have, and I want to help you." Guided by the Holy Spirit, I asked him, "Could you say that you love God with all your heart, mind, soul, and strength?" He said, "No. I fear Him, I worship Him, I serve Him, but I cannot say that I love Him." Then I asked if he would let me walk with him until he could truly say that he loved God. He put his head down and began to weep. He told me that he grew up in a broken home where his dad never saw any good in him. He never heard his dad say that he loved him. He said, "I don't even know what love is, and I don't know how to love others."

About six months later he knelt with me and cried out in tears, "Lord, I love you." When he began to walk in fellowship with God, all the symptoms of bitterness and anger fell away. He became gentle and kind to everyone in the church. In fact, he no longer sought positions of power in the church; he just wanted to serve. He has since died, but until the end of his days he was a great encouragement to that church. What happened? He just needed help to walk in the Light.

What will you do to help others know the love of Christ? What will you risk because you love your brother? Do you want to see the love of God flowing through your church? Then begin to love others as God has first loved you. Do you want God to be generous to your church? Then demonstrate a generous attitude to others in your church. You don't have to make *koinonia* happen; you need to walk with God and let Him produce *koinonia* in and through you.

What has been the most meaningful statement or verse you read in your study this week? Write it in the margin and explain why. What has God called you to do in response to His word?

God's Covenant Relationship

Know therefore that the Lord your God, He is God, the faithful God,
who keeps His covenant and His lovingkindness to a thousandth generation
with those who love Him and keep His commandments.
DEUTERONOMY 7:9

Ernie and Debbie are what is known as church hoppers. At the slightest whim, they leave one church and join another. Perhaps the music program is better, or the new church has a better children's program. They are constantly seeking the best possible experience for each member of the family. Neither Ernie nor Debbie feels the slightest obligation to the new congregation. Church affiliation means nothing more to them than getting the best bargain for their time and money.

Crystal is a single young professional with a sincere desire for a godly life. She finds the Bible study in one church better than in another, but she likes the worship service better in the second church. So, she goes to Bible study at one and drives several miles to the other worship service. Crystal has met people at both churches she would like to get to know, but she doesn't choose to get too involved. After all, she's out of town a lot on weekends.

Ernie, Debbie, and Crystal are consumer Christians. They pick their churches like someone picks a new doctor or Internet server. They don't have a concept of being in covenant with a local body of believers.

This week we will examine why Christians are to be in a covenantal relationship with each other. What harm comes from a consumerism model of church? How would you rate yourself as a covenant-keeping Christian? As you read, focus on these questions:

1. Identify the differences between the Old and New Testament covenants.
2. How does a violation of the covenant with God affect the church?
3. How can a local church help its members walk in the covenant relationship? What are some practical things you can do to build up the body?
4. How does the new covenant affect the "back door" of the church and become a greater incentive to care for God's people?

A Covenant with God

A few years ago I had a life-changing experience at Indian Falls Creek Assembly in Oklahoma. It left an indelible mark on my heart and a fresh understanding of covenant. On the final evening at a gathering of 23 hundred Native American Christians, a revered elderly man called me to the platform. I was taken by surprise.

As I moved toward the platform, a lifetime of prayers flooded my mind. As a young boy, the Lord had given me an unusual love for Native American people. I had made a covenant with God to be available to help bring a sweeping revival among native peoples across Canada and the United States. This covenant, a costly burden to me, had now brought me to this moment in my life.

As I walked onto the stage, several men were ceremonially folding a large wool blanket decorated with many native artifacts. The older man held out his arms to me. He announced loudly, "Henry has been and is a spiritual warrior to the native peoples. We honor him tonight!" As the man carefully draped the folded blanket over my shoulders, he held me tight, looked deep into my eyes, and said, "This is the highest honor the native peoples can ever bestow on any man. Welcome into the native peoples of America!"

I began to weep uncontrollably, and the Holy Spirit reminded me of the cross, where God demonstrated His love for us: " 'This cup is the new covenant in My blood' " (Luke 22:20). As I stood there with the blanket over my shoulders, I sensed the devastating pain of the native peoples and knew that the cross was the only answer to bring healing to their communities. The cross, once and for all time, demonstrated that God loved all the people of the world.

Entering into a relationship with God through Jesus Christ is not a legal contract, but it is a binding covenant with far-reaching implications. Blessed are those who know God and His covenant promises, for they will have confident expectation and security in such a relationship, knowing that God will always act according to His promises within the covenant.

Did you know that your decision to become a Christian was at the same time a decision to enter a covenant with God through the blood of Christ? ❑ Yes ❑ No

WHAT IS A COVENANT WITH GOD

1. *The covenant is based on trust.*
Simply stated, a covenant is a sacred pledge based on trust between two parties. The trusting relationship between the two parties becomes

A covenant is a sacred pledge based on trust between two parties.

the most important factor, the basis from which everything else flows. The significance of this relationship can't be understated. We must yield our willing consent as free spiritual beings and entrust ourselves to God. Let me explain.

God chose to create people in His own image and likeness so that they might live as spiritual beings with the freedom to enjoy a loving relationship with Him. In that relationship they would be the fortunate recipients of all God's blessings. The one secret to their happiness was the trustful surrender of their lives to the will and purposes of God.

As long as people would remain dependent on God in all things, they would enjoy an intimate relationship with Him and all the benefits of His presence. But sin entered the world through Adam's disobedience, and the intended relationship to God was destroyed. Adam's sin introduced fear to the human experience, and the trust relationship was broken. Adam lost so much!

Adam soon learned that people cannot save themselves from the power of sin. God must be the one to initiate and complete all that is necessary for salvation and a restored relationship.

Read the hymn in the margin by John Sammis. Circle the benefits you receive when you respond to Christ with trust and obedience. Underline the phrases that indicate how you are to relate to God.

2. *The covenant is received through faith.*

Faith is the heart of a covenant. God desires that people believe and trust in Him, for what a person believes will move and direct his entire life. Salvation, therefore, could only be by faith. God restoring the relationship that was lost by sin, and man in faith yielding to God's work in his life is now what had to take place.

When we examine God's dealings with individuals or groups of people, we understand that His primary desire is to get people to trust Him. God can do anything through people who trust Him. When unbelief is present, God chooses to do nothing through His people. Unbelief always leads to disobedience and sin.

Read Matthew 13:54-58 in your Bible. Check the reasons Jesus didn't do many miracles in his hometown.
- ❑ He was embarrassed around His relatives.
- ❑ He decided to teach them a lesson for being offended by Him.
- ❑ The people didn't believe in Him.
- ❑ He didn't have enough power.

Read Hebrews 11:6 in the margin. The emphasis of a covenant relationship is our faith in God and our subsequent obedience to Him and His will. The covenant becomes an anchor whereby Christians can

When we walk with the Lord
In the light of His Word
What a glory He sheds on
    our way!
Let us do His good will;
He abides with us still,
And with all who will trust
    and obey.

But we never can prove
The delights of His love
Until all on the altar we lay;
For the favor He shows
And the joy He bestows
Are for them who will trust
    and obey.

Then in fellowship sweet
We will sit at His feet
Or we'll walk by His side
    in the way;
What He says we will do,
Where He sends we will go;
Never fear, only trust and obey.

Trust and obey, for there's no
    other way
To be happy in Jesus,
But to trust and obey.[1]

Without faith it is impossible to please God, for the one who draws near to Him must believe that He exists and rewards those who seek Him.

♣ HEBREWS 11:6 ♣

hold on to God's faithfulness even in the midst of confusing circumstances. Our covenant-keeping God is unchanging and faithful to do all that He has promised.

3. *The covenant reveals His purposes.*

God's covenant with His people always includes a revelation of His purposes, describing a definite promise that God desires to accomplish in and through His people. In addition, the covenant serves as security and guarantees that God will care for His people.

> **Read Isaiah 54:10 in the margin. Can you recall a time when your life was shaken yet you were able to stand firm because of God's faithfulness? Briefly describe how God's covenant was your anchor.**

_____

_____

4. *The covenant is God-centered.*

God chose to initiate the covenant and willingly entered into the relationship with Israel so that He could accomplish His purposes through them and demonstrate to the world what He is like. The purpose of the covenant was to draw all people to Himself. He would be the One in whom they put their complete trust and the One in whom they would find abundant life.

Because our covenant is with the holy God of the universe, we choose to establish a serious agreement. The deeper we enter the covenant relationship with God, the more significant eternity becomes; and as eternity begins to affect our hearts, the closer we are to revival. Understanding what it means to have a covenant with God is crucial for a church, as well as every individual.

THE OLD TESTAMENT COVENANT

The Old Testament covenant was built on God's individual covenant with Abraham. God promised that from him He would build a great nation, and this nation would bless all nations of the world.

Exodus 19—20 describes the first covenant relationship between God and the Israelites. This covenant began at God's initiative when He encountered His people on Mount Sinai. At the center of the agreement were the Ten Commandments, the guiding requirements of the relationship.

The commandments were not for the world in general, but for God's people in particular. They were for the people who had chosen to enter into a covenant with Him. This covenant determined how God would relate to the people from that day forward. If they kept the covenant, they would be blessed. If they broke the covenant, they

"The mountains may be removed and the hills may shake, But My lovingkindness will not be removed from you, And My covenant of peace will not be shaken," Says the Lord who has compassion on you.

❧ ISAIAH 54:10 ❧

would be cursed. This is clearly seen in passages such as Deuteronomy 30:15-20 where God said, " 'I call heaven and earth to witness against you today, that I have set before you life and death, the blessing and the curse. So choose life in order that you may live, you and your descendants' " (v. 19). (See also Deut. 28; Lev. 26).

Read Deuteronomy 30:15-18 in the margin and complete these instructions.
1. Underline God's expectations of the Israelites.
2. Bracket how God would bless their obedience.
3. Circle the consequences if the people chose disobedience.

The people of God were given the standard by which they must relate to God. He was holy; therefore, they were to be holy. It was a covenant they had chosen to enter. If they remained true to the covenant, God would bless everything they did. He would bless them when they went in and when they went out. He would bless their children, their cattle, their crops, and anything they put their hands to accomplish. He would go with them in battle and defeat the enemy, demonstrating to the entire world that they belonged to God. God would reveal Himself to the world through His people who were in covenant with Him.

The opposite was also true. If the people of God broke the covenant, they would experience the cursing of God. He would curse them when they went in and when they went out. He would curse their children, their cattle, their crops, and anything they put their hands to accomplish. Their enemies would defeat them in battle, and all the people of the world would see how God deals with those who break the covenant. Whether they were true to the covenant or they violated it, God would show the world how He deals with people in a covenant relationship with Himself.

THE OLD COVENANT IS BROKEN

The covenant had tremendous benefits when kept and enormous consequences when broken. The conditions were clearly established and known to the people of God, and they were expected to live according to the agreement. To be in a covenant with Almighty God was a privilege beyond imagination. Because God was the initiator of the covenant, no obedience was too demanding, no dependence too absolute, no submission too complete, and no confidence too certain. Of all the peoples of the earth, God chose to enter a covenant with the Israelites, His chosen people.

Yet God's people continually struggled to fulfill their part of the covenant. In fact, the covenant exposed the futility of mankind to live according to God's law. Listen to the terms of the covenant: "If you

"I have set before you today life and prosperity, and death and adversity; in that I command you today to love the Lord your God, to walk in His ways and to keep His commandments and His statutes and His judgments, that you may live and multiply, and that the Lord your God may bless you in the land where you are entering to possess it. But if your heart turns away and you will not obey, but are drawn away and worship other gods and serve them, I declare to you today that you shall surely perish. You shall not prolong your days in the land where you are crossing the Jordan to enter and possess it."

❧ DEUTERONOMY 30:15-18 ❧

will indeed obey My voice and keep My covenant, then you shall be My own possession" (Ex. 19:5). " 'Obey My voice, and I will be your God, and you will be My people' " (Jer. 7:23). Obedience was the condition of blessing, but sinful mankind was bent toward disobedience. The old covenant was faithful to set a clear standard that would always expose sin in God's people and reveal His holiness.

The result was that God's people became convinced of their sin and were humbled to confess their inability to live according to the standard of God's law. Mankind was awakened to the need for a new covenant, the fullness of God's grace that would be completed in the work of Christ. Everything in the Old Testament covenant pointed to the coming of Christ.

Fill in the blanks to review the four characteristics of a covenant with God (see pages 54-56).

1. The covenant is based on _____.

2. The covenant is _____ through faith.

3. The covenant reveals God's _____.

4. The covenant is _____ _____.

How seriously have you taken the covenant you chose to establish with the Holy God of the universe? Check one.
❑ Is a covenant where nuns live?
❑ I didn't realize a covenant even existed.
❑ I have lived as if the covenant is not very important.
❑ I'm growing in my understanding of my covenant with God.
❑ I'm committed to the covenant God established with me.

DAY TWO

A New Covenant in Christ

What mankind could not achieve according to the law in the old covenant, Jesus Christ came to fulfill in the new covenant. In the new covenant of His blood, Jesus would accomplish all the requirements of God's law on our behalf. In Christ we have everything necessary for life and godliness, and we literally become partakers of the divine nature.

The difference between the old covenant and the new covenant is enormous. Look at the contrasts in the chart on page 59.

OLD COVENANT	NEW COVENANT
God's people failed to fulfill their part of the covenant.	God enables us to fulfill our part of the covenant.
God's laws were written on tablets of stone.	God's laws are written on our hearts.
God's laws brought conviction of sin.	God forgives sin and cleanses us from all unrighteousness.
God's laws revealed a corrupt heart that resists God's will.	God provides a new heart that is responsive to His heart.
God's laws gave His people no power to keep the laws.	Christians have the Holy Spirit to empower them to know and do God's will.

Look carefully at the new covenant prophetically described by Ezekiel, " 'I will give you a new heart and put a new spirit within you; and I will remove the heart of stone from your flesh and give you a heart of flesh. And I will put My Spirit within you and cause you to walk in My statues, and you will be careful to observe My ordinances' " (Ezek. 36:26-27).

Can you see the difference? In the old covenant God said, *"If you obey,* you will be blessed." In the new covenant God said, "I will put My Spirit within you and *cause you to walk in obedience."* Both covenants deal with the heart, but the new covenant includes the power of God working in our hearts, which causes us to obey His commands. Incredible!

Inside the first outline write descriptive terms of a person who lives under the old covenant. Inside the second outline, record all that God gives a person who lives under the new covenant.

CONDITIONS OF THE NEW COVENANT IN CHRIST

The old covenant, established on Mount Sinai, was clearly understood though not always followed. As a result, the people of God experienced the blessing or the cursing of God according to how they lived within the established covenant. The questions come today: What are the conditions of the new covenant? Are blessing and cursing involved in the new covenant as in the old covenant?

Circle the number that depicts how well you know God's covenant promises.

0   1   2   3   4   5   6   7   8   9   10
not at all   completely

Let him ask in faith without doubting. For the doubter is like the surging sea, driven and tossed by the wind. That person should not expect to receive anything from the Lord. An indecisive man is unstable in all his ways.

❧ JAMES 1:6-8 ❧

Truly, the terms of the covenant are the title deeds of our inheritance, the promises of God for His people to enjoy. This may be why many have never understood or enjoyed the greatness of God's salvation.

If Christians lack knowledge of the covenant relationship, they will be unsure or unstable in their lives. We are warned about the consequences of living the Christian life without confidence in God's promises. Read what James said in James 1:6-8.

When people understand the covenant relationship with God, they live in confidence and assurance that God will be faithful to keep His promises. These people are standing firm on the promises of God and are receiving answers to their prayers. Their strength is not in self-confidence but in absolute confidence that God will be true to fulfill the promises of the covenant.

This new covenant in Christ was not established with a nation but with anyone who would enter a relationship with God through the atoning sacrifice of Christ on the cross.

You are a ... holy nation, a people for His possession, so that you may proclaim the praises of the One who called you out of darkness into His marvelous light. Once you were not a people, but now you are God's people; you had not received mercy, but now you have received mercy.

❧ 1 PETER 2:9-10 ❧

Read 1 Peter 2:9-10 in the margin. Circle the purpose of being in covenant with God. Underline the blessings Christians receive when they enter a covenant with God.

Christians enter into a relationship with God that transforms every part of their lives. They now belong to God, for they have put their faith in Him and have chosen to follow Christ as their Lord.

THE CORPORATE IMPLICATIONS OF COVENANT

Although this new covenant with God is extremely personal, it is never private. The context of God's salvation is always in the larger purposes He has for His people. Individual believers understand that their personal relationship with God always affects all the other people in covenant with whom they associate.

Such was the case in the Old Covenant, as well. The entire nation of Israel was affected by each individual's personal covenant relationship with God. God had made them personally and collectively interdependent.

Indicate your agreement with this statement: The individual believer's personal relationship with God always affects all the people of God among whom he or she has been placed.

❑ I somewhat disagree.

❑ I'm neutral.

❑ I somewhat agree.

❑ I agree wholeheartedly.

The laws that God gave to guide the Israelites included how each individual was to keep himself in a love relationship with God, but it also included many commands to the entire nation to keep the covenant together. The nation affected every individual, and every individual affected the nation.

In the New Testament, individuals who entered a saving relationship with Christ also entered into a vital relationship with God's people in a local church. God added them to the church as it pleased Him (Acts 2:47; 1 Cor. 12:18).

THE HEART OF THE NEW COVENANT

Read 1Timothy 2:5 in the margin. Who is the mediator of the

new covenant between God and humanity? _____

There is one God and one mediator between God and man, a man, Christ Jesus.

❧ 1 TIMOTHY 2:5 ❧

The apostle Paul understood this when he said, "Every one of God's promises is 'Yes' in Him [Christ]. Therefore the 'Amen' is also through Him for God's glory through us" (2 Cor. 1:20). The new covenant with God is through Christ. In Him all the promises of God are fulfilled. In Christ our redemption was secured. At the cross Jesus paid for our sin and set us free from its consequences.

Jesus talked of the new covenant in His blood that grants us the forgiveness of sin and a relationship with God. The cross, therefore, is the heart of the covenant, forever symbolizing the love relationship God offers to people who put their faith in Him.

I love how Peter wrote his tender yet forceful exhortation: "You are to conduct yourselves in reverence during this time of temporary residence. For you know that you were redeemed from your empty way of life inherited from the fathers, not with perishable things, like silver or gold, but with the precious blood of Christ, like that of a lamb without defect or blemish" (1 Pet. 1:17-19). How awesome! The blood of the new covenant flowed from the body of God's only begotten Son, Jesus Christ, to those who believe Him and who enter into a covenant relationship with Him.

Jesus set His focus on going to the cross, for it was there that the new covenant would begin. He continually told His disciples that He must go to Jerusalem and be crucified. He knew that He must go so that the power of the cross could be exerted over all people. Much to the disciples' dismay, it was better for Him to go to the cross than to stay with them; the power of the cross, resurrection, ascension, and Pentecost could not come on all people without Jesus going to the cross.

Even today, personally and as a church, to resist the cross is to lose its power in us and through us. Jesus said we must deny self, take up our cross, and follow Him. If we try to avoid the cross, as did the disciples, we cannot go with the Lord or experience the blessings of the new covenant. If we take up our cross, we must also realize that the cross is not something for us to suffer on; it is something to die on! The cross in our lives means that the covenant is not to be taken lightly. Jesus gave everything so that we could walk in the covenant. We, too, must be willing to give our all, even our own lives, in order to walk in the covenant with God.

On the power scale in the margin, use an (x) to rank the power of the cross you experience in your personal life. Then place a (+) to indicate the power of the cross that is evident in your church.

If you indicated little power, how have you resisted the cross?

_____

_____

If you noted your church demonstrates little power, how do you think your church has resisted denying itself and following Christ?

_____

_____

List additional concerns you want to pray about for your church on the prayer list you made on day 5 of week 2 (p. 50).

on the prayer list you made on day 5 of week 2 (p. 50).

DAY THREE

Entering the Covenant

In keeping with the nature of mankind at creation, people are given the privilege to enter a covenant with God according to their own free will. Because of God's mercy and grace, He has chosen to offer this tremendous gift, the gift of a relationship with Himself. Yet we must respond to His offer and enter into a covenant relationship with Him.

God has never and will never force spiritual possessions upon us; He relies upon us to receive them. So how do we do it? How do we enter a covenant relationship with God and receive the purpose of our creation?

ENTER WHOLEHEARTEDLY

The secret of entering the covenant with God is wholeheartedness. Either you trust Him completely, or you do not trust Him at all. The first and greatest commandment is, " 'You shall love the Lord your God with all your heart, with all your soul, and with all your mind' " (Matt. 22:37). The decision to enter a relationship with Almighty God is one that demands a complete surrender of all that we are to all that He is and has promised to be in our lives and in our churches. The way we respond to God is a reflection of our belief in God. And without faith it is impossible to please Him.

Within the covenant those who give less than their whole hearts will receive much less than what they could have experienced in their relationship with God. Jesus taught this principle of giving and receiving in Luke 6:38. Read that passage in the margin.

Some churches tend to lower the standard for giving in order to attract more people and build bigger churches. Yet, in lowering the standard, many in our churches do not have a wholehearted walk with God. They were simply told how to get to heaven when they die and were not instructed in the covenant relationship with God and its inherent expectations. A love relationship with God is not merely an accessory to our lives; it is our lives.

When we enter a covenant with God and receive His great salvation, we must come prepared to give our lives to Him. All that we are and all that we ever hope to be is laid down at the foot of the cross. We can do nothing less if we desire to know God in His fullness. Paul assures us that in knowing Him fully, we are "filled with all the fullness of God" (Eph. 3:19).

> Wholeheartedness is the secret of entering the covenant with God.

> *"Give, and it will be given to you; a good measure, pressed down, shaken together, and running over will be poured into your lap. For with the measure that you use, it will be measured back to you."*
>
> ❧ LUKE 6:38 ❧

Match the references with the phrase that tells God's people what they should do wholeheartedly.

Deuteronomy 10:12	Seek the Lord with all your heart.
Proverbs 3:5	Rejoice in the Lord with all your heart.
Jeremiah 29:13	Trust in the Lord with all your heart.
Zephaniah 3:14	Serve the Lord with all your heart.

ENTER BY FAITH

The blessings that Jesus bestowed in His days on earth were often directly related to the faith of those who received them. He said to the centurion, " 'Go. As you have believed, let it be done for you' " (Matt. 8:13). To the woman who had suffered with a hemorrhage for 12 years he said, " 'Have courage, daughter. … Your faith has made you well' " (Matt. 9:22). He said to the two blind men who sought healing, " 'Let it be done for you according to your faith' " (Matt. 9:29). He said to the mother who sought healing for her demon-possessed daughter, " 'Woman, your faith is great. Let it be done for you as you want' " (Matt. 15:28).

The measure of one's faith has a direct correlation to the measure of God's response. One of the most tragic statements in the Bible is this, "He did not do many miracles there because of their unbelief" (Matt. 13:58). This is true not only for every believer but also for every church.

I was in a group of leaders who were discussing foreign missions and the task the Lord had given them. We were dealing with some challenging Scriptures when a man who was overseeing the financial side of the organization suddenly blurted out, "Well, you just need to know I'm the doubting Thomas in this group." It was clear what he meant by that statement. He was skeptical of anything that required faith.

So I responded, "Before or after you met the living Christ? Because after Thomas met the living Christ, he was not the same again. After that encounter with Christ, there is no evidence that he ever doubted again. In fact, tradition tells us that he traveled to India, shared the gospel, and was martyred for the sake of Christ."

It amazes me that Christians who have met the living Christ are unwilling to walk by faith. Let me suggest that if you are by nature a doubting person, God does not necessarily criticize you. But prolonged doubt becomes unbelief, and He does deal with that. If you have doubt, you need to move that doubt into the presence of God until He resolves it. If you choose not to believe every time you encounter Him, that is a much more grievous situation to God. He does not overlook unbelief, and your persistent doubt can have a devastating effect on your life and the lives of the people of God.

I wonder if the reason many Christians experience little blessing is that they entered into a relationship with God with little faith. Their walk with God is halfhearted, and they wonder why they are not experiencing the promises of God in all their fullness. Could it be that we are reaping what we have sown?

The measure of one's faith has a direct correlation to the measure of God's response.

Immediately the father of the boy cried out, "I do believe! Help my unbelief."
❧ MARK 9:24 ❧

Has prolonged doubt become unbelief in your life? ❏ Yes ❏ No
Read Mark 9:24. Ask God to help you overcome your unbelief so you may enter into His covenant with wholehearted faith.

A STORY FROM MEL BLACKABY

A Lesson from the Law of Gravity

Christians enjoy the benefits of a covenant relationship with God, whether we understand how it works or not. One of the amazing inventions of our time is the airplane. We take it for granted today, but consider its ability to do what at one time seemed impossible. It is parked on the tarmac, anchored firmly to the ground by the laws of gravity. Then the engine begins to rumble, and the plane starts toward the runway. The jet engines kick in, and it starts to race down the airstrip. The natural laws of gravity pull hard to keep the plane down, but soon another law begins to take effect. The laws of aerodynamics state that under certain conditions a heavy object can rise against the force of gravity and be lifted high into the air.

Although air travel means sending an enormous metal object into the sky against the laws of gravity, air travel is considered one of the safest modes of transportation we know. The laws of aerodynamics work with great efficiency! A 150-ton metal object can soar through the sky, high above the earth with relative ease.

To be honest, I don't understand the laws of aerodynamics; they are still a mystery to me. But I don't have to understand; I simply have to get on the plane, sit down, drink a Coke, eat a snack, and relax. I can sit by the window, look down on the earth, and enjoy the ride. I believe that the plane will fly, and I commit myself to that plane and get on board! In an amazing way, I enjoy the benefits of the plane's victory over gravity. Because the plane overcomes gravity, so do I—as long as I remain on the plane.

One day I was driving to the airport with my daughter who at that time was about five years old. We looked up and saw two men floating down to earth with parachutes. My daughter asked me where they came from. So we looked more fervently and spotted a small plane flying overhead. I began to explain that the plane took the two men into the air, and then they jumped out. In a way only a five-year-old could, she asked, "Dad, did they want to get out?" She knew there was safety in the plane, and to step outside also meant stepping outside of its safety.

In a similar way Jesus carries the repentant sinner right to the throne room of God, having overcome the law of sin and death. We enjoy the fruit of Christ's work on our behalf when He died on the cross for our sin and rose again. The key to that relationship is to believe in Christ and commit our lives to Him as Lord and Savior.

If we ever "step out of the plane" and try to live without Christ, we immediately begin a rapid decent away from His blessings. The covenant is still in place, but we have stepped outside of it and miss out on life as God intended.

How do people enter a covenant relationship with God?
(Hint: Review the subheads for today's lesson.)

Enter _____ and enter by _____

On the scale below, draw a stick figure of yourself to indicate where you are in covenant relationship to God.

Outside the covenant   Inside, but moving away   Inside the covenant

A Covenant to Remember

The Lord desires that we remember the covenant. In fact, He has commanded that we regularly acknowledge our covenant with Him in our lives and in our churches. So when does a person remember and acknowledge the covenant he has entered with God?

THE INVITATION

Many churches have an invitation time at the close of their worship services. This opportunity to come to the altar or to talk to the pastor allows individuals to respond to the work of the Holy Spirit as He draws them either to enter or restore their covenant relationship with God.

People may realize for the first time their need for a Savior and respond to God's invitation for salvation. Others may sense God leading them to serve Him in a new direction. During the invitation they may respond to God publicly, committing their lives in obedience. People may need the opportunity simply to come and pray, restoring the relationship that has been broken by sin.

Whatever the case, the invitation given in the corporate worship service affords the opportunity for people to begin or renew the covenant relationship.

> **If your church observes an invitation time, which of the following best describes your actions during the invitation? Add other responses in the margin.**
> ❏ I leave.
> ❏ I put on my coat and get my things together.
> ❏ I sing the invitation hymn and wonder how many more verses we're going to sing.
> ❏ I pray for others to respond to the pastor's message.
> ❏ I pray in response to the Holy Spirit's leading in my life.
> ❏ I often go forward to pray or speak to the pastor.

BAPTISM

A second place the covenant is established occurs in the ordinance of baptism. Baptism helps us remember the new covenant as we observe the symbolic reenactment of the death, burial, and resurrection of Christ. The cross is the central picture in this powerful act of obedience in a believer's life. Just as Jesus died for our sin and rose again, so the new believer dies to sin and rises to live a new life with Christ as Lord.

Baptism was a part of God's plan to cause all believers to acknowledge publicly what Christ has done for them. Just as Christ identified with sinful humanity through baptism, so we now identify

What a wretched man I am! Who will rescue me from this body of death? I thank God through Jesus Christ our Lord! Therefore, no condemnation now exists for those in Christ Jesus, because the Spirit's law of life in Christ Jesus has set you free from the law of sin and of death.

✤ ROMANS 7:24-25; 8:1-2 ✤

with Christ, the Holy One, through the same ordinance. In that moment we are acknowledging before a watching world that we willingly enter the new covenant in Christ.

The act of baptism will not save a person; it is an outward expression of what God has done on the inside of a person to transform one's heart and cause one to be born again. It is symbolic but so much more than just a symbol. It is an act of obedience to the commands of our Lord. Jesus commissioned His disciples to, " 'Go, therefore, and make disciples of all nations, baptizing them in the name of the Father and of the Son and of the Holy Spirit, teaching them to observe everything I have commanded you' " (Matt. 28:19-20).

We were buried with Him by baptism into death, in order that, just as Christ was raised from the dead by the glory of the Father, so we too may walk in a new way of life. For if we have been joined with Him in the likeness of His death, we will certainly also be in the likeness of His resurrection.

✤ ROMANS 6:4-5 ✤

What is the purpose of baptism? Mark through any responses that are not true.

It is an act of obedience.

It saves people from their sins.

It is a symbol of Christ's death, burial, and resurrection.

It is an outward expression of an internal reality.

It is an acknowledgement of a believer's covenant with God.

Have you been baptized as a believer in Christ? (circle) Yes No

JOINING A LOCAL BODY OF BELIEVERS

Receiving members into the church family is another moment when individuals are challenged to live in covenant with God and His people. When a person feels God is leading him to join fellowship with a local congregation, he is entering a covenant.

I always asked those who came to our church three questions. First, "Have you personally repented of your sin and surrendered your life to Jesus Christ as Lord?" Second, "Have you followed the Lord in believer's baptism by immersion, picturing death to the old life and resurrection to the new life in Christ?" And third, "Do you believe that God is clearly adding you to this body?"

If they responded positively to those questions, I would then ask, "Would you then enter into a covenant with God and His people, allowing Him to work through you to strengthen and build up this body?" Next, I would turn to the church and ask them to enter a covenant with the new person(s), committing themselves to pray for them, walk with them, and help them to become all that God wanted for their lives. Those were special times; we would renew our covenant together as a church that we might walk in harmony with God and one another, ready to fulfill God's purpose for our church. We reminded ourselves that we were a covenant people.

There are a thousand different ways to walk with the people in your church. My wife and I have five children. When our children were young, not many people were brave enough to invite our family of seven over for a meal. But gathering around the table with other believers is a wonderful way to keep connected, and it encourages others in the Lord. If you know some single parents who are struggling with their children, ask them to come for a meal in your home. You have no idea what that will do to encourage that parent and those children.

Take time along the way to encourage people at any stage in their Christian lives. For what God is doing in their lives touches you as a part of the body. You don't always have to wait until there is a crisis or until someone has completely fallen away from God. Don't let other believers in your fellowship struggle alone; intercept their lives before they get discouraged and fall away. Why? You have made a covenant with God and with them to walk together.

The children of a single mother in your church have been acting up during worship services and it's rumored they are hanging with a wild group at school. Check all of the responses that describe how you can express your covenant relationship with this family. Add further ideas in the margin.
- ❏ Tsk-tsk disapprovingly. Say, "People reap what they sow."
- ❏ Sit in a different spot during worship so the children won't disturb you.
- ❏ Smile kindly at the mother as you drive out of the parking lot.
- ❏ Offer to watch the children while the mother attends a week-night Bible study.
- ❏ Invite the children to accompany your family on an outing.
- ❏ Offer to assist in home maintenance chores or help the children with homework.
- ❏ Tactfully give money to relieve the family's financial strain.

COMMUNION, OR THE LORD'S SUPPER
The covenant is acknowledged when a believer observes communion (the Lord's Supper). Christians are in a new covenant, sealed in the blood of Christ, and the communion service is remembering, or renewing, that covenant.

As you read 1 Corinthians 11:23-25 in the margin, underline the reason the Lord told His followers to eat the bread and drink the cup.

In 1 Corinthians 11:28 the apostle Paul urged us to examine ourselves before taking communion. A broken relationship with Christ is paramount to a broken covenant with God. A holy God will not bless a people who have broken the new covenant, and communion is our

The Lord Jesus took bread, gave thanks, broke it, and said, "This is My body, which is for you. Do this in remembrance of Me." In the same way He also took the cup, after supper, and said, "This cup is the new covenant in My blood. Do this, as often as you drink it, in remembrance of Me."

❧ 1 CORINTHIANS 11:23-25 ❧

opportunity to examine our relationship to Christ and to be restored to the blessings of a covenant relationship.

As a pastor, I always helped our people understand that communion was a reminder of the incredible cost to God for us to enter the new covenant. People needed to examine themselves, because if one member of the body was out of fellowship with God, it affected the whole body. That is the nature of the covenant.

Knowing that God's Word shows us the ways of God and how He deals with His people when they are out of fellowship with Him, I was determined to lead our people to renew the covenant and confess their sins regularly. In the Old Testament the sin of Achan and his family caused the Israelites to be defeated when they went to battle against the city of Ai (see Josh. 7—9). In the New Testament the sin of Ananias and Sapphira was jeopardizing the entire work of God in the early church, so God dealt with them severely (see Acts 5:1-11). The communion service was established for such an occasion.

To remember the cross and the new covenant in Christ's blood will make a deep impact on those who take it seriously. Some of the greatest revivals in history came as a result of God's people participating in communion. In 1727, the Moravian Brethren were so impacted by the sacrificial death of Christ that every member of the church was drawn back to God and His purposes for their lives.

They saw their relationship to one another and to Christ in such a way that they felt the need for repentance and cleansing. Immediately, God heard their cry and brought revival to the congregation. Through a revived people, God made an impact that literally reached every corner of the earth.

In England, churches used to take a whole week for Communion. They thought it took a significant amount of time to examine themselves thoroughly and get right before God. Why? Because they were a covenant people.

Choose two of the questions to answer and share with your small group. Make any notes you need in the margin.
1. How has today's study changed the way you will respond during your church's invitation time?
2. Briefly describe your baptism experience. How does the memory of your baptism help you acknowledge your covenant with God?
3. Compare your understanding of church membership before this study with the insight you have gained into what it means to join a local church.
4. How will you partake of the Lord's Supper differently as a result of this study?

The Covenant Includes God's People

We can't understand the covenant relationship with God without also understanding that the covenant relationship includes God's people. When God established a covenant with His people in the Old Testament, it was corporate. All the people stood together and willingly entered the covenant, accepting all of its conditions and resultant consequences.

AN EXAMPLE FROM THE LIFE OF DANIEL

The life of Daniel illustrates how our lives are linked with one another as the covenant people of God. Early in Daniel's life he made a commitment to God that he never broke.

> **Find the book of Daniel in your Bible and keep it open for the activities to follow. In Daniel 1:3-5,8 check Daniel's commitment.**
> ❏ Not to eat meat.
> ❏ To be all he could be.
> ❏ To exercise twice daily.
> ❏ To pray twice daily.
> ❏ Not to defile himself.

Even though people around him were compromising, Daniel would not. Because of his faithfulness, God granted him favor in the eyes of the ruling officials in Babylon. King Nebuchadnezzar himself promoted him to be ruler over the whole province of Babylon and the chief prefect over all the wise men. As much as Daniel found favor in man's eyes, he was more concerned with finding favor in God's eyes, even if it meant being thrown into the lions' den.

The people of God as a whole did not follow the ways of God. They had turned away from God, but Daniel did not separate himself from them. Quite the opposite, he identified with them and pleaded to God on their behalf. Because they were all in the covenant relationship together, Daniel became the instrument through whom God would bring restoration to all of His people.

Daniel 9 contains one of the greatest prayers in the Bible. Daniel prays to God, pleading for mercy on behalf of the Israelites. Look at a portion of the prayer in verses 4-6 and notice how Daniel prays.

> **Read Daniel 9:4-6. Underline the characteristics of God that Daniel praised. Bracket the sins of the people mentioned by Daniel.**

I prayed to the Lord my God and confessed and said, "Alas, O Lord, the great and awesome God, who keeps His covenant and lovingkindness for those who love Him and keep His commandments, we have sinned, committed iniquity, acted wickedly, and rebelled, even turning aside from Thy commandments and ordinances. Moreover, we have not listened to Thy servants the prophets, who spoke in Thy name to our kings, our princes, our fathers, and all the people of the land."

❧ DANIEL 9:4-6 ❧

Read Daniel 9:16-19 in your Bible. In your own words, what was Daniel asking God to do?

_____

What an amazing prayer! Had Daniel sinned? Had he committed iniquity, acted wickedly, rebelled, and turned away from the commandments of God? No! Yet you would never know it if you only read this prayer without knowing the details of his life. Daniel completely identified with the rest of the people of God. Their sin became his sin, and his righteousness became their prayer. And because he stood with God's people in their time of need, they were all spared from the wrath of God. Read the answer to Daniel's prayer (Dan. 9:21-23) in the margin.

Incredible! Because of Daniel's upright character, as soon as he began to pray, Gabriel was dispatched from the throne room of God to go meet with him. What would have happened if Daniel had left the people on their own? What would have happened if he had not interceded on their behalf? Fortunately, we won't know the answers to those questions, for Daniel understood what it meant to be in a covenant relationship with God and His people.

While I was still speaking in prayer, then the man Gabriel, whom I had seen in the vision previously, came to me in my extreme weariness about the time of the evening offering. And he gave me instruction and talked with me, and said, "O Daniel, I have now come forth to give you insight with understanding. At the beginning of your supplications the command was issued, and I have come to tell you, for you are highly esteemed."

❧ DANIEL 9:21-23 ❧

EXPERIENCE THE COVENANT CONNECTION

When your church is in a time of trouble, what should you do? Go to a more healthy church? Criticize them and stand aloof? Because you are in a covenant relationship, you should stand with them and intercede on their behalf. What happens to them, happens to you. Romans 12:5 says, "We who are many are one body in Christ and individually members of one another."

We are connected to one another in the body of Christ. Whether we find ourselves in good times or times of trials, we must walk together before God. How we live affects all the rest of the body. How the body responds to God also affects our lives. How then do we encourage each other in the Lord? How do we pray for each other?

In retrospect, what have you done in the past when your church was in a time of trouble?
- ❑ Sat still as a mouse
- ❑ Stopped attending until the controversy passed
- ❑ Loudly made your viewpoint known
- ❑ Gossiped about it
- ❑ Went to another church
- ❑ Confessed sins of church to God
- ❑ Prayed both publicly and privately for your church

How will you commit to be a "Daniel" for your church in the future? Write your response in the margin.

COVENANT WITH EACH OTHER

The New Testament views Christians who have entered into the new covenant as a "chosen race, a royal priesthood, a holy nation, a people for His possession." Why? "So that you may proclaim the praises of the One who called you out of darkness into His marvelous light" (1 Pet. 2:9). Can you see how God views Christians today? We are chosen by God and belong to God. Therefore we are under the new covenant and must walk together as His people.

I mentioned in day 4 that our church members would enter into a covenant with each person whom God led to join fellowship with our church. We recognized that God had taken the initiative to move within a person's heart to obey Him in all things. We, therefore, made a pledge before God to be a good steward of every life God added to the body. Knowing that God had added the new member to the body and knowing that He saw what lay before this person in the days ahead, we were committed to helping each person become God's best, whatever that might require.

This covenant we had with God and with one another allowed us to keep those who came to the church. We were determined not to let them slip through the cracks. If a person's attendance began to slip, we knew something was wrong. To us nonattendance was a symptom of a deeper problem, and we were committed to care for one another's needs. If the person started to wander and fall away, we pledged to remain faithful and not let go.

I see an alarming trend in churches today. When a person is not walking in line with the vision of the church, often the church in effect cuts him off and sends him elsewhere. Or, if a person has fallen away from God and is living in sin, he is quickly criticized and put outside of the church body. We have become so driven by evangelism that we have forgotten to take care of the people of God.

FOCUS THE CHURCH ON THE PEOPLE OF GOD

One of the Scriptures often used for evangelism is Luke 19:10. Jesus said, " '[I have] come to seek and to save the lost.' " That verse is taken from Ezekiel 34, referring to the people of God. It condemns the shepherds who have let the flock scatter into the mountains, exposing themselves to the elements and danger from wild beasts. The Lord chastised those who would not go after the sheep, bring them back, feed them, and care for them. God said that He would raise up a shepherd who would seek and save that which was lost. That shepherd is Jesus. The sheep are the people of God.

We are in trouble if we have more concern for the unbeliever than we do the believer. God's heart always looks to His own first, for as go the people of God, so goes His purpose to redeem the rest of the world. My wife and I are currently members at a large church. A significant

You are a chosen race, a royal priesthood, a holy nation, a people for His possession, so that you may proclaim the praises of the One who called you out of darkness into His marvelous light.
Once you were not a people, but now you are God's people; you had not received mercy, but now you have received mercy.

❧ 1 PETER 2:9-10 ❧

part of our service is a time for people to come and pray at the altar. One Sunday I watched a young man go forward to pray, and I could tell that he was shaking. I got up from my seat, went down to the front, and knelt beside him; then I proceeded to pray for this young man. His head turned around, and he interrupted my prayer. "Dr. Blackaby, you have come to pray with me! You don't know what that means to me and the decision I am wrestling with today."

I discovered that he was a college student studying law, and he sensed God was calling him into the ministry. He responded to God's call on his life and is now preparing to serve the Lord.

What I did is called encouragement. When we are walking in a covenant relationship with other people, we must find ways to help them become God's best. Whether it is a college student seeking direction for his life, a young girl who feels the call to missions, or an older man who has wasted many years but now wants to make his remaining days count—people need someone to encourage them.

In Matthew 12:30 Jesus said, " 'Anyone who is not with Me is against Me, and anyone who does not gather with Me scatters.' " If we are not actively trying to gather together with Him, we are scattering. When you are in the body, you are either positively building up the body, or you are negatively tearing it down. Be careful that you don't let a divisive spirit remain in your life or in your church. Examine your life. Have you positively contributed to God's work by encouraging others in the Lord?

Give yourself a grade, ranging from A+ to F, on how well you are obeying the admonition in Hebrews 10:24-25. How is God prompting you to pray in response to your "report card?"

Grade _____

Prayer _____

_____

Let us be concerned about one another in order to promote love and good works, not staying away from our meetings, as some habitually do, but encouraging each other, and all the more as you see the day drawing near.

❧ HEBREWS 10:24-25 ❧

---

[1]John H. Sammis, "Trust and Obey," in *The Baptist Hymnal* (Nashville: Convention Press, 1991), 447.

The Head of the Church

He [God] demonstrated this power in the Messiah by raising Him from the dead and seating Him at His right hand in the heavens—far above every ruler and authority, power and dominion, and every title given, not only in this age but also in the one to come. "He put everything under His feet" and appointed Him as head over everything for the church, which is His body, the fullness of the One who fills all things in every way.

❧ EPHESIANS 1:20-23 ❧

Hank, Fred, and Leon are the trustees of their church. Everyone knows that to get something approved you have to go through them. If they don't like the idea, you might as well forget it.

Even the pastor is obliged to cater to their views. After all, the previous pastor tried an end run around them, and you know what happened to him.

What's wrong with this picture of church life? This week we will be studying the biblical pattern for authority and decision-making. As you read, ask yourself these questions:

1. Is Christ truly the Head in every church, or is He merely a figurehead?
2. How does God shape your church for His purposes?
3. How important is unity in the body as it follows Christ the Head?
4. How important is it that the members are healthy for the whole body to respond to Christ as the Head?
5. What role do leaders play in ensuring unity in the church family?

Christ, the Head

The first church I pastored in California was in a rough city in the greater San Francisco area. God had strategically placed our church in that area to say to a hurting community, "I love you." I knew almost everyone involved with major crimes, before or after the incident. I was in and out of most prisons, including San Quentin.

We heard that a new youth gang had been formed in a low-rent district where some of our church members lived. Called the Untouchables, they soon began to terrorize that area. One Sunday evening 25 of the gang members walked noisily into our service, folded their arms, and leaned their metal chairs back against the rear wall of the auditorium.

Little did they know that I grew up familiar with gang warfare, and their grand entrance didn't bother me. Not only was I not afraid of them, but inside I was shouting, *Got you! You will now hear from God!* God began to work in their lives, and within 6 months our church rejoiced that 23 of the 25 had been saved.

Later I was invited to a law enforcement banquet. During the program, an officer who worked with young offenders asked me to stand. He said, "The area of our city that used to have the highest calls of crime now has the lowest. This young man (I was 26 at the time) and his church have made the difference." In reality, it was Christ working through our church to impact the community.

God places His people in a church in the most strategic areas to demonstrate His presence and power to a watching world. The saving presence of Christ will then be manifest through the church that is willing to be used of God. The key is Christ in us, for He will always fulfill the purposes of His Father to bring the peoples of the world into a relationship with Him.

> The key is Christ in us, for He will always fulfill the purposes of His Father.

The greatest truth a church must understand, if it wants to be used by God, is that Christ is the Head of the church. We may believe this truth theologically; it is quite another thing to live it practically. How does a church function under His headship? I pray, as did the apostle Paul, "that the eyes of your heart may be enlightened so you may know what is the hope of His calling" (Eph. 1:18) for the church. When we follow Christ as the Head of our churches, we will be overwhelmed at what He will accomplish through us.

In the margin rewrite the following statement from the author to make it true.
God places His people in a church in the most strategic areas so the church can reach its greatest potential for growth.

THE CHURCH: A LIVING BODY

The fullest description of how God forms the local church into a living body of Christ is found in Romans 12:3-21; 1 Corinthians 12; and Ephesians 4:1-16. Christ is described as the Head of the body.

What portions of your body are controlled by your head?

_____

List all the bodily systems that are not controlled by the head.

_____

Did you write anything on the blank line above? ❏ Yes ❏ No
What does this truth teach us about Christ as the Head of His body?

_____

Speaking the truth in love, let us grow in every way into Him who is the Head—Christ. From Him the whole body, fitted and knit together by every supporting ligament, promotes the growth of the body for building up itself in love by the proper working of each individual part.

♣ EPHESIANS 4:15-16 ♣

The Head controls, directs, instructs, guides, motivates, and keeps the body functioning according to His purposes. Read Ephesians 4:15-16 in the margin. Note how Paul described the body to the Ephesian church.

In 1 Corinthians 12:24-25 Paul described the nature of the church to the Corinthian Christians: "God has put the body together, ... that there would be no division in the body, but that the members would have the same concern for each other."

The key to a healthy body is our relationship to Christ. When members faithfully relate to Christ, the Head, His life flows to them and through them to the rest of the body. When members function where God placed them in the body (see 1 Cor. 12:18), the body grows in love. When every member is responsive to the Head, the body can obediently carry out the will of the Father.

How would you diagnose the health of your church body? Underline your response.
On life support
Gasping for breath
Moderately healthy but out of shape
Suffering from paralysis
Chronically fatigued
Brimming with health and vigor

If you diagnosed your church as unhealthy, what is the key to restoring your church to health? Write your answer in the margin.

What is your personal responsibility in restoring and maintaining your church's health?

_____

While Jesus was in the flesh, He always knew the will of His Father. He never misunderstood the Father, for the Holy Spirit was directing His life. Once He knew the will of the Father, Jesus was always quick to obey Him. We need a firm grasp of how Jesus functioned in the first century, for He will function in the same way in the church today.

Draw a line from each reference to the statement Jesus made about Himself and God's will.

John 4:34   " 'I have come ... not to do My will,
                   but the will of Him who sent Me.' "

John 5:30   " 'My food is to do the will of
                   Him who sent Me.' "

John 6:38   " 'I always do what pleases [the
                   One who sent Me].' "

John 8:29   " 'I do not seek My own will, but
                   the will of Him who sent Me.' "

CHRIST: THE LIVING HEAD

The same Jesus who always knew the will of the Father and always obeyed the Father now has a new body through which to work. The Father fashioned together a church with Christ as the Head and each believer as a part of the body. Now the living Christ will lead the rest of the body to fulfill the purposes of God. When a church yields completely to Christ, there is no limit to what God will do through that church.

Everything the Father accomplished in His great salvation has been given to Christ. Everything that sin has done, God fully defeated and placed under Jesus' feet. In His letter to the church in Colossae, Paul affirmed this: "He erased the certificate of debt [caused by sin], with its obligations, that was against us and opposed to us, and has taken it out of the way by nailing it to the cross. He disarmed the rulers and authorities and disgraced them publicly" (Col. 2:14-15).

Christ the Head directs the body, instructs the body, and motivates the body according to the sovereign will of the Father. While Jesus ministered on earth:

1. He never failed to *hear* the will of the Father.
2. He never failed to *understand* the will of the Father.
3. He never failed to *do* the will of the Father.

The same Jesus who always knew the will of the Father and always obeyed the Father now has a new body through which to work.

"If anyone wants to come with Me, he must deny himself, take up his cross, and follow Me. For whoever wants to save his life will lose it, but whoever loses his life because of Me will find it."

❧ MATTHEW 16:24-25 ❧

As a result, the Father could perfectly accomplish His will through Jesus during His life on earth. Now Jesus is doing the will of His Father through the local church.

Do you believe this? ❑ Yes ❑ No
Will you respond obediently as the Head instructs you in your place in the body? ❑ Yes ❑ No

---

A STORY FROM MEL BLACKABY

The Greatest Blessings

Seminary life was winding down, and Gina and I knew God was preparing us for ministry in Canada. Several churches contacted us, but as we prayed about God's will, He directed us to a small, struggling church in British Columbia, Canada. In fact, it was in the worst condition of any church that had talked with us. But God is the Master, and we are the servants, so we pursued it.

This small congregation had merged with another struggling church so that they could call a new pastor together; that made a total of 19 members. When we flew up to meet with the people and confirm God's direction in our lives, the situation looked worse than we first thought. I was the only pastoral candidate willing to talk with them about coming. The bleak financial situation made it apparent that even the salary they promised was mostly in faith that God would provide it from somewhere.

The building was falling apart and infested with termites. It had no sound system, computer, photocopier, nor equipment of any kind. The congregation had only a couple of children and no youth or young adults. We looked at the housing market and were disappointed that we wouldn't be able to buy a home. The closest church in our convention was 2 1/2 hours away, and they were averaging about 40 people. We would soon discover that many people in the community were convinced our building was demon possessed and needed a cleansing.

As I began to compare the place of service I was leaving to the situation I was considering, I thought of the pastoral experience I had gained and the Ph.D. I was completing. I quickly surmised that I deserved a larger church with better pay! Wrong! Nothing could be further from the truth! I didn't deserve anything from God. Serving anywhere in the kingdom of God was far more than I deserved. It was an honor and privilege to serve as a pastor of any church.

As my wife and I talked about what we were walking away from and what we were about to get into, she began to weep. As she held our baby in her arms, she asked, "Mel, do we really want to do this?" It broke my heart. So we prayed and sought the face of God together.

As we did, the Lord seemed to guide our thinking. He said, "Mission work is hard! If you don't go, who will?" He left us with the realization that sacrifice is all right.

God's will is often hard work, but somebody must go. The Lord gave us no assurances that He would bless the work and cause the church to grow. He simply said, "Mission work is hard, but will you follow me anyway?" Then the Holy Spirit brought a familiar passage to our minds. Read it in the margin at the top of the page.

That night we knelt and prayed to God, committing to follow Him whatever the cost. As soon as we made the decision to accept this difficult assignment, the Holy Spirit brought peace and assurance that if we step out in faith, He will be faithful. That is indeed what happened. What we thought was a sacrifice turned out to be one of the greatest blessings of our lives.

DAY TWO

The Body Connected to the Head

By definition, a Christian is a follower of Christ. Being a church is also nothing less than being a follower of Christ.

FOLLOW CLOSELY IN JESUS' STEPS

How do we follow Christ as the Head of our church without getting sidetracked? Many false "heads" vie for our attention. First, we must learn to follow closely in Jesus' steps (1 Pet. 2:21).

He is also the head of the body, the church.

❧ COLOSSIANS 1:18 ❧

A STORY FROM MEL BLACKABY

Following the Right Trail

I pastored a church in British Columbia, Canada, a place filled with beautiful mountain ranges, trees, and rivers. A member of our church worked for the federal government in the area of water conservation and flood control. One day in the middle of winter George asked me if I wanted to go with him to check the readings at one of their remote stations. Heavy snow had already arrived, so we drove as far as we could in the truck, and unloaded two snowmobiles to ride another 45 minutes. Now George had spent most of his career working in harsh, Canadian weather. He hit the gas and aggressively raced off into the woods. Still getting used to the snowmobile, I launched out with caution, trying to get the feel of the machine I was riding.

I quickly realized that George was leaving me behind. The tracks of other snowmobiles in the area were my biggest concern. There seemed to be a thousand trails going every direction through the woods. The thought crossed my mind, *If I lose George, I will never find my way back to civilization!* So I hit the gas, lowered my head to get more streamlined, leaned into every corner, and kept my eyes firmly fixed on the man I needed to follow. If I was going to die that day, it would not be from getting lost—though hitting a tree was a very real possibility.

Do you see the lesson God taught me? Many roads lead through life. Others have left trails that lead away from the destination God has for me. As a pastor, I must keep my eyes firmly fixed on Jesus, or I will be hopelessly lost. I must help others see Him and encourage the church to follow Jesus with all their hearts. Unless our church is determined to follow Him, we will neither reach the destination He has for us nor fulfill His purposes for our lives.

Is your church following Christ or have you gotten sidetracked? Mark an X on the map on page 80 to indicate where your church is in relation to God's purpose. If your church is on the wrong road, can you identify the reasons you became sidetracked from following Christ? If so, write that reason in the margin.

If you feel your church is heading away from God's destination, what will you do to help your church get back on the right track?

FULFILL YOUR ASSIGNED ROLE

As Mel's story illustrates, churches can stay on track by following closely the footprints of Jesus. Second, we can follow Christ more faithfully by fulfilling our assigned role in the body. One of the most beautiful and practical Scriptures describing how the church body relates to the Head is Ephesians 4:7,11-13.

Who gives believers the gift of grace? _____
Underline what believers are to do with the gifts they are given
Circle the ultimate goal of building up the body of Christ.

Grace was given to each one of us according to the measure of the Messiah's gift. ... And He personally gave some to be apostles, some prophets, some evangelists, some pastors and teachers, for the training of the saints in the work of ministry, to build up the body of Christ, until we all reach unity in the faith and in the knowledge of God's Son, growing into a mature man with a stature measured by Christ's fullness.

❧ EPHESIANS 4:7,11-13 ❧

The body is composed of people who have been called out of the world and gathered together by God Himself. Members are directly related to the Head by God's great salvation. He teaches them about their new relationship with the Heavenly Father and His eternal purposes that are being worked out in the world around them. He instructs them about their lives in the body and how they fit into the greater purposes of the Father. He fills them with His love so that they might share His love with every other member in the body. He gives them everything they need to edify and build up the body.

MAINTAIN A CLOSE RELATIONSHIP WITH CHRIST

Individual Christians can't participate effectively in the life of the church unless their are participating in a deeply personal relationship with Christ. Nothing substitutes for a personal walk with Him. Good biblical preaching and teaching aren't adequate by themselves if you want to do your part in the body (Eph. 4:15-16). Our relationship to God doesn't come from the church but from an encounter with Him.

Let us lay aside every weight and the sin that so easily ensnares us, and run with endurance the race that lies before us, keeping our eyes on Jesus, the source and perfecter of our faith.

HEBREWS 12:1-2

ENJOY GOD'S PRESENCE

As Christians, we have the ability to draw near to God and enter into the holy place. We have access to God's presence and fellowship. We can make His presence our dwelling place, enjoying all the benefits of such a relationship and learning directly from Him.

Read Hebrews 10:19,22 in the margin. Counter the false beliefs below by writing true statements.

People have no hope of ever approaching God.

_____

Since we have boldness to enter the sanctuary [holy place] through the blood of Jesus, ... let us draw near with a true heart in full assurance of faith.

❧ HEBREWS 10:19-22 ❧

Christians should be terrified of God.

_____

Christians can't be assured of their standing with God.

_____

The relationship to God is far more than just enjoying life with Him. To enter the holy place is a call to—

* come out from the world and into the presence of God and the people of God;
* stop wandering around and enter into the promised land of God's blessing; find purpose within the will of God;
* stop lingering in the outer court of the temple, the fringes of religious life, and enter into the heart of the Christian faith in the middle of God's activity;
* cease doubting and thirst for a better life; believe that Christ will bring abundant life;
* dwell in the full light of God's countenance; live your life with meaning and significance. When you do, God pours into your life the blessings of heaven, filling you with His Spirit and allowing you to walk with Him.

Believers were added to the Lord in increasing numbers—crowds of both men and women.

❧ ACTS 5:14 ❧

Read Acts 5:14, Acts 6:7 and Acts 9:31 in the margin. Underline all that occurred when the early church in Jerusalem responded to Christ with one heart and mind.

So the preaching about God flourished, the number of the disciples in Jerusalem multiplied greatly, and a large group of priests became obedient to the faith.

❧ ACTS 6:7 ❧

WITNESS BOLDLY

Another way we can keep from getting sidetracked is to obey the command of our Head to be His witnesses. The Lord does not want "any to perish, but all to come to repentance" (2 Pet. 3:9).

God is merciful and long-suffering toward His people. He wants every person to hear the gospel and have an opportunity to repent and be saved from his or her sin. But too often churches become self-centered and are not willing to look beyond themselves to the needs around them. When a church becomes selfish, it will inevitably begin to have quarrels within the body. As a result, the lost world around

So the church throughout all Judea, Galilee, and Samaria had peace, being built up and walking in the fear of the Lord and in the encouragement of the Holy Spirit, and it increased in numbers.

❧ ACTS 9:31 ❧

them suffers grievously because His people stop taking the gospel to others who need it so desperately.

God has no Plan B. He purposed that His churches take His good news to the world. If we are not doing it, He demonstrates his great mercy by not judging us immediately as He could. Instead, He is long-suffering and patient in working with His people to repent. Too much is at stake. Withholding judgment from His people, however, will not be delayed forever, and "the day of the Lord will come" (2 Pet. 3:10).

The reason for His patience? He is not willing that any should perish. So He works with and warns His people as He does with the church at Ephesus in Revelation 2:1-7. When a church loses its first love, it has lost its reason for being and is of little use to God.

As a pastor, I was particularly concerned if we were in danger of losing our first love. I saw this dramatically in a deacons' meeting when one of our men said, "Pastor, you should assign us people to visit." He was asking for prodding or additional motivation to go out and do his job. I said, "I won't do that. If love does not compel you to visit, I won't use any other substitute for love." I then taught them from 1 Corinthians 13, 2 Corinthians 5, and Revelation 2. God was gracious and brought every heart to unity. I never had to assign them someone to love. They did it out of pure hearts before God.

Consider the activities you are involved in at your church. Have you been acting on assignment or out of love? Mark your answer with an X on the line below.

assignment   love

If God is not willing that any perish, He will lay His heart on our hearts; the love of Christ compels us. We must always guard our hearts and the hearts of the people in our churches. Keep before you Jesus' words in Mark 16:15-16 (in the margin).

At the beginning of today's study, you were asked, "How do we follow Christ as the Head of our church without getting sidetracked?" Write statements and Scriptures you read today that help you answer that question.

_____

_____

_____

The day of the Lord will come like a thief; on that day the heavens will pass away with a loud noise, the elements will burn and be dissolved, and the earth and the works on it will be disclosed. Since all these things are to be destroyed in this way, it is clear what sort of people you should be in holy conduct and godliness.

❧ 2 PETER 3:10-11 ❧

How to keep from getting sidetracked
1. Follow closely in Jesus' steps.
2. Fulfill your assigned role.
3. Maintain a close relationship with Christ.
4. Enjoy God's presence.
5. Witness boldly.

"Whoever believes and is baptized will be saved, but whoever does not believe will be condemned."

❧ MARK 16:15-16 ❧

❧ A STORY FROM MEL BLACKABY ❧

The Other Side of the Gospel

Not long ago God began to draw a young couple to our church and to stir their hearts toward spiritual things. The wife had virtually no religious background. She soon prayed to receive Christ as her Lord and Savior.

She made an appointment to talk with me about following the Lord in believer's baptism. She asked, "If what I have heard is true, and I believe it is, then that means my mom and dad will not be with me in heaven." She began to weep. I then knew that she understood both sides of the gospel. Those who believe in Christ will be saved, but those who don't believe will perish. *Perish!* What an awful word! Separated from God eternally as a consequence of sin.

We must carry this burden in our churches and never lose it! Each Sunday school teacher must not only teach a lesson but also know personally if every member of the class is saved. He or she must seek to enlist them to " 'go out into the highways and lanes and make them come in, so that my house may be filled' " (Luke 14:23).

Soon after D. L. Moody, the great preacher and evangelist, was saved, he was under such conviction about the lostness of the poor children and youth that he started his own Bible class. Quickly it grew to hundreds in attendance, and many were saved. Would the heart of God have you do this, as you seek to be on mission with your Lord to touch a lost world?

DAY THREE

The Body Shaped for His Mission

As God begins to work through His Son to accomplish His purposes, each church must respond immediately to what He is doing. He has a plan for every church and the power to complete His purposes. Paul assured the church in Corinth that "God has placed the parts, each one of them, in the body just as He wanted" (1 Cor. 12:18).

Each New Testament church was unique. Revelation 2—3 describes their uniqueness of membership, location, and assignment. The Lord knew them better than they knew themselves and was present to guide them according to His purposes.

CHURCHES HAVE UNIQUE ASSIGNMENTS

I have often thought of each church being unique, according to God's assignment, in the light of sports. A person trains his body to match his assignment. A sprinter trains his body differently than does a power lifter. Their bodies look and function differently because their bodies are asked to perform two completely different tasks. Even in football an offensive lineman trains differently from a wide receiver. Although they are working together to win the game, one trains for power and strength while the other trains for speed and agility. Each trains his body for maximum efficiency. The goal for all the team is to win the game, but each player must be equipped and function in the position assigned by the coach.

Even so, God has the assignment for each church. He adds members who help the body fulfill its assignment and places each member in the body by His design for maximum efficiency. Each member is vital to the body. Each has a special place in the body to help the entire body function at its greatest ability.

When God adds a new member to your church body, you begin to see a new assignment being given by God, simply because He chose to add that particular member. New members indicate to the rest of the body what God is seeking to do through them. When God began to add college students to our church, we realized several things:

1. God does not add members accidentally but as it pleases Him.
2. God was alerting us to His intentions, so we watched carefully to see what He was doing.
3. God was calling into the ministry many of the young adults He had added.
4. The church adjusted its activities to help them fulfill their call from God.
5. God wanted us to establish a training center to equip those whom He was calling.
6. As the church provided training, God began to bring people from many other places to study there.
7. As the Head led us to do the will of the Father, God's purpose for our church was accomplished.

The ones God added to our church family were not only to help us fulfill our unique assignment but also to add to and clarify our assignment in greater detail. Many of those who attended our training center are now serving faithfully across the nation, fulfilling the purposes of God through their lives.

Bethlehem Church has had several active retired senior adults join their church this year. In the margin list what possible assignments God might have for Bethlehem Church?

The Smith family joined First Church last month. Their child has several developmental challenges. What would you challenge First Church to do in response to this new family God added to the body? Write your answer in the margin.

Can you identify possible new assignments God is giving your church through members He has added recently? Be prepared to share your thoughts during the small-group session.

MEMBERS HAVE UNIQUE ASSIGNMENTS

Paul instructed the church in Corinth that the whole body is not an eye, for the body also needs the ear to hear. It needs the nose to smell. It needs the hand to touch. One member of the body is not the whole body. Each part is important, but only as it is functioning along with the rest of the body parts.

God shaped the church to function as a living organism that must work together to realize each member's potential. We in the church are interdependent. We need one another and are needed by one another.

In one church I pastored, the Lord added a wonderful couple who had a teenage son in prison. This was a first for us, but I alerted the church to God's activity when the couple joined. Sure enough, it wasn't long before the church saw one of our ministries was to the youth and later the adult prisons in our city.

God added a young woman with a great burden for the physically challenged. As she began to teach us and equip us to care for this special group of people, we began a ministry to those who are often neglected but precious to God.

We had been praying about starting a ministry on some Native American reserves, but we had a hard time getting accepted by them. When God added nurses and doctors to our congregation, the doors opened for us to minister there. We didn't copy what was successful in other churches. We let God shape us uniquely for the assignment He had for us.

Which of the following items best illustrates your church's approach to new ministries? Add other descriptions in the margin.
- ❑ An immovable boulder
- ❑ A copy machine
- ❑ A cookie cutter
- ❑ A sprinter at the starting gun
- ❑ A moldable ball of clay

If each church let God build and fashion its body, He would have somebody to take the gospel to every person. If we copy others' successes, we will try to reach the same people with the same methods, and many will go untouched as a result. That is why churches are often so different from one another. But when we all do our part, we find that God's strategy to reach every person in our communities is realized.

No one should be turned aside or neglected because you don't feel he or she fits into your church. God has the sovereign right to add to your church as it pleases Him, and He doesn't need to ask your permission! He knows what He is doing, and it is always linked directly to His purpose for your church.

We who are strong have an obligation to bear the weaknesses of those without strength, and not to please ourselves.
❧ ROMANS 15:1 ❧

God shaped the church to function as a living organism that must work together to realize each member's potential.

If each church let God build and fashion its body, He would have somebody to take the gospel to every person.

A manifestation of the Spirit is given to each person to produce what is beneficial. But one and the same Spirit is active in all these, distributing to each one as He wills.

❧ 1 Corinthians 12:7,11 ❧

Read 1 Corinthians 12:7,11. How does God equip the body? Underline it.

Members Help or Hinder the Church's Mission

The Holy Spirit is the power behind each member and the life of each church. We will see this more clearly in week 5. When one part of the body is not functioning as it should, the rest of the body cannot perform to its potential.

❧ A STORY FROM MEL BLACKABY ❧

Limping Forward

I love sports, and when I was younger I had the privilege of playing on some championship teams. Soccer was one of my favorite sports. Our team had a great coach and many talented players who worked together as a unit. Because of our success, we had the opportunity to travel and play in some international tournaments.

On one occasion we played in an invitational tournament that brought many teams from across North America. The competition was fierce, and the athletes gave their all to win. Unfortunately, as I stretched to make a play, another player kicked me in the back of the leg with all of his force. Immediately I felt my calf muscle tighten and pain surge through my body.

My initial reaction was to crumble and attend the injury, but my desire to win wouldn't let me stop. I reasoned that I needed to keep the muscle stretched and not let it cramp up on me. So I limped on into battle, unwilling to take myself out of the game. The injury became apparent to everybody, especially my coach. I wasn't making plays I would normally make. I didn't have the speed I once had. I didn't have the concentration I needed, because I was distracted by the pain. Even though I was determined to play through the injury, my coach, who was determined to win, decided I was more of a detriment than a benefit to the team. He pulled me off the field.

As much as the rest of my body wanted to play, it was hindered because of one part that was injured. The same is true in a church. The church body may be determined to limp forward, but it will be ineffective in doing the will of the Father unless it helps all the members to function where God has placed them. No matter how badly a church wants to go forward and fulfill the purposes of God, if it doesn't take care of all its members, it will be severely hindered.

What statements reflect your thoughts after reading Mel's story?
- ❏ We might as well give up now because that task is too hard.
- ❏ What if some members don't want to function where God has placed them?
- ❏ It's better to limp forward than not go anywhere at all.
- ❏ I want to discover my role in caring for those in my church body.
- ❏ This calling deserves serious prayer.
- ❏ God wants to do something glorious in our church.

We must also be aware that the Father has the right to remove us from our position in the spiritual battles we are fighting if we are not doing what He called us to do. Envision the Lord as He walked through the churches in the Book of Revelation. He checked to see if they were doing what He asked them to do.

If we are not able to fulfill our purpose, this same Lord calls us to repent and return to Him. Unless He brings healing and wholeness to our lives, we are of little use to Him. We must take special care of one another. The health of the body is crucial because the purposes of God are at stake.

DAY FOUR

The Body Responsive to the Head

Your deepest desires as a church member should first be your relationship with Christ and second the maturity of every other member of the body where God has placed you. Seek to know how Christ will bring others to maturity through you. It may be by encouraging, teaching, helping, exhorting, giving, or ministering. God's goal is for every member of the church to be greatly blessed through His life in you.

> **Underline the gifts you use to bless your church. In the margin, add additional ways you are serving God and His people.**
>
> encouraging   teaching   singing   helping   cooking
>
> praying   giving   writing   ministering   serving

Since God adds to the body as it pleases Him, the first thing the church must respond to is the people He sends to them. They must receive people with the utmost care and sensitivity, knowing that they are part of God's purposes for the church. Jesus said, " 'The one who receives whomever I send receives Me, and the one who receives Me receives Him who sent Me' " (John 13:20). A church's response is most significant, therefore, to God.

HOW GOD REVEALS HIS MISSION FOR THE CHURCH

In week 3 I explained that we tried to receive new members by a solemn, covenanting process. We spent time teaching the church what it meant to respond to God in this manner. We gave careful exposition of Scripture (especially Matt. 16:13-27) and traced how the early church in Jerusalem lived out its relationship with Christ in the Book of Acts. We helped them see how a church responded to Christ by studying Romans 12, 1 Corinthians 12, and Ephesians 4. We helped them see how Christ was present and personal in His relationship with us as described in Revelation 1—3.

The church had to see the heart and purposes of God as revealed in Scripture in order for us to respond adequately as God worked in our church. Much was at stake for us and for the kingdom of God.

❖ A STORY FROM MEL BLACKABY ❖

Following the Wrong Direction

While serving my first church in a small, west Texas town, I discovered that being the pastor of the only Baptist church in town meant that I was automatically drafted into the volunteer fire department. Apparently all the men in town had real jobs to attend to during the day, and the pastor and the retired men had plenty of time to fight fires. I mostly chased grass fires.

The other interesting part of living in a small town was the intense rivalry between the towns in the area. I was drawn into the rivalry because the volunteer fire departments often competed against one another—not just in sports but also in getting better equipment and training.

One day the volunteers in the town down the road were having an elaborate training exercise. They were to practice putting out a house fire in an abandoned home in the country. The house was set on fire, and the blaze was spectacular. They followed procedure to the letter and put the fire out with great efficiency, except for one minor detail—it was the wrong house!

Somehow they misunderstood the details of the assignment. They had the wrong directions. The people in charge of the training exercise had failed to communicate clearly the job to be done. They did a great job, just the wrong job.

Churches are in danger of doing a great job but the wrong job. We may be enthusiastic, creative, and effective in what we do, but we better know what the Heavenly Father wants us to do. Jesus told us that the Father is not impressed with doing good things well; He is looking for obedience to His will (see Matt. 7:21-23).

"Not everyone who says to Me, 'Lord, Lord!' will enter the kingdom of heaven, but the one who does the will of My Father in heaven. On that day many will say to Me, 'Lord, Lord, didn't we prophesy in Your name, drive out demons in Your name, and do many miracles in Your name?' Then I will announce to them, 'I never knew you! Depart from Me, you lawbreakers!'"

❖ MATTHEW 7:21-23 ❖

Read Matthew 7:21-23 in the margin. What did the people in this passage do in an attempt to impress Jesus? Underline it.

Who did Jesus say would enter His kingdom? Circle it.

The only way our church will know what the Father wants is to consistently listen to His Son, the Head of our church. Unless Christ directs us, we will never know the will of the Father. Consequently, we may be burning down the neighbor's house!

HOW GOD REVEALS HIS MISSION THROUGH EACH MEMBER

As God added new members to our body, the rest of the church pledged to help them to fulfill all that God desired for their lives and challenge them to minister to the body to which God had just added them. Those who joined our church were challenged to let God work through them to help the body become all that God desired it to be. This had a significant effect on them and on our church family.

This watch care of the members included the children and the youth as well. Since we loved our Lord, we loved each one He gave us. A church will be entrusted with more if we are faithful to care for the ones He has already given. In fact, church growth is in the hands of Christ, and He bases it on the response of the members to the Father's activity in their midst. After all, each one who comes is choosing to become a disciple of Christ.

Does your church make adjustments in how to respond to God's assignments through those He adds as He shapes your church?
❑ Yes ❑ No ❑ Occasionally

How do you as an individual receive those Gods adds to your church? Check all that apply.
❑ I do nothing.
❑ I shake their hands after the worship service.
❑ I seek ways to form relationships with them.
❑ I try to help them grow into Christlikeness.
❑ I help them find ways to fulfill their ministry to our body.

What are you doing personally to ensure new members are bonded to Christ and following Him as faithful disciples?

_____

Too often all we do is encourage new members to be faithful in attendance to all the church's activities. We push them to give faithfully and be soul winners. This may be a natural by-product of being a disciple of Jesus, but it is not what Jesus meant by "make disciples" (Matt. 28:19). The heart of making disciples is really seen in the final part of the Great Commission, " 'Teaching them to observe everything I have commanded you' " (Matt. 28:20). That is, help believers practice the commands of Christ until it has become a spontaneous and authentic lifestyle.

Read Acts 2:41-42 in the margin. What did the new believers do in the early church to grow as disciples of Christ?

_____

Notice that it was the apostles, the leaders, who ensured that every believer knew and lived out what it meant to be a disciple of Jesus.

Does this statement mean the rest of the church membership has no responsibilities in making disciples? ❏ Yes ❏ No

What do you see as the working relationship between the church's lay people and staff in developing committed disciples of Christ?

_____

_____

Often members within the church are greatly underused, while only a few carry the load. Each member must be taught that God has a purpose in mind for every member in the body. Great effort should be made to see that each one is strategically integrated into the body so that the whole body may function to its greatest efficiency.

Include the children and youth, giving them an opportunity to grow as they contribute in whatever way God has gifted them. It is God's pattern to build up each member of the body so that Christ may have a healthy and strong body through which He can touch the world.

In the margin list some ways that children and youth bless your church.

DAY FIVE

Leaders in the Body

How can the church follow Christ and know when He is speaking to them and guiding them to do the Father's will? How does Christ, the Head, communicate with each member of His body, and how does He unite them into one heart and mind to follow His leadership? These are not only proper questions; they are practical questions. When pursued, they can guide a church to live together under Christ their Lord.

The answers to these questions begin with the leaders. Since Christ is the Head of every church, what place does the pastor have? Christ is not just a figurehead. He is present and active in His body as the people function as a church. The pastor, then, is an undershepherd who obeys Christ as the Shepherd and Head of His own people.

The pastor is an undershepherd who obeys Christ as the Shepherd and Head of His own people.

THE ROLE OF THE PASTOR

When God adds a particular pastor to a church, does He specifically place him in that body? If we take our answers and guidance from the culture around us, we may see the pastor as a religious chief executive officer, leading a religious organization. But a church is not merely a religious organization (though it is highly organized as a body). It is a living body of Christ—a living organism. God adds a pastor to help

His people be all He has purposed for them to be! Knowing the condition of His people, He will add a pastor uniquely qualified in his relationship to Christ to take His people from where they are to where God wants them to be.

If God's people are greatly discouraged and brokenhearted, He may bring a Barnabas to encourage and strengthen them. If they are spiritually sick, He may bring a spiritual physician to bring healing and to deal with the sin that caused such trouble. If His people are mature and ready to go on mission with Him, He may bring a pastor with a great missionary heart. If a church is broken and divided, He may bring a pastor with a shepherd's heart, who has a strong gift of reconciliation. If a church has been thoroughly discipled and is growing in Christ, God may bring a pastor with a heart for evangelism to help the people bear witness to the Christ they have come to know. If the church has been immersed in evangelism for many years and has many people hungering to be fed the Word of God and discipled to grow toward Christlikeness, He may bring a pastor with a great heart for teaching and discipling.

The pastor must be a servant of God and submissive to the Head. The church is not his church; it is Christ's church. God Himself has been shaping the church for His purposes since before he became the pastor. The pastor, therefore, must be a man given to prayer and the ministry of the Word (see Acts 6:4). God's people must not only know about Christ but also be connected to Him in everyday life. This is the great task of the pastor, helping the people walk in a vital union with the Lord.

Every pastor must himself be passionately striving to be mature in Christ. This does not come through college courses or a seminary degree but by a constant personal relationship with his Lord. The command given to him by the Lord is still " 'make disciples … baptizing them … teaching them to observe everything I have commanded you' " (Matt. 28:19-20). And the Lord promises He will be with them to help carry out the command, even to the end of the age.

Some churches see the leader's task as primarily evangelism or soul winning, but that is not true in the New Testament. Leaders, especially the apostles, taught every believer. The apostles insisted that they devote themselves "to prayer and to the preaching ministry" (Acts 6:4). Leaders, however, must understand that you can't teach the people what you don't know. You can't lead the people where you haven't been. You can't take the people beyond your own walk with God.

One grave danger in God's churches today is of a pastor becoming merely an administrator of an organization. This is not his primary role as defined and given by Jesus. Even if he is greatly gifted in this area, he must strenuously resist this temptation or even the demands of the people. Others can do the administration, but only the pastor can be the pastor.

God will add a pastor uniquely qualified in his relationship to Christ to take His people from where they are to where God wants them to be.

Leaders must understand that you can't teach the people what you don't know. You can't lead the people where you haven't been. You can't take the people beyond your own walk with God.

Most people want and need a genuine pastor. I talked with a pastor who had just moved from a small church to a church that runs over 2500 in attendance. In making the adjustment, the Lord gave Him some clear directions in the priorities of His ministry. He said, "I have had to ask myself, what are the things that only the pastor can do? I must do them well. What are the things I am doing that others could do? I must let others do them." He was right! Pastor, you must be the pastor!

The pastor's role is not to get everyone to follow him; his role is to help the members of the church to follow Christ as their Lord. He will encourage every member to function in the body where the Father has placed him or her and to live their lives to their maximum potential in Christ. He will be a spiritual catalyst in the body for Christlikeness. What a joyful assignment the pastor has been given!

After reading about the role to which God has called him, how are you compelled to pray for your pastor? Add those prayer requests to the list you made on a separate sheet of paper. Will you commit to pray daily for your pastor? ❑ Yes ❑ No

THE ROLE OF OTHER LEADERS

Likewise, the other leaders in a church (staff, deacons or elders, teachers, administrators, musicians, and so on) are primarily to help God's people grow to Christlikeness. This is every leader's first and primary responsibility. It is not merely setting goals and efficiently organizing and running activities for church growth. God will add to the body (i.e., take care of church growth). That is what Christ promised to His disciples from the beginning: " 'I will build My church' " (Matt. 16:18).

Every leader, whatever the place of responsibility, is first assigned to edify. When I served as pastor, I had an instruction time at the beginning of each church year for our church leaders. I reminded them *not* to put their ministry assignment first. Their primary assignment was to assist each member under their care to be like Christ.

Although the finance committee handled the financial matters of the church and the missions committee guided the church's ministries, the primary task of each leader was to help each member of his or her committee to grow toward Christlikeness. It was in the context of their ministry responsibility that their primary assignment of building up the body could happen. If they were faithful to the primary assignment, they would get their work done.

Write the primary ministry responsibility of these church leaders.

Sunday School Director _____

We proclaim Him, warning and teaching everyone with all wisdom, so that we may present everyone mature in Christ. I labor for this, striving with His strength that works powerfully in me.

❧ COLOSSIANS 1:28-29 ❧

Women's Ministry Leader _____

Nursery Coordinator _____

Youth Council Chairperson _____

Deacons _____

In your group be prepared to discuss practical ways leaders can fulfill their primary task.

Every leader must use everything God has placed within him or her to edify (instruct and inform) the members of the body for the purposes of building up the body. This is clearly established in Romans 12:8-21 and 1 Corinthians 12—14. In many ways these passages are a spiritual plumb line and a standard by which the leaders must function.

Thank God for the leaders He has placed in your church. How will you express your appreciation and support to those leaders?

_____

_____

LEADERS WORKING TOGETHER UNDER CHRIST'S LORDSHIP

As leaders seek to follow and obey their Lord, they must ask the right questions. If they ask the wrong questions, they will get the wrong answers every time.

Instead of asking, What should we do this year? we need to ask, What is God doing this year and how can we join Him? What adjustments do we need to make in our lives in order to fulfill God's purposes for us? What does God want to accomplish in and through our lives this year? What has He been saying to us as a church that we must carefully obey?

God's goal for the body is Christlikeness—individually and as a body. Those who develop their relationship with Christ will be guided to do the Father's will, as Jesus did in the days of His flesh.

As we close this week's study, may I ask about your church?

1. **What evidence is there to you and the world around you that your church, a living body of Christ, has His mind guiding you?**

_____

[He] made himself of no reputation, and took upon him the form of a servant, and was made in the likeness of man.

♣PHILIPPIANS 2:7, KJV♣

2. Are you seeking to have a reputation or are you making yourselves of "no reputation" (Phil. 2:7, KJV)? What is the difference between the two?

_____

_____

3. In what ways are you willing to pay the price of obedience to Christ?

_____

_____

4. Is God therefore highly exalting and using your lives together as a church?

_____

_____

5. Have you ever been asked to dream big for what you imagine God doing through your church? How is this idea different from listening and watching to see what God will do through your church?

_____

_____

The Spirit-Empowered Body

While He [Jesus] was together with them, He commanded them not
to leave Jerusalem, but to wait for the Father's promise. "This," He said,
"is what you heard from Me; for John baptized with water, but you will be baptized
with the Holy Spirit not many days from now. ... But you will receive power
when the Holy Spirit has come upon you, and you will be My witnesses
in Jerusalem, in all Judea and Samaria, and to the ends of the earth."
ACTS 1:4-5,8

Amy and Dave joined a local church soon after moving to town. Although they had served in several leadership roles in their former church, they felt the need to get settled in before they took on any ministry tasks.

Weeks turned into months, and finally the nominating committee stopped asking. Amy and Dale are now nominal members of the church. They have established a pattern that could eventually lead to their becoming church drop-outs.

Neither Amy nor Dave feels close to the Lord. Sometimes it worries them and occasionally, the Holy Spirit convicts them of their lifestyle choices. But hey, they have their health and creature comforts. They'll worry about religion when they find the time.

This week we will focus on the biblical pattern for renewing and revitalizing your church life—being filled with the Holy Spirit. As you read, consider these questions:

1. How important is it for every member of the body to be filled with the Holy Spirit?
2. Is your church experiencing the necessary power of the Holy Spirit? What is the evidence?
3. Are you allowing the Holy Spirit to work in your life and through your life to build up the body and impact the lost community around you?
4. Have you relied more on your natural abilities than you have the Holy Spirit to work through you? What is the difference?

The Role of the Holy Spirit

God's great salvation for His people includes these two major truths: Each church has the presence of His Son, Jesus Christ, as Head of the church. And each church has the presence of the Holy Spirit as His enabling power to work in and through the church. The Holy Spirit is God's essential gift to the church.

THE HOLY SPIRIT IN THE MINISTRY OF JESUS

Long before the day of Pentecost, when the Spirit came in great power, the disciples heard John the Baptist bear witness of Jesus saying: "He whom God sent speaks God's words, since He gives the Spirit without measure. The Father loves the Son and has given all things into His hands" (John 3:34-35). More than the verbal testimony, they beheld the mighty acts and awesome powers of the Spirit through Jesus' life.

Peter witnessed to the place and work of the Holy Spirit in Jesus' life. He said to Cornelius and his household, " 'You know the events that took place throughout all Judea, beginning from Galilee after the baptism that John preached: how God anointed Jesus of Nazareth with the Holy Spirit and with power, and how He went about doing good and curing all who were under the tyranny of the Devil, because God was with Him' " (Acts 10:37-38). Peter was not talking about something he heard; he walked with Jesus and saw the many miracles that were performed.

Jesus announced to His disciples the coming of the Holy Spirit, revealing the provision God had made for His people when He saved them.

"Don't you believe that I am in the Father and the Father is in Me? The words I speak to you I do not speak on My own. The Father who lives in Me does His works. Believe Me that I am in the Father and the Father is in Me. Otherwise, believe because of the works themselves.

I assure you: The one who believes in Me will also do the works that I do. And he will do even greater works than these, because I am going to the Father. Whatever you ask in My name, I will do it, so that the Father may be glorified in the Son. If you ask Me anything in My name, I will do it."

♣ JOHN 14:10-14 ♣

As you read John 14:10-14 in the margin, underline the assurance Jesus gave His disciples. Circle the number(s) that best expresses how you feel about His statement.

1. Not possible
2. Highly unlikely
3. Has happened in the past
4. Have experienced it myself

In this same passage Jesus began to describe the awesome presence of the Holy Spirit who would be available to them. The Holy Spirit would be God's life in His people, the churches. He would teach them all things, bring to their remembrance all that He had said to them, guide them into all truth, and glorify Him in them. Read John 14:16-18 in the margin.

This same Holy Spirit, who had been present in the life of Jesus during His ministry, would now be in them, too! Jesus was not going to leave them helpless but would provide for them through the sending of the Holy Spirit.

What empowered Jesus to perform miracles (Acts 10:37-38)? Check one.

❑ Sound biblical teaching   ❑ The Holy Spirit
❑ Strong church programs   ❑ Leadership skills

What empowers believers to continue Christ's work (John 14:16-18)?

_____

THE HOLY SPIRIT IN EARLY BELIEVERS

At His ascension, Jesus had given the Great Commission to the apostles concerning world redemption, but it is obvious by what happened next that the entire church in Jerusalem would be involved. Jesus said, " 'You will receive power when the Holy Spirit has come upon you, and you will be My witnesses in Jerusalem, in all Judea and Samaria, and to the ends of the earth' " (Acts 1:8).

When the Holy Spirit came upon the apostles, He came upon all believers who were present. "When the day of Pentecost had arrived, they were all together in one place. Then they were all filled with the Holy Spirit" (Acts 2:1,4). By the time of Acts 4 the believers numbered five thousand men plus their families. Then we read, "When they had prayed, the place where they were assembled was shaken, and they were all filled with the Holy Spirit and began to speak God's message with boldness" (Acts 4:31).

Who was filled with the Holy Spirit in these instances from Acts? Cross out any incorrect responses.

Only the apostles   Only the men   All the believers

What a tremendous moment as the church was set on fire to fulfill its purpose, sharing the gospel with a lost world. As persecution arose under Saul of Tarsus, the Scripture tells us that as the dynamic power of the Holy Spirit came upon all the believers, they became a channel through which God would bless all people.

Recall a difficult time in your life. Did you respond by 1) allowing the Holy Spirit to fill you with His power or 2) did you withdraw and suffer? Underline your answer.

How can you respond differently in your next struggle so the Holy Spirit can bless others through you? Write your answer in the margin.

"I will ask the Father, and He will give you another Counselor to be with you forever. He is the Spirit of truth, whom the world is unable to receive because it doesn't see Him or know Him. But you do know Him, because He remains with you and will be in you. I will not leave you as orphans; I am coming to you."

❧ JOHN 14:16-18 ❧

Just as Jesus had commanded them to be on mission, the testimony continues in Acts 9:31, "So the church throughout all Judea, Galilee, and Samaria had peace, being built up and walking in the fear of the Lord and in the encouragement of the Holy Spirit, and it increased in numbers." The church began to spread from Jerusalem and multiplied itself in the surrounding regions.

THE HOLY SPIRIT IN GOD'S CHURCHES

The Holy Spirit, who was with Jesus, was to be the life of God in the churches. Each church would have Christ as their Head and the Holy Spirit as their power to know and carry out the commands of Christ.

> **Read John 14:26 in the margin. How are Christians able to know and carry out Christ's commands?**
>
> _____

"The Counselor, the Holy Spirit, whom the Father will send in My name, will teach you all things and remind you of everything I have told you."
❦ JOHN 14:26 ❦

The church experiences a dynamic relationship between the persons of the Trinity. This is why God gathers followers together into a congregation. The church is not just another organization. It is a functioning body, active and alive.

> **What is the source of life in your church? Check all that apply.**
> ❏ What life?   ❏ Socials
> ❏ Coffee before Sunday School   ❏ Great music
> ❏ Dynamic preaching   ❏ The Holy Spirit
> ❏ Sports teams   ❏ Other _____

THE HOLY SPIRIT IN MEMBERS OF THE BODY

With Christ as Head of the body, the Holy Spirit is His life in the body. First Corinthians 12 tell us "a manifestation of the Spirit is given to each person to produce what is beneficial [to the body]" (v. 7). "We were all baptized by one Spirit into one body—and we were all made to drink of one Spirit" (v. 13).

God composes the body as it pleases Him, and the Spirit enables every member to function where God has placed him or her to assist every other member of the body. God's provision, as a vital part of His salvation, is the Holy Spirit working in every member for the good of all. This is the key to a healthy body; the Spirit was given for the building up of the entire body.

> **Read 1 Corinthians 12:14-24 in your Bible. Imagine you have the opportunity to interview Paul about church life. Next to each question on page 99, write the verse or verses that contain Paul's answers.**

1. I know Jesus commanded His disciples to be united. Does that mean believers in Christ should be identical in looks, speech, opinions, and responsibilities? 1 Corinthians 12: _____

2. How do you answer believers who refuse to serve because they feel inferior to the highly gifted members in the church? 1 Corinthians 12: _____

3. How are members assigned their roles and given their abilities? 1 Corinthians 12: _____

4. If you had to eliminate three of the least necessary positions in the church, which ones would you choose? 1 Corinthians 12: _____

5. What do you believe is the most important position in the church? 1 Corinthians 12: _____

6. Which church members do you think God honors the most? 1 Corinthians 12: _____

Church life is literally the life of the Spirit. Paul makes clear that there are no unimportant members in a church (vv. 14-24). This truth has tremendous implications for life in our churches today. No one, including the pastor or any other leader, can say in word or deed, "I don't need you!" Paul said emphatically, "The members would have the same concern for each other" (v. 25). To lose one member means that the entire body suffers, and life in the body (local church) is deeply affected. You can never say, "Our church is better off because they left," and then wash your hands of any responsibility to redeem them.

If the Father adds a member, He has something in mind for him or her, and the new member is therefore important. If, however, a church merely becomes a religious organization, using the methods and attitudes of the business world, individuals can be fired or let go in order for the church to be more efficient and to be able to reach its goals. This should never happen in a church, which is a living body of our Lord Jesus Christ! Read Ephesians 5:25-27,32 in the margin.

What a statement! Each member is deeply loved by Christ, the Head. The Word of God is being used to bring members to health and life as they function with one another in the life of the body. This is so Christ can present to Himself a glorious church! This is indeed what Christ is now doing with your church. Do you treat church members as Christ is treating them? Or are you letting some go and feeling good about it?

God forbid that this would ever happen in His sight! Life in the body is precious and significant to God. Life in the body is given and maintained by the Holy Spirit. We are the recipients of this incredible life that can only be found in the local church.

Husbands, love your wives, just as also Christ loved the church and gave Himself for her, to make her holy, cleansing her in the washing of water by the word. He did this to present the church to Himself in splendor, without spot or wrinkle or any such thing, but holy and blameless. This mystery is profound, but I am talking about Christ and the church.

❧ EPHESIANS 5:25-27,32 ❧

Unity in the Body

Now the multitude of those who believed were of one heart and soul, and no one said that any of his possessions was his own, but instead they held everything in common. ... For there was not a needy person among them, because all those who owned lands or houses sold them, brought the proceeds of the things that were sold, and laid them at the apostles' feet. This was then distributed to each person as anyone had a need.

✤ ACTS 4:32-35 ✤

I, therefore, the prisoner in the Lord, urge you to walk worthy of the calling you have received, with all humility and gentleness, with patience, accepting one another in love, diligently keeping the unity of the Spirit with the peace that binds us. There is one body and one Spirit, just as you were called to one hope at your calling; one Lord, one faith, one baptism, one God and Father of all, who is above all and through all and in all.

Now grace was given to each one of us according to the measure of the Messiah's gift.

✤ EPHESIANS 4:1-7 ✤

humility_____

gentleness_____

patience_____

loving_____

peaceful_____

full of grace_____

Unity in the body is paramount in God's strategy to touch a world. Unity allows the body to function together as God intended. It ensures that people are functioning where God has placed them. It is the visible evidence that the members of the body are all following Christ as the Head of the body. Only the Holy Spirit working in each member can bring such unity. It is impossible otherwise.

Unity is what the living Christ and the Holy Spirit developed in the churches in the New Testament.

Read Acts 4:32-35. In this account, how did early churches express their unity?
❑ They held hands and sang "The Bond of Love."
❑ They voted unanimously at every church business meeting.
❑ They gave up their rights to personal property so none in the church body were in need.
❑ They held nightly prayer meetings.

Literally, "all the believers were together [unity] and had everything in common" (Acts 2:44). There were difficulties (see Acts 6), but the apostles and the members vigorously maintained the unity in the church family, and we must do the same. The name of our Lord is at stake, and convincing our lost world is in our hands.

Read Ephesians 4:1-7. Beside each Christian virtue in the margin, write the name of a person who exemplifies that trait.

Members of the church are to walk worthy of their calling. With all humility and gentleness, with long-suffering, they are to bear "with one another in love" (Eph. 4:2, NIV). Each member of the body is significant as we strive together to keep the unity with the Spirit. This is God's great provision for every member, causing a dynamic interaction for the good of the body. Each one is enabled through the working of the Holy Spirit in their lives.

If all members walk in union and harmony with the Holy Spirit, they won't be tempted to fulfill the lusts of the flesh, which will destroy a church. When a person causes dissension in the church and has a divisive spirit, he or she is not walking in the power of the Holy Spirit. When every member is filled with the Spirit, as was Jesus, the Holy Spirit will maintain the unity in the body.

Rate on a scale of 0 to 10 how each of the following truths motivate you to submit to the Holy Spirit. 0=This doesn't motivate me at all. 10=This truth highly motivates me.

___ When every member is filled with the Spirit, tithes and offerings are up.

___ Unity in the body is vital in God's strategy to touch the world.

___ Unity is the visible evidence that church members are following the pastor.

___ Unity in a church body will convince a lost world of the truth of the gospel.

___ A lack of unity in a church reflects negatively on the name of the Lord.

___ If all members walk in unity and with the Holy Spirit, they won't be tempted to fulfill the lusts of the flesh which destroy a church.

___ Believers who walk in the Spirit are peaceful, not divisive.

___ Deacons are charged with the responsibility to maintain peace.

THE KEY TO A UNIFIED BODY

God's people need to know how to experience what God has commanded. Each member is to help other members, so that Christ is honored in their midst. Paul said, "Be filled with the Spirit: speaking to one another in psalms, hymns, and spiritual songs, singing and making music to the Lord in your heart, giving thanks always for everything to God the Father in the name of our Lord Jesus Christ, submitting to one another in the fear of Christ" (Eph. 5:18-21).

The works of the flesh are obvious: sexual immorality, moral impurity, promiscuity, idolatry, sorcery, hatreds, strife, jealousy, outbursts of anger, selfish ambitions, dissensions, factions, envy, drunkenness, carousing, and anything similar, about which I tell you in advance—as I told you before—that those who practice such things will not inherit the kingdom of God.

But the fruit of the Spirit is love, joy, peace, patience, kindness, goodness, faith, gentleness, self-control. Against such things there is no law. Now those who belong to Christ Jesus have crucified the flesh with its passions and desires. If we live by the Spirit, we must also follow the Spirit.

❧ GALATIANS 5:19-25 ❧

Read Galatians 5:19-25 and fill in the chart below.

The works of the flesh are ...   The fruit of the Spirit is ...

_____   _____

_____   _____

_____   _____

_____   _____

Why would the works of the   **How does the fruit of the**
flesh destroy unity?   **Spirit promote unity?**

_____   _____

_____   _____

Circle qualities in both columns that are evident in your church.

These responses may have prompted you to write them on the prayer list you made for your church on a separate sheet of paper. If not, add them now and spend time in prayer.

Being filled with the Spirit is the key to a unified body. In the margin on page 101, you read the *works of the flesh*. Compare them to the *fruit of the Spirit*: "love, joy, peace, patience, kindness, goodness, faith, gentleness, self-control. … Now those who belong to Christ Jesus have crucified the flesh with its passions and desires. If we live by the Spirit, we must also follow the Spirit" (Gal. 5:22-25).

Here is the true source of unity in the body: when Christ is the Head, giving to each member *His life* through the presence of the Holy Spirit, there will be unity in the life of the church. Every member in every church must be careful to maintain this unity which the Holy Spirit creates (see Eph. 4:3).

The Practice of Unity in a Church

A strong, relentless teaching of what a church is and what God can do through His church is crucial to having unity in a church. When I pastored, I taught and practiced faithfully the reclaiming of each member who was struggling. If our churches neglect the members we have, who will want to join us? If we see wholeness in each member, others will beat a path to our door just to experience this in their lives. The testimony of those who were helped and healed drew many others to want to be a part of such a church.

All the power of the cross, the resurrection, and Pentecost are still available to the church. To live this way is an authentic witness to our Lord, to our message, and to our lives together.

Church Leaders Building Unity

Jesus fully equipped His disciples. Every leader's job is to equip fully the members of the church. Jesus' instruction is clear in this matter. " 'Teaching them to observe everything I have commanded you' " (Matt. 28:20). If a leader takes this command seriously, he or she will equip the people by teaching them several things.

1. How to have a relationship with God through Jesus Christ
2. How to be filled with the Holy Spirit
3. How to love one another with the love of Christ
4. How to express *koinonia* for one another in the body
5. How to study God's Word and pray
6. How to do God's will and strive for Christlikeness

Check any of the six preceding "how to" statements you strive to teach others as you lead. Put a star by those statements you need to model in your life so you can teach them to others.

If you do not hold any leadership positions in your church, remember that someone is watching your life to see how Christ has made a difference.

The health of the body depends on the health of every member of the body. The members are absolutely interdependent with one another. If one member hurts, the whole body hurts. If there is division in the body, the whole body suffers. But most importantly, each church has the capacity to touch the world as the body of Christ. The ability of Christ to do His work effectively is directly related to the health and unity of the body. The leaders are the ones who must equip the body for such health.

Who are the leaders we are talking about? Certainly the pastor and staff. The deacons are also crucial, for their primary role is to encourage the unity and health in the body. These leaders must give personal care for every member.

Both staff and deacons can potentially drift into becoming administrators of the church organization rather than equippers of the church members. If that happens, the whole body will miss out on much that God wanted to do through them. Many other leaders help build up the body. Whether they are teachers, committee chairpersons, or whatever leaders God raises up, they have a tremendous impact on the work of the kingdom as they equip the people of God.

Do you think churches often expect their leaders to run the church organization rather than equip the church's members? (circle) Yes No
How can you help your leaders focus on equipping members? Hint: 1 Corinthians 12:27.

_____

_____

I cannot express strongly enough how important it is that leaders walk with God. Read Isaiah 65:1-3 in the margin.

I fear that this description may profile many leaders in our churches today. May we choose to run into God's arms and find wisdom for the task He has given us. And when we do, we can take courage in the Lord.

"I permitted Myself to be sought by those who did not ask for Me;
I permitted Myself to be found by those who did not seek Me.
I said, 'Here am I, here am I,'
To a nation which did not call on My name.
I have spread out My hands all day long to a rebellious people,
Who walk in the way which is not good, following their own thoughts,
A people who continually provoke Me to My face."

❧ Isaiah 65:1-3 ❧

> *" 'Do not fear, for I am with you;*
> *Do not anxiously look about you,*
> *   for I am your God.*
> *I will strengthen you, surely*
> *   I will help you,*
> *Surely I will uphold you with*
> *   My righteous right hand.' "*
>
> ❧ ISAIAH 41:10 ❧

Circle any needs that you will commit to pray for your church leaders. Add these requests to your prayer list so you can petition for your leaders daily.

Our leaders will not fear.

Our leaders will not be anxious.

Our leaders will be strengthened.

Our leaders will remember God is with them.

Our leaders will keep God as their focus.

Our leaders will know God is lifting them up.

If you are a church leader, thank God for the marvelous promise of help He has given you in Isaiah 41:10.

DAY THREE

Power in the Body

There is an old tale that teaches a great truth. It is a story of a captain who was valiant in battle. So dominant was the warrior in battle that his sword was greatly feared among the enemy. Word about his sword became legendary among the people. Soon the king himself had heard of the infamous sword, and he sent a messenger to find the sword and bring it back for him to examine.

When the messenger returned with the sword in hand, he presented it to the king. But the king was taken back; he didn't understand the stories he had heard. "Why are the people afraid of the sword? It appears very common, very ordinary." The messenger replied, "Sir, I brought you the sword, but nothing more. If I had brought you the hand that wields the sword, you would fully understand the fear."

GOD'S POWER IS GIVEN TO ORDINARY PEOPLE

The key is never our abilities, but the power of the Holy Spirit working in and through us to accomplish God's will.

Do you understand that the hand of God through the Holy Spirit wields power in a Christian's life? We may be common or ordinary in the eyes of men, but when Christians are filled with the Holy Spirit, God can bring down strongholds through our lives. When a church is filled with the Holy Spirit, God can turn a world upside down. The key is never our abilities, but the power of the Holy Spirit working in and through us to accomplish God's will.

Mark an X on the line below to indicate how much you depend on your own abilities or the Holy Spirit to accomplish God's will.

0% Holy Spirit   100% Holy Spirit

The Spirit at Work

As a pastor, I love to share the good news of Christ. I remember the day I used my vast educational training to argue with a lost person about the existence of God. At that time I was completing a Ph.D. with a major in theology. I was ready, I thought, to overwhelm this unsuspecting lost person with an irrefutable argument. He would plead with me to help him have a personal relationship with God.

As you might imagine, the results were not what I had hoped. The best I could get out of him was a blank stare that equaled the stone faces on Mount Rushmore! The poor fellow didn't have a clue about what I was so eloquently telling him. As much as I value education, it will never substitute for the Holy Spirit.

That realization was proven true recently when I shared the gospel with a young couple. This particular night I was out of sync, tired from a long day filled with meetings. I took another young man with me to show him how it was done.

The visit didn't start well. After ringing the bell and banging on the door for some time, we figured out that we were at the wrong house. We regrouped, and found the right street and house. The reception the couple gave us was less than warm. They were courteous, but we sensed a distance that was a bit awkward.

In the kitchen we sat down with a cup of coffee and made small talk to break the ice. When I was ready to move the conversation toward spiritual things, I realized I had forgotten my Bible! I apologized and asked if I could borrow one. Like most people they had one somewhere in the house. I began to inquire about their church background.

The wife sounded a little guarded as she began. She was baptized as an infant, but her family never took her back to that particular church. She and her mother tried a Catholic church when she was older, but it was confusing to her and she didn't last long there either. When she married, they went to a few evangelical churches but didn't like any of them. She said, "Religion is so confusing. I have a lot of questions that I need answered."

I decided to cut to the chase and ask her one simple question. "With all the various religious experiences you have had, has anybody ever told you how to become a Christian?"

She said, "No, nobody has told me that."

I asked her another simple question, "Do you want me to tell you right now how you can have a relationship with God and become a Christian?"

She said, "Yes."

As I stumbled through a gospel presentation, I heard the Holy Spirit say to me, "Just make this short and get to the point; if you talk too long, you may ruin the moment!" Knowing that my mind was not sharp, I readily obeyed the Holy Spirit, and within a few minutes she prayed to receive Christ. The next Sunday she came forward in church professing her faith in Christ and requesting baptism. Her husband was at her side, rededicating his life to Christ and requesting church membership.

As my friend and I left the house that night, we remarked, "God was determined to save that woman in spite of our incompetence!" The Holy Spirit worked through one of the worst presentations of the gospel ever told!

The real story was what preceded our visit. A man in our church had been prayer walking that neighborhood for months. Another member had met this couple through their children and was praying for them. Before I left to witness that night, I had called a prayer warrior to intercede on behalf of the couple. The Holy Spirit was at work in their lives and used an unworthy vessel like me to complete His work. We can do nothing without Him (John 15:1-8).

GOD'S POWER IS GIVEN TO DO HIS WILL

The power in the body is the presence of God, actively at work accomplishing His will. He doesn't release His power for us to use as we will. He gives it to accomplish His purposes in our lives and church.

Check how you most often seek God's power.
- ❑ The attainment of my desires
- ❑ Strength to get through my day
- ❑ Ability to accomplish all my responsibilities
- ❑ Patience to deal with others
- ❑ The fulfillment of God's purposes in my life and my church

To Him who is able to do above and beyond all that we ask or think—according to the power that works in you—to Him be glory in the church and in Christ Jesus to all generations, forever and ever. Amen.

❧ EPHESIANS 3:20-21 ❧

In the Old Testament He sent His Spirit to enable His servants to accomplish His calling in their lives. He worked through them! Now He has poured out His Spirit on all flesh (not just selected individuals). This is an amazing truth! The Spirit of God is resident to perform *everything* the Lord wants to do. Ephesians 3:20-21 (in the margin) reminds us that God Himself is the power working in us. The world is waiting to know our God not by word, but by demonstrated power.

Check words that describe how you proclaim Christ to this world.

| effectively | wisely | fearfully | frequently |
| in weakness | with trembling | persuasively | rarely |

Read 1 Corinthians 2:1-5 in your Bible and complete the following:

1. Star the words above that describe how Paul proclaimed Christ.
2. Fill in these sentences:

The Corinthians came to know Christ as Paul came with a

d_____ of the S_____ and of p_____.

The world can know Christ as we come, not with words, but with a

d_____ of the S_____ and of p_____.

Imagine a bright sunny day as you prepare to launch out into the deep waters of the sea. You have a sailboat with all the trimmings. You and your crew have made all the necessary preparations. Your rations are stocked for the journey. The boat is up-to-date on its maintenance log. You have the finest of equipment and the most talented crew available. You raise the anchor, loose the moorings, and raise the sails. You are ready to sail, but nothing happens. The sailboat remains motionless in the harbor. Why? Because there is no wind to power the boat.

Your church may have all the trimmings, but without the wind of the Spirit, there will be no power. You may have all the necessary equipment and have gone through a checklist of the necessary components for a healthy church. You may have built a beautiful building and attracted many talented people who are willing to work hard for God. But your church will not have the power to sail without the presence of the Holy Spirit.

Interestingly, the Greek word for Spirit can also be translated wind. We need the wind of the Spirit in our sails. I have found that when the wind is blowing and the sails are full, people are so busy at their jobs that nobody has time to argue or bicker with one another. But when the sails are drooping and there is no activity, we tend to stare at one another and begin to complain. Oh that we would be used by the Spirit to touch our world.

Circle the picture in the margin that best illustrates your church.

SIX PRINCIPLES OF GOD'S POWER
Prayerfully evaluate your church on the six principles of God's power.

1. The Holy Spirit will never work contrary to the Father's will.

   Is any activity or attitude in your church contrary to the Father's will? ❑ Yes ❑ No

2. The Holy Spirit is never free to work where sin and unbelief are present.

   Are sin and unbelief present in your church? ❑ Yes ❑ No

3. The Holy Spirit works where God's name is honored.

   Is God's name honored in your church? ❑ Yes ❑ No **How?**

   _____

4. The Holy Spirit chooses to work through the local churches.

   Does your church want the Holy Spirit to work through you? ❑ Yes ❑ No

5. The Holy Spirit's work in the churches is always God-sized (beyond all we can ask or think).

   Does your church attempt to accomplish only what is reasonable according to budget and personnel, or do you attempt God-sized tasks? Underline your response.

6. When the Holy Spirit works in the church, it always brings honor and glory to God.

   Does your church give glory and honor to God for all that happens within the body? ❑ Yes ❑ No

Be prepared to respectfully share your evaluation in your small-group time. If your analysis burdens you, ask God's Spirit to renew your church, beginning with you.

A Functioning Body

The Holy Spirit empowers and enables a church to function as a living body of Christ. He brings to the body a caring heart and the ability to work together for a common purpose.

I have lived this message for 30 years as the pastor of several churches, and Mel has now pastored 3 churches. When we sought to live according to the Scripture, every member was challenged to grow toward Christlikeness. God then did wonderful works through each of these churches, and we believe God was honored as a result. This can, and must, be true of every church in our day. Revival would come quickly if each church and each member in the churches lived his or her life as God designed and purposed.

In one of the churches I pastored for 12 years, the Holy Spirit impressed a significant Scripture upon our church—John 6:39.

Read this verse in the margin. When speaking about His own ministry, what did Jesus state was God's will?

_____

"This is the will of Him who sent Me: that I should lose none of those He has given Me but should raise them up on the last day."

❧ JOHN 6:39 ❧

Jesus took seriously the watch care over those the Father gave Him. Each person is important in His eyes and has a significant role to play in the purposes of God.

Jesus also said, " 'Everyone the Father gives Me will come to Me, and the one who comes to Me I will never cast out' " (John 6:37). God is the One who sends people to us, and we must receive all He brings our way. Our church, therefore, made a conscious decision to receive all we believed God sent to us. We listened to their testimonies and publicly entered into a covenant with them, promising to watch over them and to teach them as Christ had commanded us. It was always a meaningful time in our church.

God sent us many different people, often with many different problems, and in the 12 years I pastored that church, we did not lose people. It was a choice we made to receive, care for, and hold on to those God gave us.

In your opinion, what would be a top priority of a church that took John 6:39 seriously? Write your answer in the margin.

_____

_____

HOW DOES A CHURCH FUNCTION AS GOD INTENDED?

The Holy Spirit's presence in the church is, in fact, the very life of the church. Each member is joined to Christ! Each member is joined to the Spirit! Each member is joined to each other! Each functions *in* the body and *with* the body. As each part functions where God put it, the whole body responds to Christ and the Father's will is accomplished in the world through His people.

The apostle Paul said as much when he wrote to the Corinthian church. Paul said that he planted, Apollos watered, but God gave the increase (see 1 Cor. 3:6-7).

Read 1 Corinthians 3:5-8. Using the analogy from these verses, complete the phrase under each picture.

Paul _____ Apollos _____ God _____

So, what is Apollos? And what is Paul? They are servants through whom you believed, and each has the role the Lord has given. I planted, Apollos watered, but God gave the growth. So then neither the one who plants nor the one who waters is anything, but only God who gives the growth. Now the one who plants and the one who waters are equal, and each will receive his own reward according to his own labor.

❧ 1 CORINTHIANS 3:5-8 ❧

Another way we might think of the parts working together is one built a loving relationship, another spoke a witness, yet others welcomed and ushered when they came to worship, the pastor preached, the music inspired, many prayed faithfully, then God gave the increase, and all rejoiced together. God works through the entire body, all members functioning where God has placed them. The Holy Spirit enables each by working in them to bring a lost person to faith in Christ. This is the body functioning in evangelism.

The same could describe the church on mission—reaching youth; caring for seniors; encouraging business people; ministering to jails, hospitals, schools, or any other place God desires to work. The body functions together with one heart and one mind, responding to Christ who is guiding them to do the Father's will.

Underline one of the ministries listed in the previous paragraph that you believe the Lord has given your church. Use the space below if you believe God has chosen a ministry that is not listed.

_____

_____

Be prepared to discuss these ideas with your group.

❧ A STORY FROM MEL BLACKABY ❧

Who Gets the Credit?

The Lord has given me a burden for the church to function as a living body with Christ as the Head. So I have encouraged members to be connected to Christ and involved in serving Him. I have come to realize that the Lord's activity is much more important than our activity. In one church I pastored, a group of us asked the Holy Spirit to show us individuals in whom He was working; we set about to join Him in His work.

I went to one member who obviously had been gifted as an intercessor, and I gave her a list of 21 people to pray for in the days ahead. She took that list and prayed through it every day, pleading for God to work in their lives. We enlisted many others to build relationships and discover how they might let God use them in bringing these individuals to Christ.

Six months later every person on the list had made a public decision for Christ. On one occasion, as an individual came forward, I asked the congregation, "If you have prayed for Rick to make the decision he has made today, would you please stand?" It seemed like three-quarters of the people stood and rejoiced together. Who brought that young man to salvation? The Spirit through the body.

HOW DOES GOD WORK THROUGH THE BODY?

God does His work through the body of His Son. All the resources the church needs to do all that God asks of it are available through the Holy Spirit. In one of the greatest pictures of a church in the Bible, Paul confirms that the Spirit manifests Himself to every member (1 Cor. 12:7).

There are different gifts, but the same Spirit. There are different ministries, but the same Lord. And there are different activities, but the same God is active in everyone and everything. A manifestation of the Spirit is given to each person to produce what is beneficial.

❧ 1 CORINTHIANS 12:4-7 ❧

Read 1 Corinthians 12:4-7 in the margin. Then read the definition of manifest. What do you think it means for the Spirit to manifest Himself to believers?

_____

Why does the Spirit reveal Himself to each believer?

Manifest—to make clear or evident; show plainly; reveal

_____

Every member of the church will experience the Holy Spirit's enabling presence and power. Every member must, therefore, be encouraged, taught, and assisted to live out the Spirit's life in them in the midst of their church.

A major purpose of the Holy Spirit within every believer is to help the rest of the body grow into Christlikeness. Each member has a vital role to play in God's plan for the church and must be treated as significant. This can be done at the time a person first becomes a believer or when they are first added by God to the body. Jesus saw the radical significance of each believer when He said to His disciples, " 'I assure you: The one who receives whomever I send receives Me, and the one who receives Me receives Him who sent Me' " (John 13:20). Every church, therefore, must see its church growth as an act of God and treat new members as a gift from God.

In other words, the entire church must see each new member as though they were receiving both Jesus and the Father. How would we treat them? Perhaps with great joy, with great care, and with great anticipation of how their presence will bless the congregation. How are we treating each member He sends us?

Think of persons who have joined your church recently. Did you receive them in the same manner you would have received Jesus if He physically had stood before your church body? ❑ Yes ❑ No

Honoring each member is not a suggestion, a convenience, or even a preference. This is a divine command! The spiritual health of the church is greatly affected at the moment new members are received. At this point a church will function as a living body or merely as a religious organization. Each new member is either related to Christ in His living body or merely added to the church roll.

When God adds members to the church, He adds them to the body of His Son. Each person has a special relationship to Christ as the Head. The Holy Spirit immediately enables every member to relate to the Head and to each member He adds to the body. This is the enabling work of the Holy Spirit in each church.

DAY FIVE

Life in the Body

The Holy Spirit equips every member to edify and build up the body. As we help each member grow into maturity, Christ will then have a healthy body through whom He can accomplish the Father's will. The Holy Spirit, therefore, must make us sensitive to what is happening in the body. When one member hurts or is sick, the entire body marshals to his or her aid in order to maintain health in Christ's body, the local church. That is how our physical bodies function and how God desires for our churches to function.

HELPING MEMBERS WHO ARE HURTING

Many times one of the members of a body has a burden too heavy to carry alone, and it affects the life of the church in an ever-increasing way. Or perhaps a member is overtaken or caught in sin. Read

Galatians 6:1 in the margin. Burden bearing is a law of Christ. It is therefore not a optional but necessity in maintaining the unity in a body.

When one of the members experiences a great loss because of a death or some other crisis, the body is affected. If the body is healthy, the other members will come alongside this one, sharing faith, comfort, inner strength, finances, or other help until the member is through his or her pain. This show of love and care not only maintains the unity in the church, but it strengthens and enlarges it. The body is stronger after the crisis than before it occurred. This demonstration of love always has a tremendous effect on the watching world. It can be used of God to draw others to Christ, for Christ Himself has orchestrated such love.

Read 1 Corinthians 12:26-27. Write an experience your church has had in ministry to someone suffering and to someone who has recently received good news.

_____

_____

Our church had many opportunities to help members who were hurting over a death in their families. We were able to lead several other members of those families to Christ. The lost family members had never experienced such oneness and caring; they were now open to hear the gospel because the good news of God now made sense to them as they saw it lived out in the church.

When a couple in our church was struggling in their marriage and it appeared they could be headed toward divorce, I would marshal the entire church family to help. The women would carefully and thoughtfully walk with the wife; the men would gather around the husband with counsel and strength. If needed, the Sunday school teachers would pay special attention to the children or youth involved until healing came to this marriage and health was restored. In 30 years of pastoring, I only saw one divorce in the churches I pastored. I simply helped the church members care for one another.

Our unity and health honored Christ. All the resources for reconciliation were present in our church. The Lord had committed to us this "ministry of reconciliation" (2 Cor. 18-19).

Read 2 Corinthians 5:18-19. What message did God give the church?

_____

In the margin on page 113, list ways you can apply this message.

Unfortunately some feel we can neglect the saving of marriages and homes *in* our churches and still have a message of integrity to a lost world. We still feel we can ask God to bless us when we dishonor Him by refusing to draw upon His presence and power to bring healing in our families. Further, we feel we can continue to function as a religious organization in spite of such utter brokenness in the body. When marriages are not healed, the church family is deeply affected, especially in its *unity*.

If the church family and I did not actively pursue healing for struggling marriages, it made the rest of the members nervous. They knew that if their lives or homes became threatened in any way, we probably would not pursue them either! One saved marriage strengthens the unity of the body and gives great confidence in witnessing to a lost world. We experience the presence and power of our living Lord, and joy becomes the order of the day.

What happens in your life when someone in the church is hurting?
❑ Nothing, I go about life as usual.
❑ I pray for them in Sunday School and worship.
❑ I intercede for them in my private devotional time.
❑ I find ways to minister to them personally through phone calls, cards, and other appropriate ways.
❑ I contact them regularly in an effort to encourage healing.
❑ Other: _____

Two important factors must be in place for this ministry of reconciliation to be implemented by a church. First, we must be free to share our hurts within the body. Often, members suffer in silence and refuse to let anybody help them grow to maturity. Unless we provide the forum for people to share their needs, our churches will be filled with hurting people who will continue to suffer in silence.

Second, we must intentionally look out for one another.

Read Philippians 2:3-4 in your Bible. Complete the chart to contrast what Paul said believers should and should not do within the church body.

Do Not   Do
_____   _____

_____   _____

_____   _____

Which side of the chart best describes you?
❑ Do Not   ❑ Do   ❑ I go back and forth.

Can you see how important it is for members to be investing their lives in the lives of other members in the body? As we are each filled with the Holy Spirit, we then begin to function where God has placed us. His assignment is to help us serve the Lord as we serve one another and maintain the health of the body.

HELPING MEMBERS GROW IN HOLINESS

The greatest priority of the Holy Spirit is to enable each person to know Christ and to love Him with all his or her heart. As a result, each member will also desire to serve and obey Him, and to relate deeply to the members of His body. Without holiness we cannot relate to God as He intended.

Pursue peace with everyone, and holiness—without it no one will see the Lord.

❧ HEBREWS 12:14 ❧

Read Hebrews 12:14. Underline what believers are to pursue.

The Holy Spirit speaks to us by convicting us of sin and righteousness, so that we might progress in our relationship with the Holy One. The Holy Spirit will convey to us what He hears from the Lord. The Lord desires that we become like Him as a body so He can do the Father's will through our churches.

As obedient children, do not be conformed to the desires of your former ignorance but, as the One who called you is holy, you also are to be holy in all your conduct; for it is written, "Be holy, because I am holy."

❧ 1 PETER 1:14-16 ❧

Read 1 Peter 1:14-16 in the margin. Mark an X on the road below to indicate where you are on the road to holiness.

What is God calling you to do so you may progress forward in your relationship with Him? Write your response in the margin.

HELPING MEMBERS FIND PLACES OF SERVICE

Some churches struggle with helping members find their place of service. Most have a nominating committee to help in the process. But committees should not primarily try to fill positions in the church organization. They are to see that every member is functioning in the body where God has placed him or her and where the Holy Spirit is enabling the member to serve. They must be sensitive to what the Holy Spirit is doing and help people recognize what He is doing in and through their lives.

For example, some are gifted with an instrument or with vocal abilities and use them to bless God's people as they worship. A skilled musician, however, may not be spiritually able to edify. His pride and skill may actually detract and hinder what God is doing in the midst of the church. A soloist may have a good voice, but she may have quenched the Spirit by ungodly living. Such a person should never be enlisted to sing merely for his or her voice.

The Holy Spirit enables some to be leaders of others, and they should be asked to lead a committee or a ministry. Yet others are faithful to serve where there is a need, but not necessarily the ones to lead the effort. Others have a Barnabas spirit as encouragers. Still others have a tremendous burden for missions. Since the Spirit equips every member for the common good, a nominating committee must be alert to the Spirit's equipping of every member, and they must assure that every member is actively helping the body to grow in Christ. We encouraged the children to do their part in welcoming people and assisting the elderly. Some mentally challenged young adults blessed others by their joy-filled lives.

Often senior adults feel they can't contribute much, either because of health issues or financial limitations. But they can be prayer warriors in all decisions, ministries, and activities in the church. A widow may offer her home for a Bible study, even if she cannot teach it. She can open her home to visitors or provide a room for a college student. She can write cards or make phone calls. She can make a significant contribution to the growth of the others in her church. All this won't just happen. It has to be done intentionally, as the church is obedient to God through His Word.

> *Now God has placed the parts, each one of them, in the body just as He wanted. And if they were all the same part, where would the body be?*
>
> ❧ 1 CORINTHIANS 12:18-19 ❧

Write the names of three church members, young or old, who contribute to the church body in ways that primarily go unnoticed.

1. _____   2. _____   3. _____

How will you express your appreciation to these persons this week?

_____

Because the Spirit enables every member and all believers, there are two principles that automatically follow. I have recapped them for you from our study this week.
1. Members are to be honored.
2. Members are to be included in the work of the church, each functioning from the place God has put him or her in the body.

As you have studied week 5, what changes in your attitudes or actions will you make in response to God?

_____

A World Mission Strategy Center

This grace was given to me—the least of all the saints!—to proclaim to the Gentiles the incalculable riches of the Messiah, and to shed light for all about the administration of the mystery hidden for ages in God who created all things. This is so that God's multi-faceted wisdom may now be made known through the church to the rulers and authorities in the heavens.

Ephesians 3:8-10

Church A is in a transitional neighborhood. Because of language and cultural barriers, the church has not ministered to the various minority groups moving into their part of town. Many of their members are retired and don't feel they can take on weekday ministries in addition to "holding down the fort" on Sundays. One church member was heard to say, "If those people want to come to our church, the schedule is on the church sign."

Church B began taking summer mission trips about five years ago. Although they've been to three continents during that time, a particular region of Mexico has captured their hearts. Every summer one team leads Vacation Bible School in the town square. Members were challenged to realize how many Hispanics were moving to their state. Now they are beginning a Hispanic mission in their facility.

Which of these churches is most like your own? Could your church be described as a people on mission with God, following with great joy Christ as your head? The Lord will use those who are trained, but He also delights in using laypersons who are willing to spread the gospel. As you read this week, keep these questions in mind:

1. Is your church a world missions strategy center?
2. Do you sense the presence of God guiding your church during congregational business meetings?
3. Is your church ready to pay the price to be obedient to Christ and touch the world?
4. How do you believe God is glorified in a church? Is He being glorified in your church? What adjustments need to be made?

God Works Through the Church

An extraordinary moment illustrates the truth that God works through churches of every size. Jack Conner, his wife Bonna, and two of their five children moved from southern California to Prince Albert, Saskatchewan, Canada. Jack had come to pastor our first mission church. We spent much time together, though Jack was 95 miles north of our location. One day Jack and I went out into the woods to pray and seek God's purposes for reaching our province and the nation.

While we walked and prayed that strange afternoon, God laid on our hearts that He would bring into being one thousand new churches and missions if we and others would be faithful. We were two small churches, and at that time there were fewer than 30 congregations in all of Canada within our fellowship. Was this possible? Wrong question. Would we believe God and set out to do all He laid on our hearts?

Two pastors could not do an assignment of that nature by themselves. If this was truly God's vision, He would lay that on the hearts of others as well. As soon as we set our hearts to plant churches, young and middle-aged adults began to respond to God's call to ministry. So many responded from our churches and others in the area that we began what we called the Christian Training Center (later the Canadian Baptist Theological College). In total, more than four hundred students were trained in a few short years.

Today the Canadian Convention of Southern Baptists has endorsed a goal of establishing one thousand new churches by the year 2020. Their vision is to see "a church for every person across Canada and around the world." They have a fully accredited theological seminary with many students preparing for church planting. The Lord has also been gracious to allow my oldest son to be the president of that seminary, giving leadership to the next generation of pastors and church planters.

Can you imagine what God wants to do and therefore can do in and through a church yielded to Him? God's strategy is to work through His churches to extend His kingdom. Have you considered how God can use your church in kingdom work, far beyond the immediate community of which you are a part?

Do you know a small group of people who together have made a difference in the world for Christ? Be prepared to tell this story

in your group session. _____

_____

GOD'S STRATEGY

God's strategy to extend His kingdom on earth is through the local churches that He establishes. Immediately after Peter declared his understanding that Jesus was the Christ, Jesus announced to Peter and the other disciples that no person would ever understand who He was unless the Spirit of God revealed it to him. Read Jesus' words from Matthew 16:17-19 in the margin.

In other words, if a person's mind has been enlightened to know the things of God, God is actively working in his life. When God begins to draw people to Himself, He has a purpose in mind.

So Jesus could say, "I will build My church on the activity of My Father working deeply in the lives His people. And I will give them the keys to the kingdom of heaven. For through them, the church, the kingdom will grow." With that declaration, the church became a world mission strategy center.

God implements His strategy and activity through every church He establishes, empowers, and guides to go into the entire world. With the keys to the kingdom, the churches preach the gospel, and all heaven is open to those who hear, believe, and receive Jesus Christ as Lord.

Reinforce your understanding of God's world mission strategy for your church by filling in the blanks:

My church was es _____ by God.

My church is em _____ by God.

My church is g _____ by God.

As a result, my church preaches the g _____.
Heaven is open to those who

h _____, b _____ and r _____.

Jesus understood that when the Father gathered the people together into a church, nothing could stand in that church's way. The God of the universe was the Author and Creator of that church, and He would accomplish His mighty purposes through them just as He desired. The gates of hell itself could not prevail against those people, called out and gathered together by God.

In the eternal plan of God, the New Testament reveals that each church is to be a center for world missions. They are a fountainhead of God's activity that flows into every corner of the earth, giving the opportunity for all people to hear the good news of God's great salvation.

In the eternal plan of God, the New Testament reveals that each church is to be a center for world missions.

GOD'S TASK

Jesus told the disciples that He would build His church, that He would give them the keys to the kingdom of heaven. Then He commanded all those gathered at His ascension to " 'go ... and make disciples of all nations, baptizing them in the name of the Father and of the Son and of the Holy Spirit, teaching them to observe everything I have commanded you' " (Matt. 28:19-20).

He also told them how His plan would unfold. They would start in Jerusalem, move into Judea and Samaria, and on to the ends of the earth.

Read Acts 1:8 in the margin. Identify your

Jerusalem (your town)_____

Judea (your country)_____

Samaria (a neighboring country)_____

"the ends of the earth" _____

"You will receive power when the Holy Spirit has come upon you, and you will be My witnesses in Jerusalem, in all Judea and Samaria, and to the ends of the earth."

❧ ACTS 1:8 ❧

The Book of Acts spells out God's plan in detail. First, Peter preached in Jerusalem (Acts 2:14), and the entire city was shaken. Then the Holy Spirit led Philip to go to Samaria to preach the gospel in that region (Acts 8:4-8), where a revival broke out. The church at Jerusalem sent Peter and John to see all this activity, and "they traveled back to Jerusalem, evangelizing many villages of the Samaritans" (Acts 8:25).

Then Philip was led by the angel of the Lord to go down on the road that leads to Gaza, a desert town, and he preached the good news to an Ethiopian eunuch who was returning to North Africa (Acts 8:26). The kingdom of heaven was again opened by Philip's preaching, and the Ethiopian ruler was saved and "went on his way rejoicing" (Acts 8:39). But Philip continued to preach in all the villages from Azotus to Caesarea.

All this activity was strategized by God's Spirit from the center of His activity in the church in Jerusalem. The Lord continued to make the church a mission strategy center by granting Peter, who was in Joppa, a vision to reach the Gentiles. An angel had spoken to Cornelius and by divine providence brought the two together. Peter obeyed God, went to Cornelius's house in Caesarea, and began to preach the gospel to them. While preaching about God's great salvation, Cornelius and all those who heard the Word entered into the kingdom. Peter baptized them all, and the Holy Spirit suddenly came upon each one. Peter returned to Jerusalem to tell what God had done. (See Acts 10.)

"Repentance for forgiveness of sins would be proclaimed in His name to all the nations, beginning at Jerusalem."

❧ LUKE 24:47 ❧

When they heard this they became silent. Then they glorified God, saying, "So God has granted repentance resulting in life to even the Gentiles!"

♣ ACTS 11:18 ♣

Read Acts 11:18. How did the church in Jerusalem respond when they realized God intended to save Gentiles?(Check one or more.)
❑ They were stunned into silence. ❑ They were angry.
❑ They refused to believe it. ❑ They glorified God.
❑ They accepted it with resignation. ❑ They rejoiced.

The remainder of the Book of Acts demonstrates that every local church was designed by God to be a center for His activity to spread to other parts of the world. The church in Antioch began to function with the same mission awareness. The Holy Spirit instructed them: " 'Set apart for Me Barnabas and Saul for the work that I have called them to' " (Acts 13:2).

Thus began one of the greatest church-planting movements in all of history. Each congregation seemed to multiply into other churches as their members went everywhere preaching the gospel and establishing churches. We read in Acts 16:5, "So the churches were strengthened in the faith and were increased in number daily." The new believers traveled as far as Phoenicia, Cyprus, and Antioch, preaching the Word. Every church God established had become a world mission strategy center.

GOD'S STRATEGY TODAY

The Canadian church I pastored had been a traditional church performing religious activities since the late 1920s. Now it was obvious that God would do much more. As the pastor, I sought to prepare the members to obey and follow their Lord. The members had never begun new mission churches, but they were ready when God spoke and began to lead them. So we mapped out our province and asked God to let us begin a church in each area, teaching each one that they then had the responsibility of taking the gospel to every person. Through one little church God began many new churches during those years.

The week I arrived, God sent five men from a city of 30,000 people, 90 miles north of us, to ask us to come to them and preach the gospel. Twice a week we went, and a church was born. Soon other communities were asking if we would come to them also. Still others asked our missions if they could help establish churches in their areas as well.

This pattern of God making *every* church and mission a world mission strategy center continued for the 12 years I pastored in that area. When I left, we had about 38 new churches and missions, plus several other towns and villages with new Bible studies that had the potential of becoming churches. We believed God when He told us in His Word to take the gospel to every person.

When has your church started a new mission church?_____
If not, why? Write your answer in the margin.

Are You Ready?

Are you ready, as a church and as an individual member, to have God work through you to accomplish His saving purposes in your world? What a question! In God's kingdom this question is life or death. Others have faced this life-deciding moment. Are you ready?

Read Joel 3:14 in the margin. Do you sense you are in a "valley of decision" at this point in your life? ❑ Yes ❑ No. If so, what decision is God calling on you to make? Write your response in the margin.

Multitudes, multitudes in the valley of decision! For the day of the Lord is near in the valley of decision.
❧ JOEL 3:14 ❧

When God commands a church to do what it has never done before or go where it has never gone before, every church must be ready! Christ said He had come from heaven not to do His own will, but " 'the will of Him who sent Me' " (John 6:38). This is still what He is doing as Head over each church. Are you ready for God to do His will through you as a church?

When God led the Saskatoon church to minister on the University of Saskatchewan campus, neither they nor I had ever done this type of work before. Soon we were not only reaching students and professors, but many of them were sensing God's claim on their lives. As you read in day 1 (p. 117), scores of young adults responded to God and pursued a lifelong call to ministry and missions. We began a theological college to train many who were being called of God.

Our church was ready when God led us to attempt things we had never done, but obedience required huge steps of faith in the process. The people came to experience more of God than they had ever known. As a result the church steadily grew toward Christlikeness. During this time the church added staff, started ministries among the mentally challenged, began a ministry in the jails, and started several ethnic Bible studies. Readiness to obey is crucial to experiencing God doing His work through the church.

Readiness to obey is crucial to experiencing God doing His work through the church.

IF YOU ARE NOT READY ...

Many churches are not ready for God to work through them. I led a series of meetings in a church in Atlanta, Georgia. The church could seat more than 2,500 people, but they were having only about 50 in attendance. I challenged them to look at their changing white community and to ask God to give them a heart of obedience to follow Him with any challenge He might put before them. At each challenge the church said no! Soon the challenges from God ceased; they sold their buildings to another church and disbanded. Interestingly enough, the new church was ready, and in a few months the church building was packed with people God wanted to touch.

Check the following reasons you might give for saying no to a challenge from God.

❑ I'm not gifted in that area.

❑ Those kinds of people make me uncomfortable.

❑ That challenge might bring more responsibility, and I'm already overworked.

❑ I like things just the way they are.

❑ That's just not fiscally responsible.

❑ I wouldn't say no; I'm ready to go.

SPIRITUAL READINESS

In everyday life readiness is vital. A lighthouse must be ready for the storms that arise and the floundering ships that seek a safe harbor. Firemen need to be ready to face many emergencies where their readiness will save lives. Policemen and doctors need to be ready, alert, awake, and prepared to carry out their assigned tasks.

How much more should churches be ready when the eternal destinies of multitudes are in the balance? God may be ready to bring revival to a church so that through it many could be reached with the gospel.

Readiness means the entire church is in a deep and real love relationship with the Head, Jesus Christ, and the members God brought together as a body for His Son. In Revelation 2, Jesus warned the church at Ephesus that they had many good qualities, but they had lost their first love. They were no longer ready to be of use to God. He warned them to " 'remember then how far you have fallen; repent, and do the works you did at first. Otherwise, I will come to you and remove your lampstand from its place—unless you repent' " (Rev. 2:5).

> Readiness means the entire church is in a deep and real love relationship with the Head, Jesus Christ.

What must you do to be ready to obey God when He calls?
Read these Scriptures and fill in the blanks to complete the acrostic: 2 Timothy 2:21, Titus 2:14, 1 Peter 1:13, and Revelation 2:5.

R _____.

Be E _____ to do good works.

Get my mind ready for A _____

Be Self – D _____

P _____ Y myself so I can be set apart to God.

Spiritual readiness is a mark of God's people. Abraham was ready when God called him to leave everything and go where God would show him. His ready obedience influenced the rest of God's people from that time forward. Joseph was ready, in spite of hardships, and God put him second only to the Pharaoh and saved his own family.

Read the Scripture references below and complete the chart to determine how God's people demonstrated spiritual readiness. Be prepared to share your discoveries with your group.

Scripture Reference	How they demonstrated spiritual readiness
Genesis 6:13-14,22	_____
1 Samuel 1:11,24-28	_____
Daniel 3:16-18	_____
Matthew 1:18-24	_____

Before the great revivals of history, God's people had a great burden for prayer, personal and corporate cleansing, and holiness. Once attention was given to these necessary prerequisites, revival came suddenly, swiftly, and with great effect. The Moravian Brethren were meeting in Hernhut, Moravia, in August 1727. For days, even weeks, the church had been praying and repenting of sin. Suddenly, during a Lord's Supper service, God was present with such power that the entire body of believers was made ready for one of the greatest missionary movements in history.

Individuals must be ready, for God may use them in their church to begin a great work. In Wales, young Evan Roberts was ready, and God began a revival through his life. It impacted his church first, then it spread over Wales, and then to the ends of the earth. In a 6-month period, 100,000 persons were converted.

GETTING READY

Two further aspects of readiness must be shared. First, a church must be ready for the enemy's schemes and attacks. A church that is not ready will let sin run unchecked, and Satan will win. If a church fails to teach its people sound doctrine, they will be vulnerable to false teachers and leaders who will leave them in ruins. Jesus warned Peter and the disciples about the enemy's plans and said, " 'Satan has asked to sift you like wheat. But I have prayed for you, that your faith may not fail. And you, when you have turned back, strengthen your brothers' " (Luke 22:31-32). They were tested, but Jesus had readied them.

Spiritual readiness is a mark of God's people.

Although they stumbled, they did not utterly fall. Instead they remained faithful to God and were greatly used to touch a world.

A **second** readiness, much needed in our day, is the readiness for Christ's return. Jesus warned us in the parable of ten virgins. Five were wise, and five were foolish and unprepared. Not being ready denied them entrance to the wedding feast. Then Jesus warned his disciples, " 'Therefore be alert, because you don't know either the day or the hour' " (Matt. 25:13). Over and over again Jesus gave this solemn warning. How much more should we be ready for God's activity in our lives?

Consider again the question posed at the beginning of today's study: "Are you ready, as a church and as an individual member of your church, to have God work through you to accomplish His saving purposes in your world?"
❑ Yes
❑ My church is ready, but I'm not.
❑ I'm ready, but my church is not.

What is your role in helping your church get ready to obey when God commands? Be prepared to share your ideas with your small group.

_____

_____

DAY THREE

Can You Imagine?

While serving as a pastor, God led me to begin work on a booklet entitled, *What the Spirit Is Saying to the Churches.* Almost at the same time God presented a mandate to begin writing *Experiencing God: Knowing and Doing the Will of God,* completed and printed in 1990. I have learned that when God initiates anything, the results cannot be measured. Ten years later the adult workbook had sold more than 3 million copies, many in other languages, and had touched lives from prison cells to the President's office. I am often asked, "Could you have imagined what God would do with your obedience?" Of course, the answer is no!

Every church member has God-sized possibilities in their lives and in their churches. Our church touched a single young man at our university, resulting in his salvation. Since then he has served as a pastor of a Native American church, finished seminary, directed all our work in Quebec, and now serves as national ministry leader for Canada. Could we, as a church, have imagined this? No! Can you even imagine what God could do through your life and your church?

THE ROLE OF FAITH

Notice this sequence of verses from the book of Jeremiah.

1. Jeremiah said to God: " ' "Ah, Lord God! Behold, Thou hast made the heavens and the earth by Thy great power and by Thine outstretched arm! Nothing is too difficult for Thee" ' " (Jer. 32:17).

2. God said to him: " 'Behold, I am the Lord, the God of all flesh; is anything too difficult for Me?' " (Jer. 32:27).

3. God invited His people to respond accordingly: " ' "Call to Me, and I will answer you, and I will tell you great and mighty things, which you do not know" ' " (Jer. 33:3).

Imagine yourself having the same conversation with God that Jeremiah had. What would you say about God?

_____

How would God answer you?

_____

How would God word His invitation in Jeremiah 33:3 to you and your church in this century?

_____

God always asks His people to approach Him with *faith!* The mind may imagine what God could do through His people, but faith believes and appropriates. Faith takes action in real life, achieving the purposes of God. Jesus said to those in His day, " 'If you have faith the size of a mustard seed, ... nothing will be impossible for you' " (Matt. 17:20). If an individual has the power to move mountains through faith, can you imagine what God can and will do through an entire church that believes Him and is fully yielded to obey Him? The church at Jerusalem was such a church, and they " 'turned the world upside down' " (Acts 17:6).

> The mind may imagine what God could do through His people, but faith believes and appropriates.

Do you think the early church turned the world upside down because of the size of their (check one)—
❑ faith?
❑ God in whom they had faith?

What's the difference? _____

_____

Obeying God one day at a time will ultimately result in seeing God do that which would otherwise be impossible. The apostle Paul assured the church at Ephesus that they would be "filled with all the fullness of God" (Eph. 3:19).

Read Ephesians 3:20-21. Imagine something, a vision you have dreamed for your church. Can you imagine this vision becoming a reality for your church?
❑ Yes! Praise God. ❑ I'm trying! ❑ No way.

I would dare to say that the vision you have for your church is not even close to what God can do and wants to do in your midst. His plans are beyond what you even have the capacity to think! Don't set goals for your church, for you may reach them and never know what God wanted to do, if you had only believed Him. Remember, the Scripture says that "without faith it is impossible to please God" (Heb. 11:6).

THE RESULTS OF FAITH

God has chosen to do the impossible through His churches, and He does it in a way that man cannot explain—except in terms of God and His impossibilities. A church in Woodstock, Georgia, is an exciting example. The members are seeing God use their church beyond what anyone could have imagined.

In the area of missions, they have used the strategy found in Acts 1:8, " 'You will receive power when the Holy Spirit has come upon you, and you will be My witnesses in Jerusalem, in all Judea and Samaria, and to the ends of the earth.' " In the year 2001, they sent mission teams to do outreach in local mission churches, and local multihousing units (Jerusalem). They sent teams to Las Vegas and other U.S.-based mission churches (Judea). They have been in Argentina, Hungary, Ukraine, Paris, Benin, Romania, Russia, and Portugal (Samaria). They have also sent teams to remote regions of Indonesia, Algeria, China, Uzbekistan, Thailand, India, Turkey, and Uganda (uttermost parts of the earth). This church has sent out 65 career missionaries, and their total mission giving for the year was $1,925,180. Incredible!

This local church is on mission with God, and they are seeing God touch a world through their church, just as God desires for each of our churches. Although this church is obviously a large one, any church, no matter what the size, can have a global impact. The key is not the members' abilities and resources; the key is God in their midst.

"Now to Him who is able to do above and beyond all that we ask or think according to the power that works in you - to Him be glory in the church and in Christ Jesus to all generations, forever and ever. Amen."

❧ EPHESIANS 3:20-21 ❧

Training "Wheels"

When I was a teenager in Saskatoon, our church began a Bible study in a small town about 32 miles east of us. The town was known as the "isle of the Prairies," and indeed, the small band of Christians there felt isolated.

A large number of youth in the town were also interested in the Lord but had nobody to lead them. Our youth group took on the assignment of reaching out to them.

I remember borrowing Dad's station wagon, piling in five or six of our youth and heading out onto the highway. Once there we would take turns giving a devotional and befriending those teenagers.

I look back and think of how moments like that mission opportunity helped shape my life. Many others were challenged to be on mission with God as well.

Paul's letter to the church at Corinth is an ultimate description of God's love through His churches and the fathomless magnitude of His love made known to each church.

Read 1 Corinthians 2:9-12. Under each picture describe what God has prepared for your church (v. 9).

What is the only possible way your church can begin to understand what God has in place for you?

_____

These verses were written to the local church in Corinth. Paul believed there was no limit to what God had in place and to what He had chosen for them to know through the Holy Spirit. Although we don't have much of this historical record, Paul's two letters—1 and 2 Corinthians—do give us an indication that Corinth, one of the most godless cities in all the Roman Empire at this time, was profoundly affected by the gospel that was shared through this church. God did an amazing work in this pagan city; Paul and the church of Corinth saw the power of God move in ways they could never have imagined.

DEMONSTRATING FAITH

God desires to do so much through every church. How should a church conduct its life with this truth in mind? **First,** every member, beginning with the pastor, must believe God. To have a thorough knowledge of the nature of the church, the church must be taught what the Scriptures say about the body of Christ, His church. The

Book of Acts is the best church growth manual I know! It relates the way in which God's salvation was spread through the early churches.

Second, church members must believe God is the same today as He was in the first century. When He chose to place Christ as the Head of our churches, He fully intended to channel all the resources of heaven through Him into our lives. It may take time for the church to move from where it has been to where God wants it to be. We should be patient with one another. God is not through with us yet!

With all humility and gentleness, with patience, accepting one another in love.

♣ EPHESIANS 4:2 ♣

Read Ephesians 4:2 and 1 Thessalonians 5:14. Circle the qualities Paul called on the believers to display.
Check the level of patience you demonstrate toward members of your church body on the scale below.

We exhort you, brothers: warn those who are lazy, comfort the discouraged, help the weak, be patient with everyone.

♣ 1 THESSALONIANS 5:14 ♣

impatient   patient

Third, members should teach one another and help others in your church body. Where some doubt, help them toward real biblical faith in God. May history record of you what David said in Psalm 40:1,3.

I [we] waited patiently for the Lord;
And He inclined to me [us] and heard my [our] cry. …
He put a new song in my [our] mouth, a song of praise to our God;
Many will see and fear,
And will trust in the Lord.

♣ PSALM 40:1,3 ♣

Make Psalm 40:1,3 (bracketed words mine) a personal prayer for your church by filling in the blanks with your church's name.

We, _____, waited patiently for the Lord; and He inclined to us and heard our cry. … He put a new song in our mouths, a song of praise to our God; many will see and fear and will trust in the Lord *because of the*

faith demonstrated by _____

DAY FOUR

The Cost of Following Christ as Head

I've had the privilege of travelling around the world, ministering to both missionaries and the people to whom they've been sent. As a result, I've seen and heard about the tremendous suffering believers endure around the world. In fact, Christian martyrs today outnumber those from any other time in human history. Most Christians in the western world don't understand the cost of discipleship.

THE COST FACTOR ABROAD

I saw a letter from a young couple that had gone to minister in a difficult area of Africa where Christians were being severely persecuted. The letter was coded so that the authorities would not understand its true meaning. Think of the persecution as you read about the Christians in terms of "potted plants."

> Out of the six plants that had been given to us, two have died. The other four are not doing so well; the heat is increasing, and the water is little. We don't know yet whether they will survive. Two new plants have been given, and they have been planted well, but it is very hot over here, and we don't know whether they will survive.

When they were home on furlough, I met the young couple who wrote this letter. They recounted some of the struggles which had affected their mission. The stories of martyrdom were so grim that I can't include them in this book.

However, in the midst of such a tremendous cost to be a Christian, the couple related how God was working in a powerful way to bring people to Christ. In fact, the night before they left to return home, a small band of Christians made their way to the missionaries' house in the middle of the night. On the roof of the home, they had a little plastic pool where they held a baptismal service for eight new believers.

I asked the couple, "Tell me about the kind of faith those new believers have." The missionaries said that when they heard about the life, death, and resurrection of Christ, they felt they owed everything to the Lord who laid down His life for them. They saw this not as a sacrifice but as a privilege. The love of Christ had captured their hearts.

Circle the words that best describe your feelings after reading this account of persecuted Christians. Add other emotions in the margin.

challenged	frightened	uplifted	unworthy
bold	ashamed	angry	motivated

THE COST FACTOR AT HOME

Jesus never hid the cost of being His disciple. He made clear that His disciple would have to deny self, take up his cross, and follow Him.

We must deal with this mark of a true disciple, for it is also the mark of a true church. Although individual believers endured suffering, the cost was experienced and shared in the context of the local church. There would be no spiritual orphans or mavericks among God's people. All God's people would share in the cost when any part of the body was suffering. The cost of following Jesus would be real,

Many of the Corinthians, when they heard, believed and were baptized.

Then the Lord said to Paul in a night vision, "Don't be afraid, but keep on speaking and don't be silent. For I am with you, and no one will lay a hand on you to hurt you, because I have many people in this city." And he stayed there a year and six months, teaching the word of God among them.

♣ ACTS 18:8-11 ♣

Now great crowds were traveling with Him. So He turned and said to them: "If anyone comes to Me and does not hate his own father and mother, wife and children, brothers and sisters—yes, even his own life—he cannot be My disciple. Whoever does not bear his own cross and come after Me cannot be My disciple.

"For which of you, wanting to build a tower, doesn't first sit down and calculate the cost, to see if he has enough to complete it? Otherwise, after he has laid the foundation and cannot finish it, all the onlookers will begin to make fun of him, saying, 'This man started to build and wasn't able to finish.' Or what king, going to war against another king, will not first sit down and decide if he is able with ten thousand to oppose the one who comes against him with twenty thousand? If not, while the other is still far off, he sends a delegation and asks for terms of peace. In the same way, therefore, every one of you who does not say good-bye to all his possessions cannot be My disciple."

♣ LUKE 14:25-33 ♣

personal, and at times deadly. The cost could only be endured faithfully in the context of God's people corporately. Unfortunately, I have found that today we intentionally avoid the cost of discipleship.

Read Luke 14:25-33. In the debit column of the ledger below, list the costs Jesus said a disciple must make to follow Him.

In addition, members deliberately abandon the people of God during times of cost in order to go to another church where they can find times of blessing instead. What a tragic misunderstanding of discipleship! What an affront to God's great salvation that our generation can be so self-centered, forsaking God's will when the cost of discipleship gets hard. Church hopping usually arises out of a selfish desire to be happy, when the Lord desires that His disciples be holy. He desires for them to make a difference where He has put them and not simply go to the place where their needs are better met.

Which desire most often motivates your life?
❑ The desire to be happy
❑ The desire to be holy

Too many people today look for shortcuts in their Christian life or substitutes for the hard, painful, and weary work of a disciple. They want instant gratification and pleasure but no cross. They look for ease and comfort in life, but they're unwilling to count the cost of following Jesus. If they don't receive honor, position, and recognition, they search out other churches that will grant recognition so they can be satisfied in their Christian lives. The thought of scars or wounds, like their Master's, doesn't enter their heads. They'll accept no pain or sorrow even though their Savior suffered greatly. They want all the benefits of God's great salvation with no costs attached.

This comfort-zone mentality too often characterizes individual believers, but more tragically it reflects the same mentality in the churches of which they are members. "Make us successful so my family and I can be happy!" "I can't afford to give financially to the ministry of the church; I have too many other obligations!" "Don't ask me to help start a mission church; it would cost our family too much!" These "disciples" are disqualifying themselves as disciples!

Jesus made clear to all of His disciples that He was going to suffer in order to accomplish the Father's will for His life. In fact, one of the most powerful images that Jesus left the disciples concerning the cost of doing the Father's will is seen in the upper room after the resurrection.

Picture the scene unfolding as you read John 20:19-21.
1. What expression would have been on your face when Jesus suddenly appeared?

_____

2. How would you have responded when He showed you His scarred hands and side?
❑ I turned my face away and grimaced.
❑ I gently stroked the scars.
❑ Tears rolled down my face as I recalled that awful Friday.
❑ I bowed at Jesus' feet in silent gratitude.
❑ I threw my arms around Jesus' neck and weep for joy.
❑ Other: _____

3. What became the mood in the room when the disciples realized Jesus meant He was sending them to suffer in the same way He suffered? Circle your responses.

fear   determination   joy   solemnity   awe

Do you feel the moment? The wounds of the Savior made a lasting impression on the disciples concerning the cost of following Jesus. Now they were being sent into the world to do the Father's will.

When was the last time you pictured the Savior's wounds?
❑ I never have.
❑ It's been years since I've considered Christ's suffering for me.
❑ It's too gruesome; I try to avoid thinking of Christ's sacrifice.
❑ I often think about Christ's sacrifice.
❑ I just now pictured the Savior's wounds and was deeply moved.

The cross for Jesus was real; it meant great suffering on behalf of sinners. If we want to impact sinners today, it will cost us, as well.

In the evening of that first day of the week, the disciples were gathered together with the doors locked because of their fear of the Jews. Then Jesus came, stood among them, and said to them, "Peace to you!" Having said this, He showed them His hands and His side. So the disciples rejoiced when they saw the Lord. Jesus said to them again, "Peace to you! Just as the Father has sent Me, I also send you."

❧ JOHN 20:19-21 ❧

"A disciple is not above his teacher, or a slave above his master."

✤ MATTHEW 10:24 ✤

THE COST OF NOT FOLLOWING CHRIST

Jesus announced that some would not be willing to pay the price. What they don't realize is that the cost of not following Jesus is far more severe. Jesus said, " 'Whoever wants to save his life will lose it, but whoever loses his life because of Me and the gospel will save it' " (Mark 8:35). If a church chooses to turn back, it may never recover from the consequences of that decision. When church members are more concerned with trying to protect their lifestyles, their comforts, or their possessions, they will lose their lives. They *will* lose the reason God chose to grant them salvation.

Your church may need to face honestly your involvement with your Lord as He seeks to be on mission in our world. Christ, the Head of your church, wants to do the will of His Father through you. When you refuse to do what He asks you to do, the Father's plan to touch the world is impaired.

Answer these questions:
1. What do you believe are the priorities for your church?

_____

2. Do these priorities move your church (check one)
❑ Closer to or ❑ Further away from ministry to the world?

2. Read Philippians 2:5-11 in your Bible. Fill in the blanks to discover the costs Jesus paid to minister to the world.

Example:	Equality with God
	E _____ Himself
	Assumed form of a _____
	Took on likeness of __ _____
Possessions	H _____ Himself
Lifestyle	O _____ to death.
Comfort	Death on a Cross

When we read passages like Philippians 2:5-11, we are forced to reconsider our reluctance not only to count the cost but also to pay the price to be involved with Him on mission in our world. Jesus didn't remain comfortable in the heavenly places. He went straight to the difficult places and became a friend of sinners.

We can't remain comfortable and go with Christ at the same time. There will be a cost when He leads us to minister to the prisons, the abortion clinics, skid-row mission projects, English as a second language classes, and so forth. Every individual, as well as the church corporately, should count the cost to follow Jesus. They must deny self and take up a real cross.

On the other hand, when a church does only what the world would do, the world never sees God, and He is denied the glory that is rightly His. For God to be glorified or honored as God in His churches, the churches must turn to Him just as He told them to do. The Scripture says, " 'Call upon Me in the day of trouble; I shall rescue you, and you will honor Me' " (Ps. 50:15).

Read John 6:66-68. What is the reward for following Jesus? Write your answer in the "Credit" column in the ledger on page 130.

Is the reward worth the costs? ❏ Yes ❏ No
Are you willing to pay the cost to pick up your cross and follow Jesus? ❏ Yes ❏ No ❏ Not yet but I'm getting there.

From that moment many of His disciples turned back and no longer walked with Him. Therefore Jesus said to the Twelve, "You don't want to go away too, do you?" Simon Peter answered, "Lord, to whom should we go? You have the words of eternal life."

♣ JOHN 6:66-68 ♣

DAY FIVE

God Is Glorified in His Churches

In day 4 we looked generally at the costs of discipleship. In day 5 we will explore specific costs of following Christ and specific blessings for those who choose to let Christ's light penetrate their darkened community and world.

SPECIFIC COSTS
In our desire to grow toward Christlikeness, in our pursuit of knowing and doing the will of God, there are some stumbling blocks along the way. I have found that they are nearly all connected to the cost factor.

As you read the following section, underline all the costs a church must be willing to pay if they want to glorify God.

For churches to accomplish the purposes God has for them, sacrificial giving will always be involved. Every time I think of sacrificial giving, I think of dear Iva Bates. She was a widowed farm lady, living on a meager pension and a modest savings account. When the Lord challenged our church to give toward a building project, she was led to participate as a member of that body. So she came and brought a check for five thousand dollars. Since I knew that she didn't have much money, I went to her only daughter and asked about Iva's situation. I discovered that she only had nine thousand dollars total in her account to live on for the rest of her life. I told her daughter that I couldn't let her mom do that; it wasn't right! Then she said something that has stayed with me ever since: "Would you deny my mother the privilege of sacrificing for her Lord?" Her words crushed me.

You know the grace of our Lord Jesus Christ: although He was rich, for your sake He became poor, so that by His poverty you might become rich.

♣ 2 CORINTHIANS 8:9 ♣

However, the Lord's promises are true; He does care for the righteous. When I was preparing to leave that church to go to another place of service, I just had to go and see Iva's daughter again. I said, "You don't have to tell me if you prefer, but could I ask a personal question? How much money does your mother have in her savings?"

Her daughter replied, "It's an amazing thing. I checked the other day and discovered that she had $11,000 in her account, and I have no idea where it came from."

Sitting across from the temple treasury, He watched how the crowd dropped money into the treasury. Many rich people were putting in large sums. And a poor widow came and dropped in two tiny coins worth very little. Summoning His disciples, He said to them, "I assure you: This poor widow has put in more than all those giving to the temple treasury. For they all gave out of their surplus, but she out of her poverty has put in everything she possessed—all she had to live on."

❧ MARK 12:41-44 ❧

Read Mark 12:41-44 in the margin.
Does your giving more closely resemble (underline)—
the rich who gave out of their surplus? OR
the poor widow who gave all she had?

Does the widow's type of giving seem fiscally foolish or irresponsible to you? ❑ Yes ❑ No

Following Christ always requires financial sacrifice. Every believer will be challenged at this point. For Jesus to be Lord of our lives, He must take precedence over our material possessions. Unfortunately, many fail this test. That's why the Scripture says, "The love of money is a root of all kinds of evil, and by craving it, some have wandered away from the faith and pierced themselves with many pains" (1 Tim. 6:10).

Another cost might be God's call on a church to reach out to the youth of their community. Some will not be willing to change their church in order to reach the young people. There might be different music, more noise, higher costs for youth activities, or the hiring of a youth minister. Some are not willing to receive unsaved youth who may look and act differently.

I was in my son Mel's church recently and noticed a large hole in the wall of the Sunday school hallway. When I asked what happened, he simply said, "Growing pains. Our youth group is enjoying tremendous growth, and our building is taking a beating. We will teach them respect for God's house, but isn't it great to see God bringing many young people to salvation?"

He also mentioned that he has had to teach the church about the cost of reaching youth. He reminded the church that he was one of those youth wrestling in the hallways just a few short years ago. In fact, some adults in his church today used to baby-sit him as a child. Mel laughs as he warns the church, "Be nice to these rambunctious youth. Someday they may be your pastor!"

If God leads the church to look toward the local college or university, it must be ready to pay the price to reach the students. They tend to have vision, energy, and faith but little money. They will often want to be a part of extensive mission and outreach projects, use contemporary music equipment, and minister in unusual ways. But if a church is willing to count the cost and sacrifice, the rewards will far exceed the costs. However, the costs are real, and some will resist the changes needed to do the will of God.

God may also remind a church, during a time of home or foreign missions study, that He wants their church to become involved with Him on mission trips, which are costly, but they touch a world that needs to know Christ. The trips will also affect those who go. Some may sense God's call into ministry or missions. Parents will suddenly realize how real the cost is to them when they give their sons or daughters lives over to God.

Starting a new mission church, close to home or in another region, may cost the loss of members and money in order to establish a strong foundation. It may take the pastor away for weeks at a time, and he may even feel called to move to the new mission or to a missionary career overseas.

Reaching language groups, such as Chinese, Laotians, Cambodians, East Indians, or Spanish can make many costly demands in churches. When churches in the Vancouver area began to reach out to different ethnic groups, I remember little things like the lingering strong odor of oriental cooking that we were not used to smelling. We had to overcome the difficulties related to communication barriers and cultural differences. I understand the real-life costs to reaching people for Christ, but if a church can remember the incredible "adjustments" God made with His Son for us, we may be ashamed of our complaints. For just as Christ made sacrifices in order that we might come to know God, so He will ask us to make sacrifices so that others may come to know Him as well.

Review the costs you underlined as you read the preceding paragraphs. Can you recall a time when your church faced inconvenience and discomfort with the introduction of a new ministry? If so, briefly describe that time.

_____

_____

How did God bless your church through that ministry?

_____

_____

SPECIFIC BLESSINGS

God's nature is revealed openly before a watching world as His followers bring glory to Him. One of many examples of this principle is Daniel. Such was the impact of his life before a watching world that the pagan King Darius made the decree that all of his dominion should worship the God of Daniel. (See Dan. 6:26-27.)

The apostle Paul understood that "the incalculable riches of the Messiah," which were a "mystery hidden for ages in God," were now to "be made known *through the church* to the rulers and authorities in the heavens" (Eph. 3:8-10). Isn't that a powerful affirmation of the church? Glory comes to God when His people live out what God has provided through His mercy and grace.

I saw this happen in a community with a large number of deaf people. When our church members voted to begin a deaf ministry, they didn't realize how this would interrupt their comfortable church life. Soon our basement was crowded with the deaf and their families. Our supplies began to be used and not replaced. We began to receive calls to help in ways we had not anticipated. Everything changed.

Fortunately God enabled us to do what He called us to do. We adjusted and were patient and kind. As a result, we saw many deaf saved, and later they found their own place to meet. But we had the joy of being on mission with God to the deaf community.

Have you been resisting costs of obedience that you are now willing to pay so you can follow Christ completely?
❑ Yes, and I'm still resisting.   ❑ Yes, I'm ready to follow.
❑ I don't know. I need to pray about that.
❑ No, I've paid the costs of obedience.

LET GOD'S GLORY SHINE

The world doesn't need to see good people doing good things for their God. They need to see God doing "above and beyond all that we ask or think" among His people. When the church allows God to fill them with His presence, the world will see and glorify Him because they have experienced Him in the lives of His people. They will know His love because the church sincerely loves all people, His power because the church steps out in faith and attempts what only God can accomplish, and His people as they let Him display His mighty work through them. When God begins to heal marriages, return wayward children, heal alcoholics and drug addicts, provide for physical needs in times of crisis, and give wisdom to business people, the world comes to know the difference God makes in our world.

How can your church reveal God's glory to a watching world? Write your response in the margin.

The world does not need to see good people doing good things for their God. They need to see God doing "above and beyond all that we ask or think" among His people.

The Church in the Kingdom

"Therefore, you should pray like this:
Our Father in heaven,
Your name be honored as holy.
Your kingdom come.
Your will be done
on earth as it is in heaven."
MATTHEW 6:9-10

My wife Marilyn and I have traveled to more than 80 countries of the world. We have often felt overwhelmed by the masses of people who need to be reached with the gospel. As we shared together, God unfolded the hundreds, if not thousands, of ways He is touching them—not through just one group but through all of His people—through missionaries and nationals alike, through personal witnessing and radio, through Bible correspondence courses and the *Jesus* film, and through compassion shown in hospitals. The message of the gospel is being spread by means of boat, bicycle, airplane, and Land Rover. His kingdom continues to be extended to the megacities and the remote villages, to the tribal chiefs and national leaders. Countless prayer warriors are on their knees supporting the progress. God is marshalling His people in a cooperative interdependence that is unprecedented in history.

How can you become a part of the larger family of God and enjoy the blessings of such a relationship? This week we will focus on our role in kingdom work through local churches. Keep these questions in mind as you read.

1. Are you seeking the kingdom of God as your number one priority?
2. Is your church diligently praying for God's mighty power to be demonstrated in their midst?
3. Have you neglected the role of the local church as the primary means of extending the kingdom?
4. Is your church cooperating with other churches in your denomination?
5. Are you and your church praying alongside other churches that God will bring revival and spiritual awakening?
6. Does your church sense its need to be involved with others to fulfill its mission to touch the world?

Thy Kingdom Come

Christians in China believed their Lord when the Communists took over their nation and all missionaries had to leave. From a human perspective the future of Christianity in China looked bleak. But circumstances, no matter how grim, cannot thwart the plans of God. At that time there were probably one million believers in China. God continued to extend the kingdom through house churches, just as He did in the New Testament during times of persecution.

When China opened up again just a few decades later, there were as many as one hundred million believers. More people are coming to Christ in China every day (around 20,000). Nothing can stop the rule of God in the hearts of His people. If God can expand the kingdom in countries where churches are not allowed to meet, what could He do through our churches in countries that are free? We need to learn about God's plan to extend His kingdom through His churches and through them to touch the world.

THE KING

Jesus preached on the kingdom of God 112 times, while He mentions the church only 3 times. The good news that Jesus proclaimed was that the kingdom had come with the coming of the King! To further understand the kingdom of God, we must have a thorough understanding of the King.

What made this kingdom different from all the other kingdoms of the world was the nature of the King. Jesus was born, not only as the Savior, but also as the King. Matthew 2:2 records that the wise men came from the east asking, " 'Where is He who has been born King of the Jews?' " They were aware of the prophecies concerning the coming Messiah who would rule over the kingdom. They knew that Jesus fulfilled those prophecies, and they came to worship Him.

Christ was born King simply because He was King before He was born. He was called the Son of David, the Son of man, and the Son of God, all of which were names identifying the Messiah. In the Gospels, He was called King of the Jews and King of Israel, indicating that the people had identified Him with the coming kingdom of God.

The message Jesus preached was " 'Repent, because the kingdom of heaven has come near' " (Matt. 4:17). Other translations of this verse say the kingdom of heaven "is at hand" (NASB), or "is near" (NIV). In a new sense, the kingdom of heaven had arrived on earth with the coming of Jesus. The kingdom had always been, for the King had always been. Jesus made the statement, " 'If I drive out demons by the Spirit of God, then the kingdom of God has come to you' " (Matt. 12:28).

> The good news that Jesus proclaimed was that the kingdom had come with the coming of the King!

Jesus never applied the term *King* to Himself. Not only was it politically dangerous in the Roman Empire, but also His followers had an incorrect understanding of His kingship. This, however, does not detract from the fact that He is King and that He has a kingdom.

Read John 19:19-21 in your Bible. Complete the sign Pilate had placed on Jesus' cross.

JESUS THE NAZARENE

The _____ ____ ____ _____

How did the Jewish leaders react to the title Pilate gave Jesus? Check all that apply.
❑ They protested Jesus' kingship.
❑ They questioned Jesus' kingship.
❑ They ignored Jesus' kingship.
❑ They accepted Jesus' kingship.

Read Revelation 19:16. Underline the title God gave Jesus. How does your lifestyle reflect your reaction to Jesus title?
❑ I protest Jesus' kingship over my life.
❑ I question Jesus' kingship over my life.
❑ I ignore Jesus' kingship over my life.
❑ I accept Jesus' kingship over my life.

On His robe and on His thigh He has a name written: King of Kings and Lord of Lords.

❧ REVELATION 19:16 ❧

He fulfilled all the prophecies of the coming King and was determined to teach the people what the kingdom was all about. The kingdom will continue its growth until Christ returns at His second coming. At that time the King will judge once and for all those who refuse to follow His rule in their lives, and the number of subjects in the kingdom will be complete. Until Christ returns, the number of true believers will grow as the church proclaims the gospel of the kingdom.

THE KINGDOM
Everyone who has been born into the family of God and now bears His image belongs to the kingdom of God. That's where Christ rules. The kingdom of God, then, is found wherever Christ reigns.

Jesus taught important principles about His kingdom to a Roman political leader and a Jewish religious leader. On the next page, read John 3:5-7 and John 18:36. Summarize what each man learned about the kingdom of God.

Jesus answered, "I assure you: Unless someone is born of water and the Spirit, he cannot enter the kingdom of God. Whatever is born of the flesh is flesh, and whatever is born of the Spirit is spirit. Do not be amazed that I told you that you must be born again."

❧ JOHN 3:5-7 ❧

"My kingdom is not of this world," said Jesus. "If My kingdom were of this world, My servants would fight, so that I wouldn't be handed over to the Jews. As it is, My kingdom does not have its origin here."

❧ JOHN 18:36 ❧

God created man in His own image, in the image of God He created him; male and female He created them.

❧ GENESIS 1:27 ❧

Those who bear the image of God belong to Him and should be given to Him.

Nicodemus _____

Pilate _____

The territory of His kingdom is not found in geography but in His spiritual reign that is far beyond mere physical boundaries. To be born into the world is not equivalent to being born into the kingdom. The kingdom is not fleshly but spiritual. It is not determined by land and sea but by the wind of the Spirit. Only those who have been born again enter the kingdom.

In Luke 20:20-26, the religious leaders were trying to trap Jesus by asking if it was lawful to pay taxes to Caesar. Jesus said, " 'Give back to Caesar the things that are Caesar's' " (v. 25). The Jews lived within the borders of the Roman Empire. They enjoyed protection from the enemies, walked along the roads that Rome had built, and enjoyed the commerce that came from the safety of the sea. As a result, they were to pay taxes back to Rome. After all, the coin had Caesar's picture on it, so they were to give back to Caesar the things that were his.

But that's not all Jesus said. He said give back " 'to God the things that are God's' " (v. 25). Now the basis of Jesus' argument concerning money was whose image was on it. So if a coin bears the image of Caesar, it belongs to him. But that which bears the image of God belongs to God and should be given back to Him.

Read Genesis 1:27. Who bears the image of God? _____

Jesus' teaching involved more than paying taxes to Caesar and a tithe to the temple. His higher teaching was that those who bear God's image belong to Him and ought to give their lives back to Him. The people were amazed at Jesus' words and became silent.

How much of your currency would you estimate you give back to your country in taxes each day? Place an X on the line.

0% _____100%

How much of yourself, bearing the image of God, do you give back to God each day? Place an X on the line.

0% _____100%

THE KINGDOM FOCUS

The Book of Acts continues the same focus on the kingdom of God that was introduced in the Gospels. After spending three years listening to Jesus teach and observing His life, the disciples were well versed in the ways of the kingdom. As they preached about the kingdom, the early church spread. When the apostle Paul went to Ephesus, he preached the same message that Christ had preached in the days of his flesh. Acts 19:8 tells us His approach. To the end of his life, Paul's message remained the same. In the last chapter of Acts, we find Paul under house arrest in Rome. "From dawn to dusk he expounded and witnessed about *the kingdom of God*. He persuaded them concerning Jesus from both the Law of Moses and the Prophets" (Acts 28:23).

> *"He entered the synagogue and spoke boldly over a period of three months, engaging in discussions and trying to persuade them about the things related to the kingdom of God."*
>
> ❧ Acts 19:8 ❧

Read Colossians 1:13-14 in the margin.
1. **On the diagram below, identify the two realms within which a person can choose to live**
2. **On the arrow, draw a stick figure to indicate where you are in relation to God's kingdom.**

> *He has rescued us from the domain of darkness and transferred us into the kingdom of the Son He loves, in whom we have redemption, the forgiveness of sins.*
>
> ❧ Colossians 1:13-14 ❧

Domain of _____   **_____ of the Son**

We can glimpse a portion of what Paul taught about the kingdom of God in his letter to the Colossians. Salvation transfers the believer into the kingdom, for those who have not been given salvation in Christ are still living in darkness, outside the kingdom. Two people can stand side-by-side, one in the kingdom and one outside the kingdom. The religious leaders were looking for a kingdom on earth; they could not see the kingdom in their midst.

How is your vision? Do you acknowledge the kingdom, or rule, of God in your daily life?
- ❏ I'm totally blind.
- ❏ I'm nearsighted. I can only see the daily pressures that surround me. I don't focus on a kingdom of God that seems so far away.
- ❏ I'm farsighted. I know God's kingdom is near, but I focus on my goals for the future rather than God's rule now.
- ❏ I have 20/20 vision. I recognize the work and the rule of Christ in my daily life and joyfully submit to His reign.

The Work of the Kingdom

The church is God's lifeline to a lost and dying world.

Every generation of Christians must evaluate its role in God's great plan to bring salvation to the world and extend the kingdom of God. That plan is intimately related to the nature of the local church. Its role in the kingdom of God has not changed since its inception: the church is God's lifeline to a lost and dying world.

Check the statements that best describe your thoughts when you read that your church is God's lifeline to a lost and dying world.
❑ The world is going to drown.
❑ We need to quit focusing on ship maintenance and care about the souls floundering around us.
❑ We need to work on our lifesaving skills.
❑ We are humbled and willing to be used as God's lifeline.

THE ROLE OF THE CHURCH

Jesus urged people to " 'seek first the kingdom of God' " (Matt. 6:33), not the church. But He also established the church as a divine institution for the proclamation and extension of the kingdom. To emphasize the significance of the church is not to diminish the significance of the kingdom, for in the eternal plan of God, the work of the kingdom is to be accomplished through the churches.

The churches and the kingdom are naturally connected because of their relationship to Christ. Christ is the King of the kingdom and the Head of the churches. He reigns over the kingdom and leads His people in the churches. The church is Christ's new body in which He continues to do the work of extending the kingdom as He did while on earth. His message of " 'repent because the kingdom of heaven has come' " (Matt. 3:2) is still to be preached through the churches to every generation.

As you read the following paragraph, underline the many kingdom roles God has given the church.

Each church, as the body of Christ, is the witness through the ages that He is still alive. The church is the King's army sent out to defeat the enemy in the power of the Holy Spirit. The church has the unlimited power of the sovereign King to do His will on earth. Each church is a working arm of the kingdom, responsible for practically implementing God's kingdom agenda.

Read Ephesians 3:10 in the margin of page 143. Take a few moments to reflect on the enormity of this truth.

1. What is to be made known? _____
2. Through what medium will God's wisdom be made known?

_____

3. To whom does the church make known God's wisdom?

_____

4. Based on the truths you discovered, what is an amazing role God has given the church?

_____

This is so that God's multifaceted wisdom may now be made known through the church to the rulers and authorities in the heavens.

❧ EPHESIANS 3:10 ❧

❧ A STORY FROM MEL BLACKABY ❧

Who's in Control?

I had just arrived in a new city, ready to pastor a small group of people who were trusting God to do a great work. As I sought to understand what God was doing in our city, I ran into many discouraged pastors. The city had a reputation as a hard place to grow a church. Several people told me why they thought the churches were having such a hard time.

They said, "There's a native American reservation alongside the city that practices a lot of spiritualism in the hills around the area. The presence of evil spirits has made it so difficult for us Christians."

The first thing that crossed my mind was a sense of wonder. Why in the world would a Christian be worried about the teachings of a false religion when they know the one and only true God? I believe in the power of evil spirits, but I sensed that many Christians did not believe in the power of the Holy Spirit of God. As powerful as the evil one is, how does he compare to the awesome power of God?

Notice the incredible power given to those who are a part of God's church. Read these Scriptures:

A. Acts 4:33   B. 2 Corinthians 10:4
C. 2 Timothy 1:7   D. 2 Peter 1:3

Write the letter of the Scripture passage that declares each truth.

___ God gives believers a spirit of power, love, and sound judgment.

___ God gives believers the power to testify to Christ's resurrection.

___ God's power gives believers everything they need for life and godliness.

___ God's divine power enables believers to demolish strongholds.

We must never cower in fear against the enemy when we serve the King! We cannot be satisfied with serving a god who is smaller than our God.

Each church must boldly go forth in His name, "in Him the entire fullness of God's nature dwells bodily, and you have been filled by Him, who is the head over every ruler and authority" (Col. 2:9-10).

THE KEYS OF THE KINGDOM

Did you know that the keys of the kingdom of heaven have been given to His churches? It's an affront to the Holy God that in many churches the keys are hanging on the key rack and not being used. God looks for a people and a church who understand that they have the keys and are ready to use them so people will be set free.

The key to the kingdom is the Word of God being shared by the people of God. When God's Word is shared, the Holy Spirit takes that Word and sets people free with its truth. The apostle Paul said, "To those who are perishing the message of the cross is foolishness, but to us who are being saved it is God's power" (1 Cor. 1:18).

In Matthew 13, Jesus told one of His kingdom parables, the sower and the seed. He said that the Word of God is like a seed. When the seed is put in good soil, it will produce a crop: " 'some 100, some 60, and some 30 times what was sown' " (Matt. 13:8). When we plant the truth of God into a person's heart, that one truth can produce much fruit. That Word has its own life, for it will not return void (see Isa. 55:11).

> Read Isaiah 55:10-11 in your Bible.
> Circle the pictures that illustrate how God described His Word.

> Why did God compare His Word to these images?

> _____

What happens when the Word of God is in your hand? A Christian who has been filled with the Holy Spirit handles the Word of God with understanding, and in that Word is all the power of God to bring to pass what we need in this world. You will never confront a situation He has not already promised to deal with redemptively. Christians can bring wholeness to any situation, for they handle the mighty Word of God.

> **Do you know the promises of God so you can apply them to your own life?** ❑ Yes ❑ Somewhat ❑ No
> **Do you know the Word of God so you can help others in need of God's power to set them free?** ❑ Yes ❑ Somewhat ❑ No

The key to the kingdom is the Word of God being shared by the people of God.

Think of a situation you currently face. What promise of God can you apply to that situation?

_____

Check the following Scriptures that best express your relationship with God's Word.

❑ "Jesus answered them, 'You are deceived, because you don't know the Scriptures' " (Matt. 22:29).

❑ "The word of the Lord to them will become: Do and do, do and do, rule on rule, rule on rule; a little here, a little there" (Isa. 28:13, NIV).

❑ " 'You splendidly disregard God's commandment, so that you may maintain your tradition!' " (Mark 7:9).

❑ "By this time you ought to be teachers, you need someone to teach you the elementary truths of God's word all over again" (Heb. 5:12, NIV).

❑ "Be diligent to present yourself approved to God, a worker who doesn't need to be ashamed, correctly teaching the word of truth" (2 Tim. 2:15).

When Christ gave the church the keys of the kingdom, He made it the channel through which the promises of God would be available to the world. If we share God's Word with others, they will receive the blessings of God. If we don't share God's Word, we lock them out and keep them from knowing and receiving God's blessings.

Check the phrase that best describes what your church is doing with the keys to the kingdom.

❑ They're hanging on a key rack in the vestibule.

❑ We often misplace the keys and spend time looking for them.

❑ We use the keys to lock our doors against anything or anybody who causes discomfort.

❑ We use the keys to the kingdom to power up our engine so we can go out into our world and transport people into the kingdom of God.

You may feel you the need to add requests to your ongoing prayer list for your church. Spend time in prayer for your church and for your own role in helping your church fulfill its kingdom work.

How the Kingdom Grows

I listened with wonder and awe as missionaries told what was happening among the Masai peoples in East Africa. For centuries it seemed impossible to make any inroads into this large tribe. Many had tried to no avail. The missionaries turned to God in prayer and enlisted others to pray for this unreached people group with an even greater fervor. They literally prayed what Jesus told them to pray and inserted the Masai people in their prayer: "Father, may Your kingdom come among the Masai people."

Soon, an opening came to speak to one of the tribal chieftains. With much prayer the missionaries shared, and the man became a Christian. Immediately he ordered all his people to hear God's good news that was for them, too. Soon hundreds were being saved, then thousands, and now tens of thousands. Churches were immediately started, pastors were trained, and the Scriptures were taught. The heart for evangelism and missions gripped their hearts, and they sought to tell the good news to people all over the region.

Much later a friend of mine spoke to a chief who was also a pastor. As my missionary friend shared from the Book of Acts and the Great Commission, he challenged this chief and his people to take the message of God's great salvation to other people also, until the whole world had heard the news. The chief smiled and pointed to the horizon. "Do you see that smoke rising? We have already taken this good news to them. And if you get there, you will see other smoke rising even farther away. We have been there, too. We have made a promise to God that we would take the news of His salvation as far as we see the smoke rising!"

My friend was overwhelmed but not surprised. As people are saved and churches are established, they will extend God's rule, God's kingdom "as far as the smoke rises!" In God's eternal plan, His kingdom will extend and grow until His rule fills the earth.

THE POTENTIAL FOR GROWTH

Everywhere the early church proclaimed the gospel, people heard and believed. God immediately added them to His people in churches where they lived; then Christ would lead that body of believers to extend the kingdom even further through their lives. This was God's plan in the first century, and it is His plan in our generation. There is no limit to what God can do through one church willing to follow Christ in extending the kingdom. In Matthew 13, Jesus talked about how the kingdom grows.

Blessed be His glorious name forever;
And may the whole earth be filled
*   with His glory.*
Amen, and Amen.

❦ PSALM 72:19 ❦

Read Matthew 13:33. (Keep your Bible open to that passage.)
What did Jesus say the kingdom of heaven is like?

_____

Why do you think Jesus used this illustration to describe how
His kingdom grows?

_____

A little bit of yeast impacts the entire amount of dough. Where does
it start? Wherever it is placed. In the same way, what will happen if
a church is placed into a community that does not know God? That
church, if it is walking with the Lord, will begin to impact the entire
community. Its influence will be felt because of the presence of Christ
in the midst of that congregation.

**Read Matthew 13:31-32. What metaphor of transformation did
Jesus use to describe kingdom growth?**
❑ A clump of carbon into a glittering diamond
❑ A caterpillar into a butterfly
❑ A tiny seed into a tree
❑ A single musical note into a grand symphony

The mustard seed is the smallest of all the seeds, but if it is sown into
the ground and given time, it will become a large tree. As long as the
seed has within itself the potential to grow, it will. Your church may
be small, but it has all the potential of heaven to grow. For the King
of the kingdom is resident and desires to impact the community in
power. It may take time, but the steady and faithful service of a king-
dom-oriented church will be rewarded with fruit that will last. That
is the nature of the kingdom of God.

> The steady and faithful service of a kingdom-oriented church will be rewarded with fruit that will last.

**Could God take your church, like a mustard seed, and use it to
bring glory to Him and extend His kingdom? Picture your church
as a tiny mustard seed. Do you believe God can take your church
and use it to bring glory to Him and extend His kingdom?**
❑ No. We're too far gone.
❑ I want to believe, but I'm so discouraged.
❑ Yes, I believe in how great and powerful God is, not in how
   great and powerful my church is.

I believe God wants to use every church to bring glory to Him and
extend His kingdom. That's why He established churches in the first
place. He wants to extend His rule into family after family, business

after business, community after community, and nation after nation. However, He needs a people who will believe and follow Him.

Will you voice the same prayer for your church that the missionaries in our opening illustration prayed for the Masai people? Fill in the blank with your church's name and voice this prayer out loud.

Father, may Your kingdom come among _____

❧ A STORY FROM MEL BLACKABY ❧

A Transformed Life

One night a young lady came to my door just before midnight with a loaded gun in her possession. She felt her life wasn't worth living; suicide appeared to be the best option. Tragically, she would leave behind her husband and five children. As her car passed our home, she decided to stop and talk to the pastor as a last resort.

My father happened to be leading a revival in our church and was in the living room as I answered the door. The two of us began to minister to her by showing her the promises of God in the Scriptures. I will never forget the moment she not only heard the Word but also accepted it as true. Her body went completely limp as God lifted the burden from her life.

We noticed an immediate difference, and it continued in the days that followed.

She had been depressed and deeply troubled, but now she was full of joy and at peace. She had been wearing dark and gloomy clothes; now she came to church in bright cheerful dresses. But more than anything, the look on her face testified to the power of God to set her free.

I was struck by the privilege I had to see God do a miracle in her life. I thought of the apostle Paul who said, "My speech and my proclamation were not with persuasive words of wisdom, but with a demonstration of the Spirit and power, so that your faith might not be based on men's wisdom but on God's power" (1 Cor. 2:4-5).

UNLEASHING THE POWER

Biblically and historically, God has chosen to transform lives and extend His kingdom through His people.

Biblically and historically, God has chosen to transform lives and extend His kingdom through His people. Nowhere was the unleashing of the power more dramatic than in times of revival and spiritual awakening, which were nearly always accompanied by an explosion of world missions. For example, God placed His hand on John and Charles Wesley. In 1729, during their studies at Oxford, they began The Holy Club. As God worked in the lives of those who were drawn to the meetings, the power of the Holy Spirit was unleashed. All over England, wherever these men preached, thousands met the Savior.

In the newly formed churches, every believer was thoroughly discipled, and the impact of these Methodists literally changed the face of England. As God's power was unleashed through these churches, child labor laws were established, freeing thousands of children from a form of slavery in the mines. For the first time laws were passed outlawing slavery, and the beginning of a labor movement was established, bringing much-needed rights to the working-class people. The social change was an expression of the rule of God, the kingdom of God. God's people began to express the heart of God that " 'the earth will be filled with the knowledge of the glory of the Lord' " (Hab. 2:14).

Recall an instance when you saw the amazing power of God's kingdom unleashed through His people. In the margin, briefly describe that time. Be prepared to share it with your small group.

If you want to be a part of turning the world upside-down, seek first the kingdom of God and understand your role in the purposes of God. This will always lead you to link your life with the people of God. Today let me leave you with this passage that demonstrates the incredible power God desires to unleash into our world through the churches:

Read Ephesians 1:18-23 through a reporter's eyes:
WHO was the subject of Paul's prayer? (v. 19) _____
WHAT did Paul pray? (v. 18)
The eyes of your heart may be _____ .
WHY did Paul pray this? So believers would know:

1. the _____ of His calling (v. 18)

2. the glorious _____ of His inheritance (v. 18)

3. the _____ greatness of His _____ (v. 19)

HOW did God demonstrate His great power? (v. 20)

By raising Jesus from the _____

WHERE does Christ rule? (v. 21) Far _____ every ruler
    and authority
WHEN will Christ rule? (v. 21)

Not only in _____ _____ but in the _____ ___ _____ .

WHO is the body of this powerful ruler and Head? (vv. 22-23)

His _____ , the _____ of the One who fills
    all things in every way.

[18]I pray that the eyes of your heart may be enlightened so you may know what is the hope of His calling, what are the glorious riches of His inheritance among the saints, [19]and what is the immeasurable greatness of His power to us who believe, according to the working of His vast strength.

[20]He demonstrated this power in the Messiah by raising Him from the dead and seating Him at His right hand in the heavens—[21]far above every ruler and authority, power and dominion, and every title given, not only in this age but also in the one to come. [22]And "He put everything under His feet" and appointed Him as head over everything for the church, [23]which is His body, the fullness of the One who fills all things in every way.

❧ Ephesians 1:18-23 ❧

Common Misconceptions

Do you think average church members understand the kingdom of God? ❏ Yes ❏ No ❏ Not sure

Do most church members seek the kingdom as their number one priority? ❏ Yes ❏ No

If not, part of the problem may lie in five misconceptions.

1. Making the church and the kingdom identical

Many people confuse the church and the kingdom, making it sound as though the two are identical. They're not. When you're born again, you aren't born into the church; you're born into the kingdom of God. Salvation means you enter a kingdom where a King rules over His subjects as Lord. Anyone who tells you that you accept Him as Savior and later surrender to Him as Lord is speaking foolishness.

Read Romans 10:9. What verbal confession must be combined with belief to receive salvation?

_____

If you confess with your mouth, "Jesus is Lord," and believe in your heart that God raised Him from the dead, you will be saved.

✤ ROMANS 10:9 ✤

You can't enter the kingdom of God unless you submit to His rule. He is Lord by the nature of redemption. Now that God rules in your life, He impacts every part of it—the home, the workplace, and the church. When we think of salvation apart from the kingdom of God, we are disoriented to what God was doing when He chose to save us. The kingdom is essential to salvation. As soon as we confuse the two, we are in trouble.

2. Giving the church priority over the kingdom

Another misunderstanding is the belief that the church has greater significance than the kingdom. The proper question to ask is not, "Have you accepted Jesus and joined the church?" but, "Have you been born again by the Spirit of God, and what is the evidence that Christ is now Lord of your life?" When that transaction has taken place, you evidence the new life. Jesus said in Matthew 13:11, " 'To know the secrets of the kingdom of heaven has been granted to you.' " Those who are born again are now living in the kingdom and have spiritual eyes to see the activity of God, spiritual ears to hear the voice of God, and a new heart that is sensitive to know the will of God.

Once we have the priority of the kingdom in place, we then must take seriously the role of the churches within the kingdom. The church is the best place for us to grow as Christians and fulfill our roles in the kingdom.

On Day 5 of week one (page 29) you were asked to evaluate whether you have most often focused on the church or God's kingdom in your Christian journey. Now evaluate your church body. Do you, as a church family, give more priority to: (check)
❑ Your church and its needs or ❑ The kingdom of God?

3. De-emphasizing the local church

Another major confusion of the church and kingdom is a de-emphasis on the local church. Too many people see local churches as merely denominational entities and actually blame the churches for perceived failures in the kingdom. This tragic mistake has weakened the effectiveness of the local church. Each church is a sovereign creation of God, established for bringing His great salvation to the world. The churches, therefore, are absolutely essential to the purposes of God. That's the focus of the New Testament Scriptures, and that's the plan of God to touch the world.

There was a time when coming to Christ meant joining His body, but this practice has changed. "I don't have to go to church to be a Christian" is a common response among those who prefer the invisible church and thereby avoid accountability to the body of Christ. A depreciation of the local church has damaged its effectiveness to hold believers accountable to the Word of God and has left many of them detached from the people of God. Don't be fooled; God loves each and every church, and He is using them to do His purposes on earth.

While conversing with a new acquaintance, you broach the subject of church attendance. Your acquaintance says, "I'm a Christian, but I don't receive any benefit from attending church." In the margin, write your response, using Hebrews 10:24-25 as a guide.

4. Competing with other churches

One of the ways to assess the quality of your love for other believers is to observe what happens when you see positive or negative situations in other churches.

How do you react when you see the church down the street reaching people and growing by leaps and bounds?
❑ I feel jealous.
❑ I try to influence my church to copy their programs so we can mirror their success.
❑ I find fault with their way of doing things and criticize them to all who will listen.
❑ I find fault with my own church for not growing and criticize our staff.
❑ I thank God for the souls He is bringing into the kingdom.

Misconceptions:
1. Making the church and the kingdom identical
2. Giving the church priority over the kingdom
3. De-emphasizing the local church
4. Competing with other churches.

Let us be concerned about one another in order to promote love and good works, not staying away from our meetings, as some habitually do, but encouraging each other, and all the more as you see the day drawing near.

❧ Hebrews 10:24-25 ❧

Does it sorrow you to see another church experiencing disunity? OR Are you glad when persons from that troubled church transfer into your church as a result? Underline your answer.

How you respond to the blessings or the misfortunes of God's people is a direct reflection of your relationship to the God of those people. *Koinonia* is basic in the life of God's people and therefore in and among the churches. Churches, and groups of churches, voluntarily choose to cooperate to fulfill God's purposes. Christ is available to meet every need the churches encounter. As each church follows Christ, it will take its place among all churches around the world in doing kingdom work. There's no room for competition or civil war; there's a place for everyone in kingdom work. This is God's strategy to touch a world with the gospel of Jesus Christ.

It is spiritually impossible to love God with all your heart and not seek to build relationships with others in the family of God. And when God desires to impact a community, He will always bring His people to work together for the greater cause of extending the kingdom. This does not mean that churches or denominations ought to compromise their convictions; rather they must do their part in kingdom work and pray for the others whom God is using.

MISCONCEPTIONS:

1. Making the church and the kingdom identical
2. Giving the church priority over the kingdom
3. De-emphasizing the local church
4. Churches competing with other churches
5. Working in isolation from other churches

5. *Working in isolation from other churches*

You will accomplish far more in the Lord's work as you work side-by-side with other believers around the world. You can go anywhere in the world and be with your spiritual family. You will find strength and encouragement as you work together.

Let me explain what I mean with a simple illustration. War draws neighbors into a common battle. The two world wars compelled many nations to fight side-by-side for the same cause. The Gulf War drove many armies together as a united front against a common enemy. Although each nation had many capable leaders, one general was in charge to coordinate the efforts. They did not form one massive army; they fought side-by-side.

Read Ephesians 6:12 and complete the statement. (Leave your Bible open to that page; you'll return to it soon.) The kingdom of God is

at war with _____.

Each church is to fight side-by-side, taking orders from Christ the King who coordinates the combined efforts in the war with the forces of Satan. Everyone is needed in this eternally significant battle. No church can fight in isolation, for Christ desires a united front within the kingdom. Those who follow Christ as their leader will ultimately link their lives with God's people around the world.

Read Ephesians 6:14-18. Match each body part with its protective spiritual armor. Circle the one body part that is not protected.

waist   gospel of peace

chest   salvation

feet   truth

head   faith

front torso   righteousness

back

If you were a soldier and your back was not protected, what would you do? Check one or more.

❏ Stand firm and not turn my back on the enemy.

❏ Make sure I don't get separated from the other soldiers so we can cover one another's backs.

❏ Keep my eyes on the commanding officer so I know I'm facing the right direction.

❏ Other:

Consider your church as a soldier fighting the forces of evil. Do you most often struggle against ❏ Satan OR ❏ God's saints? Does your church work ❏ in isolation OR ❏ united with other churches?

The strength of God's army depends on the strength of local churches. As the visible body of Christ on earth, the church is equipped to fulfill its ministry and mission and empowered by the Spirit of God as it engages in kingdom work. The work will be complete when Christ returns at the great second coming to establish the kingdom in its fullness and turn it over to His Father. But until then each church has its role to fulfill in God's plan to touch a world—not in isolation but in a united effort with all believers.

List the five misconceptions we discussed in today's study. Check your answers on page 152 .

1. _____

2. _____

3. _____

4. _____

5. _____

DAY FIVE

Unity in the Kingdom

In 1986 when the World's Fair came to Vancouver, British Columbia, I was the director of missions giving leadership to the churches in the area. The first thing God led us to do was establish a comprehensive prayer ministry that bonded all of our work together. We felt we must also build meaningful relationships with four other Baptist groups that had not worked together for many years. As much as we desired to reach the lost, we had a greater sense of urgency to reach out to our brothers and sisters in the Lord.

God enabled us to bring the groups together and greatly blessed our times of worship. Through the Pavilion of Promise (the only Christian pavilion at the World's Fair), we had daily opportunities to witness to the throngs of people who came from all over the world. When we compiled our statistics with those of the other believers we were working alongside, together we saw more than 20 thousand professions of faith in 6 months. God blessed the nations of the world that had come to celebrate the World's Fair.

God also blessed us locally, for we saw 3 new congregations begin during this time, and we built lasting relationships with other believers. There's no way to know what God will do through your life and your church when you move outside of your particular group and serve alongside other believers in kingdom work.

In the greatest prayer ever recorded, Jesus prayed for everyone who would believe the gospel, starting from the disciples' testimony all the way down through the ages until He returns again. As Christianity spread, noticeable differences appeared among believers. Paul called on them to emphasize their commonality.

"I pray not only for these,
but also for those
who believe in Me through
their message.
May they all be one, just
as You, Father,
are in Me and I am in You.
May they also be one in Us,
so that the world may believe
You sent Me."

❧ JOHN 17:20-21 ❧

Read Ephesians 4:4-6. What did the believers have in common?

One b _____   One S _____

One h _____   One L _____

One f _____   One b _____

One G _____   and F _____

Each believer is profoundly connected with every other believer. As children of God, automatically we are spiritual brothers and sisters. God expects us to treat each other as such. Each church, in turn, has the same connectedness with other churches serving the same King.

DENOMINATIONAL UNITY

Denominations are the greatest picture of New Testament Christians because they practice unity of heart and soul for the purpose of proclaiming the gospel together. They can accomplish more together than they ever could by themselves, and the kingdom of God is extended through them. This is not just good strategy; the Holy Spirit directs the activity.

As a result, God's people have developed hospitals and health care, education through colleges and universities, training of those called into ministry and missions, missionary efforts to take the gospel to every nation, evangelistic meetings that touch entire cities, and many renewal movements that encourage all churches. I believe that unified denominations with a clear word from God are the most powerful forces in the world, but that is exactly why Satan targets them and seeks to divide them.

Churches who have linked their lives with a larger denomination are not merely following man-made institutions, which practice man's tradition and create divisions within God's kingdom. However, some people increasing perceive them as such. As God raises up His people, granting unique assignments to each, He is not creating disunity, but diversity. That strategy has always been characteristic of God's activity throughout the Bible and Christian history. More is being done to reach out into our diverse cultures than ever before. God, in His great wisdom, has specialized forces that are penetrating our world and finding ways to reach people who seem unreachable.

I have seen new leaders arise who attribute diversity to the sinful work of men or the activity of Satan. As a result they criticize and cast judgments over groups that are working together on a common goal. Watch out for those who always seem to create divisions and separate the people of God.

Read Proverbs 6:16,19. Underline how God feels about a person who spreads strife among believers.

The purpose of denominations is not to segregate Christians from one another but to reach every person within a community. One church cannot meet the particular needs of every resident.

What is your church doing in combination with other churches to meet needs in your community? Write your answer in the margin.

Just as variety exists among different people on earth, variety among churches exists so they can reach every lost person. Let's not put down others in the family of God; let's bless them and encourage them in the assignment God has given them. We have been far too concerned

There are six things which the Lord hates,
Yes, seven which are an abomination to Him:
A false witness who utters lies,
And one who spreads strife among brothers.
❧ PROVERBS 6:16,19 ❧

about people following us than about people following the assignment God has given them to do for the sake of the kingdom.

In our day, can God raise up people who are deeply sensitive to the Holy Spirit, to quicken all His people to the workings of the Holy Spirit? He can! Can God give an assignment to another group to raise up an army of men, challenging them to be spiritual leaders again? He can and He has! Can He establish a people who champion the cause of unborn children? He must! We are not to have their own self-centered ministry. Instead, they are to be used of God to quicken the churches to their responsibilities. Some seek out and press for uniformity. Uniformity is not the same thing as unity, just as diversity is not disunity!

With such diversity among churches, can there still be God-honoring unity? ❑ Yes ❑ No
Read John 17:21. What did Jesus declare was the sole basis for unity among believers? Underline one.

Same values   Same traditions

Same worship songs   Same programs

Same goals   Same relationship with the
                                              Father and the Son

---

⚜ A STORY FROM MEL BLACKABY ⚜

Partnering with Others

I know the joy of partnering with others in mission work. Many people came long distances to help our little church accomplish what God called us to do. Our building was old and run-down; some parts were unusable. So we set out to renovate the building, trusting God would help us as we worked.

A group from Tennessee brought 21 people to work on the renovation. We tore down every wall and ceiling, ran all new wiring, pulled up all the flooring, and began rebuilding. Some of the team had taken their only week of vacation and spent their own money for plane fare and other expenses. As they were leaving, I can still picture tears coming down their cheeks as they said, "Thank you for letting us come!" It was overwhelming for our people to see such love.

As the work continued and we neared the end of the renovation, we were a little short of money to add attic insulation in two buildings. We didn't know what to do but to pray and ask God to provide. I remember a Monday morning that I was feeling especially burdened about finishing the building before cold weather arrived. When my secretary brought me the mail, I noticed a letter from a church in Oklahoma. The pastor simply said, "We felt the Lord leading us to partner with you as you share the gospel in Canada." Enclosed was a check for $5,000, the exact amount we needed to finish the work.

As I read the letter during our Wednesday prayer meeting, I watched a rough old guy begin to weep. He asked, "Why are people so kind when they don't even know us?" The answer is simple. We are all serving the same King, and He chose to bring in reinforcements to help us in the battle. As a result, we began to look for churches we could bless.

Has your church been on the receiving end of help from other churches? If so, describe that instance in the margin.

Any local church can be a part of this experience with God. People, however, do not work it up; it is a sovereign work of God in its timing, nature, and place. Never does He work through a people who are indifferent, casual, or careless in their relationship with Him. He will not bring His blessings upon a people who quickly come and go from His presence. He desires that we linger before Him, crying out with a keen awareness that we need His presence in our lives. Often, he will wait to see if His people are serious about prayer for revival simply by how they persist in asking.

Check words that describe your church's attitude toward praying and doing God's work in His kingdom?
❏ Indifferent   ❏ Casual
❏ Careless   ❏ Responsive
❏ Linger before Him in prayer   ❏ Quickly come and go
                                from His presence

What then can a local church do to be a people prepared for their Lord? Wider interdependence opens up a world that some have never known. You begin to reach out to others. You'll receive more than you ever imagined. It's a law of the kingdom. If you truly deny self and seek the good of others, the Lord will always bless you far beyond what you have ever known. Because of your obedience to love your brother, the Lord will touch many through your church.

As you consider all you have discovered about your church's role in God's kingdom, what truths have particularly challenged you?

How will you turn those challenges into prayer requests for your church? Write those requests on your ongoing prayer list and spend time in prayer.

The Church: God's Perspective

Be on guard for yourselves and for all the flock, among whom the Holy Spirit has appointed you as overseers, to shepherd the church of God, which He purchased with His own blood. ... "And now I commit you to God and to the message of His grace, which is able to build you up and to give you an inheritance among all who are sanctified."

ACTS 20:28-32

The annual church planning retreat was well-attended, and each of the leaders had done their homework. After a morning of demographic studies, membership trends, and projections of growth for the city, the group began negotiating budget allocations for the coming year.

The senior pastor, a skilled administrator, managed to lead the group to complete the budgeting process with time to spare. Several of the guys decided they had time to get in a round of golf. As the retreat concluded, the pastor lead a prayer asking God to bless these plans.

When your church gears up for a new budget year, is the process pretty much a rehashing of last year's plans? If so, keep in mind these questions as you read this final week's material:

1. Does your church understand God's ideal? Is it concerned about knowing and doing God's will?
2. Do you understand the nature of the church in the plan of God?
3. Do you believe that God could use your church to fulfill His purposes? Are you praying and working toward that end?
4. How do you think the watching world sees your church? Are they attracted or turned off by what they see? What adjustments do you need to make?
5. How can you and your church maintain God's ideal of building up the body?

What Is God's Ideal

As mentioned in week 3, on August 13, 1727, God deeply touched a group of Moravian brethren in Hernnhut, Moravia. So profound was the encounter they had during a Communion service that they offered their lives unreservedly to be used by God in service to Him. They committed themselves to a 24-hour-a-day prayer ministry, and the practice lasted continuously for 100 years.

More missionaries were sent into the world from this church in those years than all the combined missionaries of all other groups of that day. Their missionaries were found in almost every corner of the earth. One of their missionaries significantly touched the life of John Wesley, whom God later used to spark probably the greatest nation-changing revival in English history.

In our day, each church must seek to know what's on God's heart at all times. The early church in Jerusalem is a role model for us because the believers were committed to obey God as He showed them what was on His heart. They soon became a people on mission with God. He used them to turn " 'the world upside down' " (Acts 17:6).

Read 2 Corinthians 5:14-15 in the margin.
What compelled the apostle Paul and the Moravian brethren?

_____

What did this compelling force lead them to do?

_____

Christ's love compels us, since we have reached this conclusion: if One died for all, then all died. And He died for all so that those who live should no longer live for themselves, but for the One who died for them and was raised.

❧ 2 CORINTHIANS 5:14-15 ❧

As you consider your schedule, spending habits, and leisure activities, what appears to be the compelling force in your life?
❏ My bank account ❏ My family ❏ My fears, worries
❏ My reputation ❏ My comfort ❏ My appearance
❏ My love for Christ in response to His love for me.

WHAT IS ON THE HEART AND MIND OF GOD?

The Moravian experience offers a taste of what God can do with any church that is released to Him. From Genesis to Revelation we have the record of the nature of God, the ways of God, the heart of God, and the eternal purposes of God.

In our generation we must seek to know how we fit into God's plan to touch a world. We ought to seek what is in the heart and mind of God. God wants to demonstrate His mighty power through

We need to come into His presence, ask Him His plans, and adjust our lives so that He can accomplish them through us.

every church that will let Him. Too often, however, we tell God our limited plans and ask Him to bless them. Oh how we need to come into His presence, ask Him His plans, and then adjust our lives so that He can accomplish them through us.

Consider your church's decision-making process. On a scale of 1 to 5, (1 being not well and 5 being very well) prayerfully evaluate how well your church follows the principles below:

___ We regularly and reverently come into God's presence.
___ We ask God to reveal His plans for our church and then patiently wait for His revelation.
___ When God reveals those plans, we individually adjust our lives and the life of our church.

Pray for your church leaders as they seek to lead your church to make decisions in a way that glorifies God and accomplishes His purposes. Add these requests to your ongoing church prayer list.

It is God who is working among you both the willing and the working for His good purpose.

❧ PHILIPPIANS 2:13 ❧

Read Philippians 2:13 in the margin. We ought to work out our salvation in all its fullness, seeking to accomplish God's purposes for our lives. "His good purpose" then, is what we strive to know and do.

We already know how God's purposes began; we read in the Book of Genesis that He created man and woman in His own image and likeness and gave them dominion over the fish of the sea, the birds of the air, the cattle, and every animal that roamed the earth. He told them to be fruitful and multiply. Finally, "God saw all that He had made, and behold, it was very good" (Gen. 1:31).

Although we were made in the image of God for the purpose of fellowship with Him, sin disrupted the relationship. Sin always does! But God's love found a way to restore that fellowship through the life, death, resurrection, and ascension of His Son, Jesus Christ. The final fulfillment of God's eternal purpose is unfolded in Revelation 21:1-7.

Read Revelation 21:1-7. Answer the question, What is the final fulfillment of God's eternal purpose? by writing in the margin words or phrases that are particularly significant to you.

These verses represent God's perspective—the big picture as God sees it! But what about in the meantime? Now that we have a glimpse of what is on the heart of God, how then shall we live?

Read 2 Peter 3:10-12 on page 161. What did Peter tell believers to do as they waited for God's eternal purposes to be fulfilled? Underline all that apply.

Camp out on a mountaintop.
Live holy lives while you wait.
Conduct yourselves in a godly manner.
Sell all your possessions and join a commune.
Earnestly desire His coming.
Forget about His second coming and get on with life.

GOD'S IDEAL: IS IT REALISTIC?

The record is before us. The Scriptures reveal God's ideal plan for His people. We must keep a God-centered approach to the Scriptures. We must keep God's position before us at all times. Is this goal realistic from His perspective? As far as God is concerned, the answer is a resounding yes! Read Paul's encouragement to the church in Philippi, italicized for emphasis, from *The Amplified Bible*:

> Therefore, my dear ones, as you have *always obeyed* [my suggestions], so now, not only [with enthusiasm you would show] in my presence but much more because I am absent, work out (cultivate, carry out to the goal, and *fully complete)* your own salvation with reverence and awe and trembling (self-distrust, with serious caution, tenderness of conscience, watchfulness against temptation, timidly shrinking from whatever might offend God and discredit the name of Christ).
>
> [*Not in your own strength*] for it is *God Who is all the while effectively at work in you* [energizing and creating in you the power and desire], both to will and to work *for His good pleasure* and satisfaction and delight (Phil. 2:12-13, AMP).

Don't miss Paul's wonderful encouragement by getting lost in the parentheses and brackets. Fill in the blanks in the following verses as if Paul is writing to your church. Use those additional phrases from the Amplified version that are particularly meaningful to you.

Therefore, my dear church at _____,
as you have always obeyed my suggestions, so now, not only with enthusiasm you would show in my presence, but much more because I am absent, _____ your own salvation with _____. Don't try to do this in the strength of your church at _____, for it is God Who is all the while _____both to will and to work for His _____ .

Paul's letter said God was at work in the church, enabling them to do His will. God gave this same assurance to the church in Ephesus (see Eph. 3:20-21 in margin). God's ideal, from His perspective, is realistic.

The day of the Lord will come like a thief; on that day the heavens will pass away with a loud noise, the elements will burn and be dissolved, and the earth and the works on it will be disclosed. Since all these things are to be destroyed in this way, it is clear what sort of people you should be in holy conduct and godliness as you wait for and earnestly desire the coming of the day of God, because of which the heavens will be on fire and be dissolved, and the elements will melt with the heat.

❧ 2 PETER 3:10-12 ❧

To Him who is able to do above and beyond all that we ask or think— according to the power that works in you—to Him be glory in the church and in Christ Jesus to all generations, forever and ever. Amen.

❧ EPHESIANS 3:20-21 ❧

The promise of God to work in every church includes your church, right now, where you are! All of God [Father, Son, and Holy Spirit] is present with every church and in every church. He is our life! All His purposes are possible and honor Him when implemented. The key is the nature of the relationship! If only our churches could understand that their potential rests solely in their relationship to God through Jesus Christ and in their ability to trust Him completely.

Read John 15:5-7 in your Bible and answer these questions:
1. What metaphor did Jesus use to describe the relationship

between Himself and your church? _____

2. Why do you think Jesus chose that analogy? Check one.
   ❏ To remind us of all the yard work we need to do
   ❏ To frighten us into being effective fruit-bearers
   ❏ No real reason; He just happened to be in a vineyard when He was talking to His disciples
   ❏ To remind us that our growth and fruitfulness come only through our relationship with Him

3. What promise did Jesus give your church in verse 5?

_____

4. What assurance in verse 7 did Jesus add to His promise?

_____

5. What is your honest response to verse 7? Check one or more.
   ❏ It's a nice thought, but it will never happen.
   ❏ It's an idealistic principle that doesn't work realistically.
   ❏ I want to believe and see that power exhibited in my church.
   ❏ I believe it because I've seen it happen. (Describe in margin.)

God's eternal purpose, God's ideal, is true for an individual, as well as a church. He wants His people to abide in Him. Any church that chooses to abide, hear, and obey His Word as He guides them will bear much fruit. If for any reason they run into difficulty in living out God's ideal, they only have to ask whatever they desire, and it will be done for them. God's ideal is absolutely realistic, given the presence of God in His people and the promises of God to His people.

How is God calling you to respond to the last statement?
Write your thoughts in the form of a prayer in the margin.

Less than Obedient: Will God Bless?

Will God bless His people when they are less than obedient? What a crucial question to face. What a necessary question to answer, especially at this time in the study of experiencing God together as His people. Will God bless His people when they are less than obedient? This question can only be answered adequately from God's perspective.

With God, partial obedience is disobedience. And disobedience to God is a grievous sin; sin withholds the blessings of God that He intends to share with His people. Let me illustrate: The picture is found in 1 Samuel 15. Saul had been anointed king over God's people. He had clearly been commanded to " 'listen to the words of the Lord' " (1 Sam. 15:1). The Word of the Lord came clearly to Saul, and he knew exactly what he was to do. So Saul *began* to obey the Lord, but his human reasoning became a fatal substitute for obedience. Read 1 Samuel 15:10-11 in the margin.

Just like many churches that are confronted by God, Saul begins to reason away and give excuses for his disobedience. Samuel asked him, " 'Why then did you not obey the voice of the Lord, … and did what was evil in the sight of the Lord?' " (1 Sam. 15:19). Saul's pathetic response demonstrates that he did not understand his radical accountability before God. He said, " 'I did obey the voice of the Lord' " (1 Sam. 15:20). He then began to explain how the people put pressure on him, convincing him of a better way. So he partially obeyed what God had specifically commanded. The consequences for Saul's disobedience were fatal.

When Saul was finished explaining to God, God then gave Saul His view on disobedience.

Read 1 Samuel 15:22-23 in the margin. Use phrases from these verses to complete these statements:

God views rebellion as _____.

God views insubordination as _____.

As far as God is concerned, any form of disobedience is serious. When He gives a command to His people, He expects them to carry it out to the letter. When we disobey, He sees our hearts as rebellious and stubborn. He considers it as serious as the sin of witchcraft and idolatry. When we choose not to follow the Lord, we are giving allegiance to

With God, partial obedience is disobedience.

Then the word of the Lord came to Samuel, saying, "I regret that I have made Saul king, for he has turned back from following Me, and has not carried out My commands." And Samuel was distressed and cried out to the Lord all night.

❧ 1 SAMUEL 15:10-11 ❧

*"Has the Lord as much delight in burnt offerings and sacrifices
As in obeying the voice of the Lord?
Behold, to obey is better than sacrifice,
And to heed than the fat of rams.
For rebellion is as the sin of divination [supernatural fortune-telling],
And insubordination is as iniquity and idolatry.
Because you have rejected the word of the Lord,
He has also rejected you from being king."*

❧ 1 SAMUEL 15:22-23 ❧

substitutes for Him and His Word. We have allowed our limited human reasoning to take precedence over the expressed Word of God.

OUR GOAL: COMPLETE OBEDIENCE

Should we then take it seriously that Jesus commands us to teach " 'them to observe everything I have commanded you' " (Matt. 28:20)? In other words, we are to help God's people keep the commands of God, practice them, and live them out in every area of their lives. A disciple is one who does what his or her Master and Teacher commands. The standard is nothing less than observing all that Jesus commanded. Not perfection but complete obedience is our goal. Knowing that God will take us from where we are to where we ought to be, we strive to implement all that our Lord asks of us. To see what God desires of our lives and then to intentionally lower the bar and settle for less than what was asked would be discounting Christ's lordship.

Let me give an example. Didn't the Lord command us to go and make disciples of all nations? To insist that we have indeed obeyed, then reason away why we have not been a part of world missions in one way or another, would bring upon us the displeasure of God. Not every person will pick up and move to a foreign country to share the gospel, but every person can be involved in missions through his or her relationship to the rest of the body. Some will literally go and invest their lives in mission work, but everyone can pray, give financially, send materials, or be involved in short-term mission projects.

> **What specific actions has your church taken in response to the Lord's command to make disciples of all nations? Write your answer in the margin.**

> **Have you responded personally to God's call to be involved in worldwide missions?**
> ❑ Yes. I obey the Lord's command by _____.
> ❑ No. I can't because _____.
> ❑ God is calling me to missions involvement by _____.

COMPLETE OBEDIENCE GLORIFIES GOD

Only in obedience will God's name be glorified. If His name is being profaned by our disobedience, He cannot and will not bless! His name is at stake before a watching world. I have known churches that began well. I know a mission church that started out well, and then sin crept in. Relationships became strained. The pastor, deacons, and other church leaders refused to deal with it. They covered it over, often by increasing their efforts in soul winning and mission projects. In their zeal to do *part* of what Christ commanded, they remained disobedient to a crucial matter on the heart of their Lord.

To see what God desires of our lives and then to intentionally lower the bar and settle for less than what was asked would be discounting Christ's lordship.

Let me say it again: In the case I mentioned, the blessings of God were withdrawn. Sin continued, and the church began a downward spiral. They would have disbanded had the church not realized their sin, repented, and returned to obedience before God. The blessings of God immediately returned, and the church began to grow.

Nothing is more serious than persistent disobedience in the lives of God's people, especially when the church tries to cover it up with partial or selective obedience. God will not bless a church that does not obey Him. Yet those who fear Him and walk in obedience can find no way to measure His blessings.

Read David's words in Psalm 24:3-5. Check the boxes to indicate the virtues that are evident in your life and the life of your church.

	MY LIFE	MY CHURCH
Clean hands	❑	❑
Pure heart	❑	❑
Complete obedience	❑	❑
Truthfulness	❑	❑

Were you able to honestly check every box for you and your church? ❑ Yes ❑ No
If you answered no, will you or your church receive God's full blessings? ❑ Yes ❑ No

As we come before the Lord in worship each Sunday, we must find cleansing from sin and present an obedient heart before Him.

Another major failure that affects a church's relationship with God involves mixing the ways of the world with their obedience to God. God commanded that His people be separated from the world so that they could be exclusively His. When the people of God were set free from Egyptian captivity and were about to enter the promised land, He warned them not to mix the culture of those in the land with the commandments He had given them. They were to be different; they were to be a people belonging to God. They were to be distinctly different from the people around them, so that the world might see the difference God makes among His people.

As you read Deuteronomy 6:12-15, underline what would set God's people apart from their surrounding culture.

The New Testament is equally strong at this point. (See Matt. 6:24; 16:24.) The difference between the ways of God and the ways of the world are as different as light and darkness. Holy people cannot act like the sinful world. Unfortunately, many churches compromise with the commands of God. Some will leave the impression that it is legitimate

Partial obedience is disobedience.

*Who may ascend into the hill
    of the Lord?
And who may stand in His holy place?
He who has clean hands and a
    pure heart,
Who has not lifted up his soul to false-
    hood [partial disobedience],
And has not sworn deceitfully.
He shall receive a blessing from
    the Lord
And righteousness from the God
    of his salvation.*
    ❧ PSALM 24:3-5 ❧

"Watch yourself, lest you forget the Lord who brought you from the land of Egypt, out of the house of slavery. You shall fear only the Lord your God; and you shall worship Him, and swear by His name. You shall not follow other gods, any of the gods of the peoples who surround you, for the Lord your God in the midst of you is a jealous God; otherwise the anger of the Lord your God will be kindled against you, and He will wipe you off the face of the earth."
    ❧ DEUTERONOMY 6:12-15 ❧

to use the ways of the world, for the end justifies the use of any means. In other words, use any means as long as a soul is saved. But God's goals are not ours. He is interested in revealing Himself and His ways by *how* He does something.

Read 2 Chronicles 16:9. Check the answer that best completes this statement: God supports those who—
❑ get the job done; ❑ have impressive personalities;
❑ do good things; ❑ stay constantly busy serving Him;
❑ live by strict rules; ❑ give their heart completely to Him.

Our world does not need to see good people doing good things for their God. The world needs to see God doing what only He can do through His people.

Our world does not need to see good people doing good things for their God. The world needs to see God doing what only He can do through His people. Is the world encountering God in the way we serve Him? Or do we use the ways of the world and conceal Him before the world?

Jesus cried out to the Father in His high priestly prayer, just before He went to the cross: " 'Sanctify them by the truth; Your word is truth.' " Then He added a significant fact: " 'Just as You sent Me into the world, I also have sent them into the world' " (John 17:17-18). The Father revealed Himself completely and exclusively through His Son. Now God desires to work through His Son's new body, the church. Don't mix the ways of the world with the ways of God.

Jesus added one more significant factor in this matter when He prayed, " 'I sanctify Myself for them, so they also may be sanctified by the truth' " (John 17:19). Oh that we would see more and more churches concerned with revealing God fully by their uncompromising obedience to the truth. Only then will God reveal more of Himself to them. May you be the example that draws many other churches to be set apart for God.

DAY THREE

Returning to God's Ideal

At this point your hearts may be longing after God. You desire to return to or to develop a deeper relationship with God. You look at your church and see its potential from God's perspective, and you long to be part of such an experience—not just for your own survival but for God's glory and name.

The constant heart cry of God to His people is, "Return to me and live" (Ezek. 18:30-32). God said to the church at Ephesus in Revelation 2:5, " 'Remember then how far you have fallen; repent, and do the works you did at first. Otherwise, I will come to you and remove your lampstand from its place—unless you repent.' "

When God calls His people to repent, He desires for us to turn around and return to our first love relationship with Him. He did not leave the relationship; we did! When you look carefully at Revelation 2-3, God calls for four of the seven churches to repent and return. The cry of God sounds throughout the Bible. You must hear the Scripture at this point to understand how much God desires for His people to return to Him. Read Isaiah 44:21-22, Jeremiah 15:19, Jeremiah 24:7, Hosea 6:1, Joel 2:12-13, and Malachi 3:7 in the margin.

As you read the verses in the margin, do the following:
1. Bracket actions God's people were to take.
2. Underline what God promised to do in response to their actions.
3. Circle the word that each verse has in common.

HOW SHALL WE RETURN?

I could take you to many more Scriptures like those you just read. But I want to stop at Malachi 3:7 because it ends with an important question: " ' "How shall we return?" ' " The Ephesian church was called to return to its first love. They were commended for right doctrine, zealous works, and their orthodoxy. However, their church was in a fatal condition because they didn't love God as they once did, so their love for one another was flawed. They were practicing the letter of the law, but it was bringing death. What they lacked was the spirit of the law.

The different churches mentioned in Revelation, however, had different issues. The church at Ephesus left their first love, so they needed to return to the love relationship. The church at Pergamum was called upon to return to the truth. The church at Thyatira was not dealing with sexual immorality in their church. They were to return to holiness or face the severe judgment of God upon the entire church, for His name was being profaned.

The church at Sardis had a name for being alive, but from God's perspective they were dead, and their works were grossly incomplete. They were not living as the body of Christ doing His work, and they needed to return to Him before God moved in and brought judgment. The church at Laodicea was lukewarm and complacent. They said to themselves that they were a rich church and needed nothing from others. From God's perspective they were an utter abomination, and He was about to cast them out of His sight. They were urged to return to God's standards for spiritual wealth and holiness.

As you ponder Christ's messages to the churches in Revelation 2—3, check on page 168 what you feel God is asking you or your church to return to in your relationship with Him.

"Remember these things, O Jacob,
And Israel, for you are My servant;
I have formed you, you are My servant,
O Israel, you will not be forgotten
* by Me.*
I have wiped out your transgressions
* like a thick cloud*
And your sins like a heavy mist.
Return to Me, for I have redeemed you."

❦ ISAIAH 44:21-22 ❦

"If you return, then I will restore you."

❦ JEREMIAH 15:19 ❦

" 'I will give them a heart to know Me,
for I am the Lord; and they will be My
people, and I will be their God, for they
will return to Me with their whole heart.' "

❦ JEREMIAH 24:7 ❦

"Come, let us return to the Lord.
For He has torn us, but He will
* heal us;*
He has wounded us, but He will
* bandage us."*

❦ HOSEA 6:1 ❦

"Return to Me with all your heart,
And with fasting, weeping, and
* mourning;*
And rend your heart and not
* your garments."*
Now return to the Lord your God,
For He is gracious and compassionate,
Slow to anger, abounding in lovingkindness,
And relenting of evil."

❦ JOEL 2:12-13 ❦

"From the days of your fathers you have
turned aside from My statutes, and have
not kept them. Return to Me, and I will
return to you," says the Lord of hosts.
"But you say, 'How shall we return?' "

❦ MALACHI 3:7 ❦

❑ Ephesus—Return to your love relationship with Me.
❑ Pergamum—Return to My truth.
❑ Thyatira—Return to holiness.
❑ Sardis—Return to true life in Me.
❑ Laodicea—Return to My standards for wealth and holiness.

_____ - _____
(Your church's name)   (What is God saying to your church?)

GOD GIVES US THE OPPORTUNITY TO RETURN

Amazingly, the Lord was giving each church, no matter how bad they had become, an opportunity to return. The opportunity would not be forever, but all had the chance to repent and return to God's ideal. I don't know about you, but that brings me great encouragement! As long as you hear God's call to return, He is there to receive you with open arms. The Holy Spirit searches our hearts. Only the Holy Spirit can show us what the Lord sees as He walks through our churches. As God's people gather to worship, true worship must focus on Him and not on self. He must be the center of every life.

I have been in many meetings where God brought cleansing to a church. If I had space, I could tell countless stories of God's manifesting His presence in a way that brought the entire church to its knees. They were weeping and crying out in the presence of a holy God. But when they rose to their feet again, they did it with renewed strength and joy beyond measure. The focus of their lives took on a new direction. The fruit of their lives from that point forward can't be measured, for when they returned to God, God returned to them in all His majesty and glory. Now He had a church through which He could touch the world.

The Lord is standing at the door of many churches. He is knocking, but He is on the outside. He is begging for someone to hear Him, open the door, and welcome Him to the spiritual table in the church. He is looking for at least one.

Could you be the one to open the door of your church and welcome Jesus inside?
❑ Yes ❑ No ❑ I want to be, but I don't see how I can make much difference in my church.

Out of a renewed relationship comes a fresh love for God that draws people to hear His voice and obey His words. It brings a renewed *koinonia* that changes the dynamics of the entire church family. You will discover that joy, love, fruitfulness, hunger for the Word of God, freedom to be on mission with God, and prayer returns with a fresh awareness of the presence of God.

Can you recall a time when God allowed you to experience a revival among His people? Make notes and be prepared to share with your group. Give God the glory.

_____

_____

REVIVAL AND AWAKENING

A believer who is thoroughly taught by the Scripture always prays, "O God, send a revival to your people, the body of Christ!" All the revivals in the Old Testament were in the midst of the gathered people of God. In the New Testament the outpouring of the Holy Spirit at Pentecost was as the believers were gathered together. History continues to bear witness to the fact that revival and times of refreshing come among God's people corporately.

When God begins to impact the land in a mighty move of His Spirit, many unusual things begin to occur that stretch God's people. He forces them out of their comfort zones. Genuine revival and spiritual awakening begin to impact all of God's people, producing incredible unity among the family of God. Together, they pray, labor for souls, worship, and sing praises to God for the wonders of His mighty works among them.

Any local church can be a part of this experience with God. People, however, do not work it up; it is a sovereign work of God in its timing, nature, and place. He desires that we linger before Him, crying out with a keen awareness that we need His presence in our lives. He will often wait to see if His people are serious about their prayer for revival simply by how they persist in their asking.

Those who are unwilling to pay the price will not know the power of God and will not experience revival! Revival has often been God's primary means of advancing the kingdom of God on earth. And He has chosen to do it through His people who have gathered together to do His will across the world.

What are you willing to do personally to help your church seek to live out God's ideal? Check all that apply.
- ❑ Offer or seek forgiveness from those believers with whom I have broken relationships.
- ❑ Obey God wholeheartedly regardless of what others do.
- ❑ Pray daily for my church to be on mission for God.
- ❑ Make needed sacrifices of money, comfort, and tradition.
- ❑ Invest myself in the care and discipleship of fellow believers.
- ❑ Return to God from the following area(s) in which I have strayed: _____

169

❧ A STORY FROM MEL BLACKABY ❧

An Unexpected Guest

As we were writing this book, Dad flew to Cochrane so that we could put the finishing touches on the manuscript. During the time he was here, the man scheduled to speak in one of our Sunday evening services had to fly home to be with his father who had just had a heart attack. We quickly put a service together. Dad spoke on the subject of revival. Then we anticipated an informal time of sharing, but God had something much different on His heart.

Near the end of the service, we asked for any questions from the congregation. There were a few comments, but there seemed to be an uneasy hush among the crowd. Finally, one young woman stood up and cried out in tears, "I can't sit still; my heart is about to pound out of my chest. I must confess my sin to the church." After she shared, several women came around her to pray. Immediately, another stood with great brokenness and shared what the Holy Spirit was doing in her life. As we gathered around her, the floodgates seemed to open, and the Holy Spirit moved among all who were present. One confessed that she had left her husband that day; another was struggling with pornography, and many others were convicted of their pride and

spirit of self-righteousness. A holy God was dealing with His people as they gathered together for worship. After several hours had passed, some went home but could not remain there. One began to tremble as he told his wife that God was at the church and he had to go back and "make things right." People remained before the Lord that night until 1:30 A.M.

God continued to work through the week, causing people to gather for spontaneous prayer meetings. In fact, several gathered an hour before the regular prayer meeting, just to pray for the prayer meeting! Many of the moms waited until their children were in bed and then met at the church on Thursday night to pray. Many things have spun out of that time of worship, and only time will tell all that God will do in the days ahead.

I would not categorize this moment as one of the classic examples of revival, yet God was reviving His people during their time of worship, just as He desires to do any time His people gather for worship. Everyone who was at the worship service that night was glad they had chosen to link their lives with the people of God. For God spoke to us clearly, and we all heard Him at the same time.

❧ DAY FOUR

Maintaining God's Ideal

Returning to God's ideal, to an intimate love relationship, produces a renewed life in the Spirit. How is this ideal maintained? What can the church do to continually renew its spirit?

What is God's ideal purpose for each believer's life?

_____

As we learned in day 1, God's ideal for an individual is the same as His ideal for the church: to abide in Him, hear and obey His Word, and bear fruit for the kingdom. In today's study, we will discover that each element of a worship service is designed to enable believers to realize God's ideal.

BAPTISM

I had the privilege of watching my son baptize his daughter. Mel has made it a part of every person's baptism for the new believer to give a public testimony. Christa was seven. She was excited about being baptized, so she rehearsed what she planned to say and had her mother type it out for her to read from the baptistry. After reading her testimony, she said, "I also want to sing a song of how I am going to serve Jesus." And she did! This was a first for me. The whole congregation was deeply touched—including the visitors. They were experiencing God's ideal for a church, and this moment of baptism was one way to maintain it.

Baptism can either become a casual, even dead, religious ritual or a significant time of renewal. It allows the church to rejoice together over one who has responded to Christ as Lord, and it challenges all who are present to review their own walk with Christ.

THE LORD'S SUPPER

Another significant time in the life of the church is Communion, or the Lord's Supper. We mentioned this ordinance when we considered the new covenant, but we want to emphasize its importance again at this point. Look carefully at how the apostle Paul described this moment in the life of believers in 1 Corinthians 11:23-26.

According to this passage, Jesus commands the church to be " 'in remembrance of Me.' " In remembering Jesus and His death on the cross, the church has the opportunity to renew its covenant of love with the Lord and to maintain God's ideal as the living body of Christ. Paul warns, however, that those who are careless or casual about the body and blood of their Lord will put the entire church in grave danger. He goes so far as to say that carelessness in this matter will be the cause of some actually dying and others getting sick.

But those who take the Lord's Supper seriously, examining themselves before partaking, have found it to be a great moment of renewal and even revival. Because of its significance, the Lord's Supper should not be tacked onto a service, merely to save time, for it will rob the people of a deep and meaningful encounter with God.

Why do you think renewal and revival comes when a church takes baptism and the Lord's Supper seriously? Be prepared to share your thoughts with your group.

I received from the Lord what I also passed on to you: on the night when He was betrayed, the Lord Jesus took bread, gave thanks, broke it, and said, "This is My body, which is for you. Do this in remembrance of Me."

In the same way He also took the cup, after supper, and said, "This cup is the new covenant in My blood. Do this, as often as you drink it, in remembrance of Me." For as often as you eat this bread and drink the cup, you proclaim the Lord's death until He comes.

❧ 1 CORINTHIANS 11:23-26 ❧

"An hour is coming, and is now here, when the true worshippers will worship the Father in spirit and truth."

❧ JOHN 4:23 ❧

WORSHIP

The supreme opportunity to maintain God's ideal is found in regular times of worship. Here believers are to stand before God, hear from God, and adjust their lives to His will. Carefully planned, worship enables the people to come solemnly and joyfully into God's presence.

The day of Pentecost was a visible example of what happens when people worship. In that encounter they were gathered together with one heart; they experienced the presence of God together; fear came upon every soul; they continued with gladness, and the Lord added to the church daily those who were being saved. Here was God's ideal experienced, enhanced, and maintained in worship.

Worship isn't for spiritual entertainment or to promote self; it's a time to honor God and give Him opportunity to speak to us. Guard times of worship carefully. If every worship service is turned into an evangelistic service, God's people will wither and die spiritually. They cannot survive without true worship.

Worship services have many opportunities for God to keep His people practicing His ideal. He speaks through times of prayer, the careful reading of His Word, the music, times of quiet meditation, the faithful exposition of Scripture, and certainly the invitation to respond at the end of the service. As the pastor guides the people through their encounter with God, he will share what God is doing. He will interpret how the body must respond to what God is doing. He will also teach the people specific truth about God and His ways.

I worked diligently to try to prepare God's people and me for each time of worship. Therefore, we had great expectations when we came into His presence. We knew that the Father, Son, and Holy Spirit were all present and active. As each person had the freedom to respond, the entire body was edified and built up as we experienced God together.

When someone came forward to pray, I encouraged people to come alongside and pray for him or her. Many times someone came under great conviction of sin and responded to God with a heart of repentance. I would often listen to them, pray with them, and then ask them to share with the church so that we could walk with them in a redemptive manner to bring full restoration into their lives. The apostle Paul said that in the body, a redemptive community, when one member hurts, they all hurt (see 1 Cor. 12:26). Too often, however, the body is never given the opportunity to know when a person is hurting, and therefore can't respond to bring healing. As a church, we sought to share and care for one another as God intended. As a result, the whole body was edified, "growing into a mature man with a stature measured by Christ's fullness" (Eph. 4:13). The unbelievers and visitors were often deeply moved by God, desiring to become part of such a fellowship.

Consider the following elements of a worship service and note how God works through each to help His people maintain an intimate love relationship with Him.

Musical Prelude _____

Prayer _____

Scripture reading _____

Congregational singing _____

Sermon _____

Invitation _____

PREACHING AND TEACHING GOD'S WORD

Another significant ingredient of maintaining God's ideal is the faithful preaching and teaching of God's Word. You can't read about the life of Christ and not be overwhelmed at the place of Scripture in His life. The Gospels consistently give examples of how Jesus' words and actions fulfilled Scriptures (John 2:22; 7:38; 13:18). With Scripture Jesus faced Satan's temptations, and with Scripture He faced the cross.

Before He ascended to the Father, Jesus interpreted the Scriptures for His disciples. (See Luke 24:27.) The life of the disciples in the early church in Jerusalem and their preaching was immersed in the Scripture concerning the purposes of God. Peter used Scripture at Pentecost; Stephen used Scripture in his defense before the religious leaders; and Philip used Scripture in Samaria.

So, preaching and teaching God's Word must be done week after week, year after year, if a church is to maintain its spiritual health. God's people need regular feeding on God's Word. To give people the great truths of God's Word will do more to maintain God's ideal for His church than any other single thing.

Write a note to your pastor assuring him of your prayers for his sermon preparation. Thank him for his impact on your life.

PRAYER

Prayer needs to be as preeminent in the life of the church as it was in the life of Jesus in the days of His flesh. One of the most obvious disciplines of Jesus' life was His prayer life. He constantly turned aside to pray. The writer of Hebrews described His prayer life as

We proclaim Him, warning and teaching everyone with all wisdom, so that we may present everyone mature in Christ. I labor for this, striving with His strength that works powerfully in me.

❧ COLOSSIANS 1:28-29 ❧

Beginning with Moses and all the Prophets, He interpreted for them in all the Scriptures the things concerning Himself.

❧ LUKE 24:27 ❧

He often withdrew to deserted places and prayed.

☘ LUKE 5:16 ☘

During those days He went out to the mountain to pray, and spent all night in prayer to God.

☘ LUKE 6:12 ☘

offering up "prayers and appeals, with loud cries and tears, to the One who was able to save Him from death, and He was heard because of His reverence" (Heb. 5:7). Jesus' life was a life of prayer—early in the morning, during the day, late in the evening, and even at times all night long, seeking to know the will and purpose of the Father in and through His life. He lived this way and urged His disciples "to pray always and not become discouraged [not quit]" (Luke 18:1). He also said, in very strong terms, " 'My [Father's] house will be a house of prayer' " (Luke 19:46).

A church must be taught and guided so that prayer is a way of life for every member, every family, and the church body as it meets together. Though every believer has a built-in desire to pray, they must be taught. They are taught by example as well as practical teaching. Leaders must strive to create an atmosphere of prayer, and the people will follow the leaders whose hearts are truly bent toward prayer.

A regularly scheduled prayer meeting can be a significant time for teaching God's people to pray. In our church, the prayer meeting was informal, allowing the body to interact and share what God was doing in their lives, including suffering together. I came to experience God and His love for the church in those tender moments of prayer.

I recall one meeting when a new believer began to weep as she spoke. "I asked you to pray for me as I told my parents about the joy of my salvation and my baptism, but they didn't take the news well. They are going to drive 500 miles to speak personally with their bishop because they believe they might lose *their* eternal salvation because I was baptized. They had vowed to God that they would raise their baby girl to be faithful to their church." As we listened to this new believer, the church began to feel her pain and to minister to her. Her Lord was real, and His encouragement through the church sustained her. She continued to be faithful to the Lord, and as a result, the entire church was inspired.

How could your church's corporate prayer life be strengthened?

Be persistent in prayer.

☘ ROMANS 12:12 ☘

_____

MISSION ENDEAVORS

One last word about maintaining God's ideal. Intentionally being on mission with God will fuel the fire for God. I'm not talking about just doing missions, though that is obviously involved. Rather, I refer to creating a heart for God and His desire that none should perish but all should come to repentance (2 Pet. 3:9). A church with the heart of God following Christ as the Head will be on mission with God in their world. When the life of the body is fully functioning, it is a dynamic experience. Whether through observing the ordinances of baptism and the Lord's Supper, gathering for worship, preaching and teaching God's Word, times of prayer, or mission endeavors, the Lord will always go before us, motivating and compelling us by His love.

Describe how your church has been on mission with God in the past six months. Explain how you were involved.

_____

_____

Do you plan to be a part of future mission endeavors?

❑ Yes   ❑ No   Why not?_____

DAY FIVE

A Church Before a Watching World

We often forget that being a Christian is more than going to church on Sunday and loving the family of God. We also scatter throughout the week in many different places for the world to see. In case you didn't know, the world is watching you. If you claim to be a Christian, you must live in a way that honors God during the week.

The world watches as you drive to church on Sunday morning. They also watch you drive to work Monday through Friday. They observe what you do on Saturdays and see how you live at home with your children. They may see you casting your vote or at the gas station, grocery store, or mall. They may be with you at a school meeting, a sporting event with your children, or a community meeting at city hall. Each believer lives his or her life before a watching world.

Can you recall a time when you became aware the world was watching you? Describe that time.

_____

What do you think the world saw in you?

_____

"You are the light of the world. A city situated on a hill cannot be hidden. No one lights a lamp and puts it under a basket, but rather on a lampstand, and it gives light for all who are in the house. In the same way, let your light shine before men, so that they may see your good works and give glory to your Father in heaven."

♣ MATTHEW 5:14-16 ♣

Who is watching you? (Name)

Relative _____

Neighbor _____

Coworker _____

Church member _____

I recall a time when trouble arose in our neighborhood. It was in part racially motivated, and tempers were high. A vigilante group, some of whom were carrying guns, called a neighborhood meeting. They were going to discuss how to get rid of the problem. I did go to the meeting, and I spoke as a Christian. The Lord was gracious to turn things around, and we were able to diffuse the situation. But long before this particular situation arose, our church had let our light shine before men. We had already gained a reputation of integrity, and because of the way God resolved the problem, some of our neighbors were drawn closer to the Lord.

God desires for us to be involved in the lives of our neighbors in order for churches to positively impact the world around them.

Have you wanted to meet the neighbors who are new in the neighborhood but just haven't gotten to it? Resolve to set a time and take someone with you. Pray that God will help you become a positive influence in your neighbors' lives.

What does the world see when they look at your church? Your church is the body of Christ, walking in your community. The world must see the difference He can make today, just as He made a difference in the world when He came in the flesh.

LIVE OUT YOUR FAITH IN THE REAL WORLD

Jesus desires for every church to live our lives in the midst of a watching world so that they may see Him in us. We cannot hide ourselves behind the walls of our church buildings; we must live out our faith in the real world among real people. When we do, the world will be drawn to Him.

Ephesians 3:8-12 is a powerful passage of Scripture concerning the church before a watching world. Every phrase in that passage is packed full of meaning for the church. We are to "shed light" in our communities so that people might see God for the first time. To the natural man, God is a mystery; He is hidden from their eyes because of sin. But His eternal purposes for the church were to show the world the wisdom of God. Let me try to outline the progression in God's plan to touch a world.

1. God purposes to use the church to reveal His wisdom.
2. All that God purposes was accomplished in Christ Jesus.
3. The church will demonstrate before a watching world the wisdom of God by the difference that Christ makes in their lives.
4. God reveals Himself by working among His people through the Holy Spirit, drawing a world to Himself.
5. God touches a world through the churches and brings glory to Himself.

This grace was given to me—the least of all the saints!—to proclaim to the Gentiles the incalculable riches of the Messiah, and to shed light for all about the administration of the mystery hidden for ages in God who created all things. This is so that God's multi-faceted wisdom may now be made known through the church to the rulers and authorities in the heavens. This is according to the purpose of the ages, which He made in the Messiah, Jesus our Lord, in whom we have boldness, access, and confidence through faith in Him.

❧ EPHESIANS 3:8-12 ❧

Read again Matthew 5:14-16 (p. 175) and Ephesians 3:8-12 (p. 176). What word is common to both these verses?

_____

How bright is the light your church is shining in your world? Check one.

❑ Night light ❑ 40 watts ❑ 100 watts ❑ Floodlight

In the margin, list some ways your church can boost the power and shine brightly in your world. Be prepared to share your thoughts with your small group.

❧ A STORY FROM MEL BLACKABY ❧

The Lifeline

One summer I had a pastor visit me while he was on vacation. He could see in our service that God was mightily at work, and he longed to see the same thing in his congregation. He began to share the trouble he was having and how discouraged he and his wife were becoming. After listening for a while, I asked one question: "Tell me about the prayer in your church."

He dropped his head and said, "I tried to have a prayer meeting, but nobody came but my wife and me. So we cancelled that program and don't have it anymore." It wasn't long before I received word that he had resigned as pastor, the church sold their property, and the people disbanded.

My heart broke. Prayer is not a program; it is our life! A church cannot survive without it. If my wife and I were the only ones praying, I would maintain a regular time of prayer and invite others to join us. Prayer is a key factor in maintaining God's ideal for a church. The early church practiced prayer constantly. Jesus prayed as a way of life. No church can maintain God's ideal without genuine and faithful prayer.

DEMONSTRATE GOD'S GLORY

To the extent that a church reflects the fullness of God in them, the watching world gives glory to God. The more they see of God, the more they will be drawn to Him. A church I was pastoring sought to live out the life of Christ unashamedly in their community. Soon, there were some college students who heard how God was changing lives. Still others, who heard and saw the difference in these students, began to attend church gatherings. In the next few years, many students were saved and began to experience the powerful presence of the Holy Spirit in their midst.

At the same time we obeyed the Lord in taking the gospel to the towns and villages across the province. In each place we encouraged the people to live out their faith before their friends and neighbors. As the communities began to see the Christians living their lives with joy, they began to notice the changes in their lives. When the town drunk was saved, the people knew only God could have done such a thing. As a result, people were drawn to God, and a church was born. When people in neighboring towns heard what God was doing, they asked if we could come help them as well. Transformed lives make a difference!

When people look at your church, do they see the difference God makes? ❏ Yes ❏ No If yes, **how?**

_____

_____

This year alone our own church in Jonesboro, Georgia, is ministering to people in Alaska, Utah, Idaho, Wyoming, and New York. They are going to Guadeloupe, Venezuela, Liberia, Romania, and Cambodia. The mission teams include children, youth, young adults, and older adults. They are sending work crews, creative arts teams, and choirs. All is being done before a watching world. In every place there are those who encounter God working through His people. As a result, many are coming to God and finding salvation in Jesus Christ.

If you're willing, God will take your church and touch the world. He will invite you to come alongside Him and be a demonstration before the world of what He is like. He isn't asking us to work hard and try to evangelize the world. He's asking us to deny self, pick up our cross, and follow Him into the world. It's amazing the places He will lead your church if you are willing to follow. Living out your faith as you go, God will touch the world through you and your church.

You have concluded the pencil and paper portion of *Your Church Experiencing God Together*. Now it's time to live out this study personally and as a church. Review the past eight weeks and complete the following on your own paper or in the margin.

1. **Record three statements, principles, or Scriptures that you highlighted as particularly meaningful.**

2. **Identify how these three principles have made a difference in your life and/or the life of your church.**

3. **How will you continue to be obedient to the Lord as you live out these principles so that you and your church can experience God together?**

HOW TO BECOME A CHRISTIAN

❧

The Bible tells us that God is a God of love. His virtues include kindness, compassion, justice, faithfulness, patience, and truthfulness. But the Bible also tells us that we all fall short of the goodness of God. Although we may do good things, nothing we can do measures up to His standard of righteousness. We all deserve to be punished.

God's remedy for this impossible situation was to send His Son Jesus to be our substitute, bearing the penalty for evil in our place. Jesus Christ's death on the cross was a gift of love from God the Father. Accepting Jesus' death as payment for our sin is the only way we can meet God's standard. When we accept Christ's sacrifice, God the Father accepts and adopts us as His children.

If you are willing to confess that you are a sinner, that you want to turn from your sin in repentance and invite Jesus to be your Savior and Lord of your Life, pray this simple prayer:

Dear God, I know I have sinned by breaking your laws. I ask for your forgiveness. I believe Jesus died for my sins. I want to receive Him as my Savior and Lord. I want to obey Him in all that I do. In the name of Jesus I pray. Amen.

Entering into a relationship with Jesus not only makes Him our Savior from our sins but also acknowledges Him as Lord of our lives. Now Jesus sits on the throne of our lives and deserves the right to rule our hearts. We now have a new nature. This new nature competes with the old nature of sin.

Fortunately, God also gives us His gift of the Holy Spirit. As we cooperate with His Spirit, He transforms us from the inside out for the rest of our lives. Becoming more like Jesus is a process that involves Bible study, prayer, and being a member of a church.

If you prayed the prayer to receive Jesus as Savior and Lord, contact your small group leader, your pastor, or a trusted Christian friend and tell them of your decision. They would be happy to pray with you. If you are not confident that you are a Christian, take the same steps. This decision is too important to leave undecided. May God bless you.

"For God loved the world in this way: He gave His only Son, so that everyone who believes in Him will not perish but have eternal life."
❧JOHN 3:16❧

All have sinned and fall short of the glory of god.
❧ROMANS 3:23❧

The wages of sin is death, but the gift of God is eternal life in Christ Jesus our Lord.
❧ROMANS 6:23❧

God proves His own love for us in that while we were still sinners Christ died for us!
❧ROMANS 5:8❧

If you confess with your mouth, "Jesus is Lord," and believe in your heart that God raised Him from the dead, you will be saved.
❧ROMANS 10:9❧

Therefore if anyone is in Christ, there is a new creation; old things have passed away, and look, new things have come.
❧2 CORINTHIANS 5:17❧

LEADER GUIDE

This leader guide will help you facilitate an introductory session and eight group sessions for the study of *Your Church Experiencing God Together.* Feel free to adapt the suggestions to fit the needs of your group and the length of your sessions.

Commit this study to God in prayer, asking Him to put together the small group He desires to participate in this study. Begin your publicity at least six weeks in advance. Send personal invitations to church leaders—deacons, committee chairpersons, Sunday School teachers, and others you feel led to contact. Announce the study in the church newsletter, worship bulletin, and hallway bulletin boards. Secure child care for each session.

Before each session arrange for a TV-VCR in your meeting room. Preview each video in order to complete your viewer guide before the session. Each week reproduce page 5 for each participant. Complete each week's assignment. The Leader Guide has more material than can be used in a one-hour session. Be prepared to choose activities.

Begin praying now—and continue praying throughout this study—that God will use this time to do a mighty work in your church as your group members discover how to experience God together.

INTRODUCTORY SESSION

Before the Session

1. Have copies of *Your Church Experiencing God Together* ready for distribution.
2. Prepare an attendance sheet for participants to sign their names, addresses, phone numbers, and email addresses. Place this on a table near the door along with pens, markers, name tags, and a basket for collecting money.
3. Read the "Introduction" on pages 7-10 and be prepared to summarize it during the session.

4. Provide a TV-VCR for your meeting place. Preview the introduction video. Position the tape at the introductory session.

During the Session

1. As participants arrive, ask them to sign the attendance sheet, prepare name tags, and pick up copies of *Your Church Experiencing God Together.* Invite them to leave payment for their books in the basket or offer to collect their money after the session.
2. Introduce yourself and, depending on the familiarity of the group, give a little information about yourself. Ask members to do the same.
3. Ask a volunteer to read aloud "About the Authors" (p. 4). If someone has participated in a study of *Experiencing God,* invite the person to share a brief testimony.
4. Encourage members to share why they chose to participate in this study and what they anticipate happening in their lives and in the life of your church as a result.
5. Invite a volunteer to read aloud the questions you will discuss as a group throughout this study (p. 7). Briefly summarize the introduction (pp. 7-10) or ask members to read it this week in addition to week 1.
6. Tell participants that group times are not to be gripe sessions about your church or staff, but rather times to pray for your church and to experience God and seek His will for your church in order for it to fulfill His purpose.
7. Distribute copies of the viewer guide. Encourage viewers to take notes as they watch the video.
8. Play the introductory session video. Then lead the group to discuss statements that were particularly meaningful to them. Note especially the decisions/actions they will take from this session.

9. Ask, When did God think of the idea of church? (from the beginning) What does church mean? (called out ones) What do you think God had in mind when He called our church into existence? If we don't know, how will we know?

10. Assign week 1 in the member book for discussion at the next group session. Explain to participants that they will receive greater benefit if they spread their study over the week rather than attempting to complete all five days at one sitting. Encourage them to complete each learning activity for greater retention of learning.

11. Close by asking God to give them open hearts to learn and grow as they commit to this study.

SESSION I

Before the Session

1. Place the attendance sheet, name tags (optional), member books, pencils or pens, and Bibles near the door.

2. Duplicate viewer guides. Provide a TV-VCR. Preview the session 1 video. Position the tape at the beginning of session 1.

During the Session

1. Welcome members. Open with prayer.

2. Introduce the week's content by reading aloud the title for week 1. Ask: What does that statement mean to you? Do you think believers need to hear and receive that truth? Why?

3. Ask members to follow along in their books as you lead a discussion of the main ideas from week 1. Use the discussion starters for days 1-5 in the right-hand column.

4. Distribute copies of the viewer guide. Encourage viewers to take notes as they watch the video. Play the week 1 video. Then allow time for learners to discuss or ask questions.

5. Add your thoughts to the video discussion by asking: How did Henry's father teach him to be a shepherd? How does standing outside the church affect a person's testimony?

6. Assign week 2 for the next group session.

7. Lead members in a time of guided silent prayer.

Ask them to thank God for placing them in a church family. Then direct them to ask God to help your church family care for one another so deeply that others will be drawn into the kingdom of God. Then, ask them to pray for unity among all Christians in your community.

Discussion Starters

Day 1

- What do you understand to be the difference between being saved and experiencing God's great salvation?

- List the first two characteristics of God's great salvation (p. 15). How would you explain those characteristics to someone who has not studied this material?

- Share a time when you were overwhelmed by God's great salvation.

Day 2

- Review the four additional characteristics of God's great salvation discussed in day 2. How do these characteristics help you gain a deeper appreciation for your own salvation?

- Do you agree or disagree that our relationship with God is not private? Why? (p. 17)

- Brainstorm ways your church cares for a new believer (p. 18). If you don't know, ask a volunteer to talk with a staff or lay leader and be prepared to report back next week.

- How have you grown in maturity from watching older believers? How can you set an example for younger Christians to follow?

Day 3

- (Ask someone to read aloud Matthew 16:15-18.) How did today's study enhance your understanding of this passage? (pp. 21-22)

- If church growth isn't the standard to evaluate the health of a church, what is? Does this concern or relieve you? Why? (p. 22)

- Share your response to the activity on page 24 in which you compared ways your church family has ministered to you to the way the early church cared for one another.

- How can you help your church care for each member in more ways (more productive ways)?

Day 4

- Why must we understand the corporate dimension of salvation in order to fulfill God's purposes for our individual lives?
- Indicate whether you agree or disagree with this statement from page 26: "If we bypass the people of God we have shut down evangelism." Explain your response.
- (Ask someone to read aloud John 17:20-23.) How do you feel when you realize Jesus was praying for you and your church?

Day 5

- Name the seventh characteristic of God's great salvation. Was the idea of "seeking the kingdom" rather than "seeking the church" a new concept for you? How do you think churches would be different if all members grasped this truth? (p. 30)
- What is the primary truth we must understand about the kingdom? (p. 29)
- How have you seen Jesus rule over sickness, nature, or other areas of life? (p. 30)
- Share your ideas from page 31 on how you can support and encourage kingdom work in places other than your church.
- Discuss any further thoughts or highlights from this week's study that you would like to share with the group. (Return to step 4, p. 181.)

SESSION 2

Before the Session

1. Write each of the five truths about *koinonia* (activity p. 36) on separate slips of paper.
2. Purchase a spiral notebook or journal to use as a prayer request journal during this study. You will add requests specifically related to your church's needs each week. Encourage participants to purchase a prayer journal for their personal use.
3. Provide a TV-VCR. Preview the session 2 video. Position the tape at the beginning of session 2.

During the Session

1. Welcome members. Open with prayer.
2. Distribute the five slips of paper defining the truths about *koinonia* to five members. Direct each of the five persons to read aloud his or her statement. Ask the entire group to identify what the statements define (*koinonia*). Lead the group to examine how these five statements and this week's study changed or enhanced their understanding of *koinonia*.
3. Ask members to follow along in their books as you lead a discussion of the main ideas from week 2. Use the discussion starters for days 1-5 beginning at the bottom of the page.
4. Distribute copies of the viewer guide. Play the week 2 video. Allow time for learners to discuss or ask questions about the video presentation.
5. Add your thoughts to the video discussion by asking what new meanings of the word *koinonia* they discovered through this study. What draws unbelievers to the church and to Christ? (our love for other believers)
6. Assign week 3 for the next group session.
7. Explain, This week's study has provided several opportunities for prayer. In day 3 you were challenged to ask God for the opportunity to seek reconciliation with a person with whom you are estranged. Pray for the strength to offer and/or seek forgiveness.
8. Ask members to turn to page 45 and identify the specific requests from Paul's prayer that they prayed for your church. Record those requests in the prayer journal.
9. Share prayer requests from the activity on page 50. Record the requests. Lead the group in a time of prayer, allowing volunteers the opportunity to pray aloud for the mentioned requests.

Discussion Starters
Day 1

- What are the most difficult parts of our lives to lay down for our brothers and sisters? (p. 33) Why is a willingness to lay them down an indication of *koinonia* or agape love?

- (Ask a volunteer to read 2 Corinthians 6:1.) What do you think it means to receive God's grace in vain? What are some practical ways we can receive God's grace and allow it to flow out of our lives to bless other believers? (p. 34)
- Do you agree or disagree with this statement from page 36: "True *koinonia*, in its fullest expression, can only be found in one place—the local church." Why?

Day 2
- What is the difference being acting right and being right? (p. 37)
- Describe a time when you experienced Christ's presence in a very real way. (p. 38)
- How did your personalized version of Romans 8 on page 39 help you appreciate God's *koinonia* love for you? How can this grasp of God's great love help us extend *koinonia* to others?

Day 3
- What did you learn about *koinonia* from the diagram you completed on page 40?
- Recall the story Henry related about his relationship with one of his teenage sons (p. 41). Did you think of a person with whom you have a strained relationship when you read, "God needed to draw me closer to Him in order that I might be closer to my son"? What if we try to walk in the light and have *koinonia* with that person but they don't care about their relationship with God or us? Is there hope for the relationship? Explain.

Day 4
- How did you answer the question on page 45, "What would happen if your church was filled with the love of Christ?"
- Share your sketch or verbal description of what a church family would look like if Christ's love was in every believer. (p. 47)
- What feelings did you identify in the activity on page 48? Why?

Day 5
- Respond to this statement: "We must learn to release our people from burdensome busyness so that they can build healthy and strong relationships." How can our church follow this principle and still keep activities running in the church?

- What did you learn about your heart from the activity on page 49?
- What reasons did you give on page 50 for why a church might lose its first love?
- How did you respond to the final activity on page 52? (Return to step 4 on p. 182.)

SESSION 3

Before the Session
1. Bring a fist-sized rock to group time.
2. Make certain you have your prayer journal.
3. Provide a TV-VCR. Preview session 3. Position the tape at the beginning of session 3.

During the Session
1. Welcome members. Open with prayer.
2. Display the rock and ask people to imagine it as their heart. Direct each participant to hold the rock a moment, weigh it in their hand, and then pass it to the next person. Ask, Does this rock remind anyone of a Scripture passage you studied in this week's lesson? After discussion, read aloud Ezekiel 36:26-27. Ask, What did God promise to give His people in place of a heart of stone? How did that promise describe God's new covenant with His people?
3. Ask members to follow along in their books as you lead a discussion of the main ideas from week 3. Use the discussion starters for days 1-5 on page 184.
4. Distribute copies of the viewer guide. Play the week 3 video. Allow time for learners to discuss insights they gained into God's covenantal relationship.
5. Add your thoughts to the video discussion by asking, How does making a covenant with new members help the "back door" of the church? What do our authors suggest we do when we see problems in our churches?
6. Assign week 4 for the next group session.
7. Ask learners to share prayer requests for your church that they recorded in response to the activity on page 62. Write those requests in the class prayer journal. Although it is important to

183

pray for health concerns and other needs, strive to keep this prayer time focused on how your church can experience the power of the cross by denying itself and following Christ wholeheartedly. To begin your prayer time, request participants pray silently, committing themselves to be "Daniels" who will stand with their church and intercede on its behalf. Then read some or all of the prayer requests aloud, giving time for members to voice a prayer regarding that request.

Discussion Starters

Day 1

- How was your understanding of the term *covenant* challenged or enhanced in day one?
- (Ask a volunteer to read Matthew 13:58.) How do you feel when you hear that verse? How can we prevent that statement from being said about us or our church?
- How has God's faithful covenant anchored you during troubling times? (p. 56)
- React to this statement: "Because God was the initiator of the covenant, no obedience was too demanding, no dependence too absolute, no submission too complete, and no confidence too certain" (p. 57). Is this still true today?

Day 2

- Recall comparisons of the old and new covenants. (p. 59)
- What are the purposes and blessings of being in a covenant with God?
- Why is the new covenant more valuable (expensive) than the old? (paid for with Jesus' blood)

Day 3

- Respectfully give an example of how "Some churches tend to lower the standard for giving in order to attract more people and build bigger churches" (p. 63). How can we maintain high standards for wholehearted devotion to God without coming across as harsh and judgmental to the non-believers and immature Christians we are trying to reach?
- How did Mel's illustration of the airplane and the parachute on page 65 help you grasp the concept of living within God's covenant?

Day 4

- If any of your group have recently joined the church, been baptized, or experienced their first Lord's Supper, ask the person to share a word of testimony. Ask the group, What other ideas do you have for expressing your covenant relationship with your church family?
- Share one or both of your responses to the activity at the end of day 4. (p. 69)

Day 5

- What did Daniel ask God to do in Daniel 9:16-19 (p. 71)? What portion of Daniel's prayer especially touched you? Why?
- (Ask a volunteer to read Hebrews 10:24-25 on page 75.) How well do you think our church does in keeping up with people who have quit coming or who are irregular in their attendance? What can we do as individuals and as a group to help our church keep people from slipping through the cracks? (Return to step 4 on p. 183.)

SESSION 4

Before the Session

1. Have note cards or stationery envelopes addressed to each of your church staff members located on a table near the door.
2. Make certain you have your prayer journal.
3. Provide a TV-VCR. Preview session 4. Position the tape at the beginning of session 4.

During the Session

1. As participants arrive, ask them to write a brief note of appreciation to each staff member on the note cards or stationery you have provided. (If you have a large staff, you may need to ask participants to write more than one staff member and/or make this a take-home activity.)
2. After the activity is completed, ask: What's the difference between being a church leader and being the Head of the church? What happens when churches get these roles confused?
3. Ask members to follow along in their books as you lead a discussion of the main ideas from week 4. Use the discussion starters for days 1-5 on page 185.

4. Distribute copies of the viewer guide. Play the week 4 video. Allow time for learners to discuss insights they gained into God's plan for the headship of His church.

5. Add your thoughts to the video by discussing the implications of Henry's statement that if each New Testament church found its uniqueness in Christ, there would be no unreached people group in any city.

6. Assign week 5 for the next group session.

7. Ask members to share prayer requests for your pastor that they recorded in response to the activity on page 92. Encourage members to share additional prayer concerns for your church that may have arisen as they considered the health or the direction of your church. Record all requests in the class prayer journal. Allow a quiet moment for personal reflection and repentance. Then invite volunteers to voice prayers of thanksgiving for your church and for your staff. Close the prayer time.

After the Session
Mail or hand deliver the notes from your group to each church staff member.

Discussion Starters
Day 1
- What is our personal responsibility in restoring and maintaining our church's health? (p. 77)
- Is church health possible if we are responsive to Christ as the Head, but other members are not?
- React to Mel's statement on page 80: "I deserved a church with better pay!" How does our attitude of what we deserve keep us from knowing and doing God's will?
- How can we live out the truth of Matthew 16:24-25? (p. 78)

Day 2
- Respectfully share your response to the "trail" activity on page 80.
- React: God has no plan B. (p. 82)
- What do you think is the result when church members act on assignment rather than out of love? (p. 82)

- How do we follow Christ as the Head of our church without getting sidetracked? (p. 82)

Day 3
- Do you believe God has a plan for our church? Do you believe He has a purpose for our church? Does He have the people to carry it out?
- Respond to the case studies on page 84.
- What assignments do you think God may be giving our church? (p. 84)
- Tell how you responded to the activity on page 86.

Day 4
- How do the questions on page 89 challenge your usual response to those who join our church?
- What do you see as the working relationship between the church's lay people and the staff in developing committed disciples of Christ? (p. 90)
- Share some of your responses describing how children and youth bless our church. (p. 90) How can we express appreciation and encourage them to continue being a blessing?

Day 5
- How did today's study help you have a greater appreciation for our pastor?
- How do you pray for our pastor? (p. 92)
- What did you record as the primary responsibility of the church leaders listed on pages 92-93?
- Share some of your ideas for expressing appreciation to church leaders. (p. 93)
- Which question on page 94 particularly challenged you? Why? (Return to step 4 at the top of this page.)

Session 5

Before the Session
1. Prior to the session duplicate four copies of the case studies on page 190.
2. Bring your prayer journal and have a marker board or poster board in your meeting room.
3. Provide a TV-VCR. Preview session 5. Position the tape at the beginning of session 5.

During the Session
1. Open with prayer. Introduce today's study by asking someone to read Acts 1:4-5,8 from page 95.

2. Ask members to follow along in their books as you lead a discussion of the main ideas from Week 5. Use the discussion starters for days 1-5 beginning at the bottom of the page.

3. Invite a volunteer to read aloud Galatians 6:1-2. Read Case Study #1 from column 1, page 187. Lead the class to discuss how Terrie and Don properly applied the principle of carrying each other's burdens.

4. Form three small groups. Give each group one of the three remaining case studies. Instruct them to determine how the persons in their case studies did not follow the principles from Galatians 6 and what those persons must do to respond biblically to their situations. Allow groups to share their responses.

5. Distribute copies of the viewer guide. Play the week 5 video. Allow time for learners to discuss insights they gained from the video presentation.

6. Add your thoughts to the video by discussing how you can grieve the Holy Spirit and ways you can identify the work of the Holy Spirit in the life of your church.

7. Assign week 6 for the next group session.

8. To begin your prayer time, review the requests you recorded during your discussion of Day 3. Encourage members to share requests from the activity on page 104. Invite someone to pray about those requests. To close your session, direct participants to use some of the printed requests from Isaiah 41:10 to voice a verbal prayer for your church leaders.

Discussion Starters
Day 1
• How did you respond to the activity on page 98?
• List ways church members silently give off the message, "We don't need you." (Write responses in one column on the poster or marker board.) Look at the list and list alternate actions that will help all members to feel valued and needed. (Record responses in another column.)
• What statements or activities in this day's study were especially meaningful to you? Why?

Day 2
• If you can share without betraying any confidences, whose names did you record beside the Christian virtues on page 100? How do they display those virtues?
• Which of the statements about unity on page 101 motivated you the most? Why?
• Which of the "How to" statements on developing unity on page 102 do you think our church does well in teaching others? In what areas can we improve in equipping our members?
• How can we help leaders focus on equipping members and thus multiplying leaders?

Day 3
• (Read Mel's statement on page 105, "God was determined to save that woman in spite of our incompetence.") Relate a time when God worked through you in spite of your incompetence. Invite volunteers to share a similar example.
• Were you surprised at Paul's description of himself in 1 Corinthians 2:1-5? How did that passage encourage you? (p. 108)
• Respectfully share your evaluation of our church from page 107. (Add to the class prayer journal any prayer requests this activity may prompt.)

Day 4
• (Ask someone to read John 6:39.) What would be some of the top priorities of a church that took John 6:39 seriously (p. 108)? Does this describe our church?
• What ministry assignment do you believe God has given our church? Share your answers to the questions that explored how our church is responding to this assignment. (p. 109)

Day 5
• What church ministry experiences did you record on page 112?
• If you can share names without betraying any confidences, whose names did you record on page 115? How did you express appreciation to these persons? (Return to step 3 at the top of this page.)

CASE STUDIES FOR WEEK 5

Read the situation assigned to your small group. Determine if the believers did or did not properly bear another's burden, based on Galatians 6:1.

1. Terrie and Don co-teach a Sunday School class. They were concerned to see one couple living far beyond their means. At a class social they carefully and privately broached the subject of credit card debt. They discovered the couple was deeply in debt and their marriage was strained. Terrie and Don connected them with a financial counselor and met with them regularly for several months for prayer and encouragement.

2. Mike and Dan were aware a member of their church had been seen around town with a woman who was not his wife. However, they didn't know how to approach him without being offensive, so they decided they should mind their own business and say nothing.

3. Megan and Carly work together and attend the same church. Megan was concerned to see Carly frequent bars with business associates after work. She began to accompany Carly to the bars in an attempt to persuade her to change her lifestyle. Soon, Megan was drinking as well.

4. Bill and Nancy have been making negative comments about the church for several months. Finally, a group of deacons visited them in their home and chastised them for causing dissatisfaction and division within the church body.

SESSION 6

Before the Session

1. Provide a TV-VCR. Preview session 6. Position the tape at the beginning of session 6.
2. Bring your prayer journal and have a marker board or poster board in your meeting room.
3. Write "Welcome to the World Mission Strategy Center" on the marker board or poster board.

During the Session

1. As members arrive, direct their attention to the sign on the board and welcome them to the World Mission Strategy Center.
2. Direct participants to name key words that describe a world mission strategy center (p. 118). Write responses on the board. Discuss how the description of a world mission strategy center helped them better understand the purpose God has for your church.
3. Ask members to follow along in their books as you lead a discussion of the main ideas from Week 6. Use the discussion starters for days 1-5 on page 188.
4. Distribute copies of the viewer guide. Play the week 6 video. Allow time for learners to discuss insights they gained into God's strategy for world missions.
5. Add your thoughts to the video by asking for reactions to the statement of the Romanian layman, "I, too, have received the blessing of being beaten," and Henry's statement, "Christians today are surprised by the cost of following Jesus."
6. Assign week 7 for the next group session.
7. Invite learners to share ways they feel your church can reveal God's glory in your community. Record these in the class prayer journal in the form of requests. Invite members to pray about these requests and other needs. Close your prayer time by asking members to read aloud the prayer from Psalm 40:1,3 that they wrote on page 128.

Discussion Starters

Day 1

- Tell about a small group of people who have worked together to make a difference in the world for Christ. (p. 117)
- Share experiences you have had obeying the Great Commission in your own Jerusalem, Judea, Samaria, and ends of the earth (p. 119).
- Discuss the missions strategy of your church. If possible, invite the chairman of the missions committee to come to this session. If not, pre-enlist a member to interview this person.

Day 2

- Relate a time when you were in a "valley of decision." How did you feel during that experience? What was the outcome of the experience? What did you look to for support as you sought to make the right decision? (p. 121)
- What must a church and an individual do to be ready to obey God when He calls? (p. 122)
- How did the biblical personalities you studied on page 123 demonstrate spiritual readiness?
- How can we help our church be ready to obey when God commands? (p. 124)

Day 3

- What is the difference between the size of our faith and the size of God in Whom we have faith? (p. 125)
- (Ask someone to read Ephesians 3:20-21.) Discuss the difference between asking God to bless our dreams and asking Him to accomplish His purposes for our church.
- What is the only way we can begin to grasp and believe what God has in store for our church? (p. 127)

Day 4

- How did you feel after reading the account of persecuted Christians on page 129?
- What did you list in the debit column as costs of following Jesus (p. 130)? What did you list in the credit column? Is following Jesus worth the cost?
- Respectfully share your responses to the activity evaluating our church's priorities on page 132. What requests for our church do we need to add to our prayer journal?

Day 5

- What costs did you underline that a church must pay if it's willing to follow Christ? Which of these costs has our church paid? Which of these costs do you think we are resisting?
- (Invite volunteers to read Proverbs 22:9, Luke 6:38, and 2 Corinthians 9:6-8.) What do these verses teach us about giving?
- How has God blessed our church through a ministry that caused us discomfort and inconvenience? (p. 135) (Return to step 4 on p. 187.)

SESSION 7

Before the Session

1. Provide a TV-VCR. Preview session 7. Position the tape at the beginning of session 7.
2. Bring your prayer journal and a ring of keys with you to the session.

During the Session

1. Thank members for their presence and continued faithfulness to the workbook study and small-group time.
2. Display your keys and ask participants how many keys they have with them. Direct them to turn to a partner and tell what they open with each of their keys. After a moment, ask: How is our church using the keys to the kingdom God has given us?
3. Ask members to follow along in their books as you lead a discussion of the main ideas from week 7. Use the discussion starters for days 1-5 on page 189.
4. Distribute copies of the viewer guide. Play the week 7 video. Allow time for learners to discuss insights they gained into the meaning of the kingdom of God.
5. Add your thoughts to the video by discussing the difference between unity and uniformity. Ask, How do the church and the kingdom work together to achieve God's purposes?
6. Assign week 8 for the next group session.
7. Ask members to share requests they listed for your church in response to the activities on

pages 145 and 157. Record these in the class prayer journal. Invite members to forms groups of two or three to pray about these requests. Close in prayer by asking members to voice aloud the prayer personalized for your church on page 148.

Discussion Starters
Day 1
• (Ask volunteers to read aloud Matthew 21:9, John 1:49, John 3:13-15, and John 11:27.) Identify the titles for Jesus found in these verses. How do all of these titles acknowledge Jesus as the Messiah?
• What did Jesus teach Nicodemus and Pilate about the kingdom of God? (p. 140)
• How can we improve our vision so we can see the kingdom of God among us?

Day 2
• What are the kingdom roles God has given the church (pp. 142-43)? Which of these roles surprised you? How do you think our church is fulfilling these roles?
• Can you identify passages other than those listed on page 143 that testify to God's great power given to believers? How have you experienced God's power in your life?
• What promise of God is especially meaningful to you? What promises of God would you like to claim for our church? (pp. 144-45)

Day 3
• What metaphors did Jesus use to describe the kingdom (p. 147)? Did you find these illustrations challenging or comforting? Why?
• Share the example of God's power being unleashed through His people that you recounted on page 149.
• (Read aloud Ephesians 1:18-23.) What did you learn about God's power when you examined this passage on page 149?

Day 4
• (Ask the two questions at the beginning of Day 4 on page 150.)
• What are the five misconceptions people have about the kingdom of God? Which of these

misconceptions did you have? How did this study help clarify your understanding of God's kingdom? Are there still some gray areas?
• Respectfully share whether you think our church focuses more on the kingdom of God or on our own needs.
• How did you respond to the question that examined your response to other churches in our community on page 151? How has this study helped you change your attitude toward them?

Day 5
• How is our church combining with other churches to meet needs in our community (p. 155)? How can we promote even stronger cooperation and unity?
• Share your responses to the first two activities on page 157. (Return to step 4 on p. 188.)

SESSION 8

Before the Session
1. Provide a TV-VCR. Preview session 8. Position the tape at the beginning of session 8.
2. Bring your prayer journal and have a marker board or poster board in your meeting room.
3. (optional) On 8 1/2 X 11 paper have someone draw a row of several buildings with a church in the middle titled "My Church." Label the picture "Our Church's Neighborhood." Make a copy for each participant and distribute it at the beginning of the session. Or, draw the buildings on the marker board with the same heading.
4. (optional) Make a copy of "A Scroll of Remembrance" for each participant. If possible, use parchment paper. On the paper type or write: We covenant together, as God's people at _____ Church, to be completely obedient to our Lord so we can be a church on mission with God before a watching world. (Leave a space for signatures.) If you are unable to provide copies, ask someone to draw this document on poster board or on the marker board in your room.

During the Session

1. Distribute copies of "Our Church's Neighborhood" as members arrive and ask them to name the blank buildings with businesses or homes they consider your church's neighbors.

2. After an opening prayer, allow volunteers to share the neighbors they identified. Discuss ways your church has been involved in those neighbors' lives. Ask: How do you think the watching world sees our church? Are they attracted by what they see? What adjustments do you think our church needs to make?

3. Ask members to follow along in their books as you lead a discussion of the main ideas from week 8. Use the discussion starters for days 1-5 beginning at the bottom of the page.

4. Distribute copies of the viewer guide. Play the week 8 video. Allow time for learners to discuss insights into God's perspective on the church.

5. Display or distribute "A Scroll of Remembrance" and read aloud Malachi 3:16. Encourage your class to sign the document as a way of covenanting with one another to be a church family on mission with God before a watching world.

6. Lead the group in a time of guided prayer. First ask them to praise God for Who He is. Allow them to voice prayers of thanksgiving for your church and leaders. Then guide them to lift up specific requests for your church. Close by asking God to strengthen your members to remain true to the covenant they signed.

7. Thank members for remaining faithful to this study and encourage them to daily apply what they learned in your church and community.

Discussion Starters

Day 1

• Respectfully share your evaluation of our church's decision-making process (p. 160). What prayer requests for our church leaders did you add to your prayer list? (Write those requests in the class prayer journal.)

• How did you word Paul's message to our church on page 161?

• Share your responses to the activities based on John 15:5-7. (p. 162)

Day 2

• How did you feel when you first read the statement, "Partial obedience is disobedience?"

• What sets God's people apart from their surrounding culture? (p. 165)

• Give examples of how churches mix the ways of the world with the ways of God and consequently hide God from the world. (Be careful to be respectful, not critical, as you discuss.)

Day 3

• To what do you feel God is calling our church to return (p. 168)? How can we return?

• Give God the glory by sharing an experience when He allowed you to experience revival among His people. (p. 169)

Day 4

• What is your understanding of God's ideal purpose for every believer's life? (p. 170)

• Share your thoughts about why renewal comes to a church when the Lord's Supper and baptism are approached seriously (p. 171). Have you personally experienced a time of revival during a baptism or communion service? Tell about it.

• Respond to this statement from page 172: "If every worship service is turned into an evangelistic service, God's people will wither and die spiritually. They cannot survive without true worship."

• Share how an element of worship on page 173 helps God's people maintain a love relationship with Him.

• How can our church's corporate prayer life be strengthened? (p. 174)

Day 5

• Who has a good relationship with your neighbors? How did you develop that relationship? Brainstorm ways we can become more involved in our neighbors' lives. (p. 176)

• What was your response to the "light" activity on page 177?

• Share a portion of your response to the concluding activity on page 178. (Return to step 4 on p. 189.)

HENRY BLACKABY MINISTRIES

❈

Henry Blackaby Ministries exists to help people experience a life-changing relationship with God that dynamically affects their home, church, and business through a message of revival and spiritual awakening.

We seek to help people experience God through preaching, teaching, conference speaking, leadership training, the production and presentation of ministry materials, and various media outlets including radio and the Internet.

For further information about Henry Blackaby Ministries, please contact us at Henry Blackaby Ministries, P.O. Box 161228, Atlanta, GA 30321

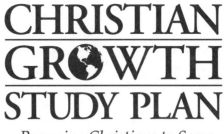

CHRISTIAN GROWTH STUDY PLAN

Preparing Christians to Serve

In the **Christian Growth Study Plan (formerly Church Study Course)**, this book *Your Church Experiencing God Together* is a resource for course credit in the subject area Church of the Christian Growth category of plans. To receive credit, read the book, complete the learning activities, show your work to your pastor, a staff member or church leader, then complete the information on the next page. The form may be duplicated. Send the completed page to:

**Christian Growth Study Plan
One LifeWay Plaza, Nashville, TN 37234-0117
FAX: (615)251-5067, Email: cgspnet@lifeway.com**
For information about the Christian Growth Study Plan, refer to the Christian Growth Study Plan Catalog. It is located online at *www.lifeway.com/cgsp*. If you do not have access to the Internet, contact the Christian Growth Study Plan office (1.800.968.5519) for the specific plan you need for your ministry.

Your Church Experiencing God Together
Course Number: CG-0808

PARTICIPANT INFORMATION

Social Security Number (USA ONLY-optional)	Personal CGSP Number*	Date of Birth (MONTH, DAY, YEAR)

Name (First, Middle, Last)	Home Phone

Address (Street, Route, or P.O. Box)	City, State, or Province	Zip/Postal Code

CHURCH INFORMATION

Church Name

Address (Street, Route, or P.O. Box)	City, State, or Province	Zip/Postal Code

CHANGE REQUEST ONLY

☐ Former Name

☐ Former Address	City, State, or Province	Zip/Postal Code

☐ Former Church	City, State, or Province	Zip/Postal Code

Signature of Pastor, Conference Leader, or Other Church Leader	Date

*New participants are requested but not required to give SS# and date of birth. Existing participants, please give CGSP# when using SS# for the first time. Thereafter, only one ID# is required. **Mail to:** Christian Growth Study Plan, One LifeWay Plaza, Nashville, TN 37234-0117. Fax: (615)251-5067.

Rev. 5-02